MEDICAL DOCTORS
A STUDY OF ROLE CONCEPT AND JOB SATISFACTION
THE EGYPTIAN CASE

SOCIAL, ECONOMIC AND POLITICAL STUDIES OF THE MIDDLE EAST

ÉTUDES SOCIALES, ÉCONOMIQUES ET POLITIQUES DU MOYEN ORIENT

VOLUME XXXIII

THERESA EL-MEHAIRY

MEDICAL DOCTORS

A STUDY OF ROLE CONCEPT AND JOB SATISFACTION
THE EGYPTIAN CASE

LEIDEN
E. J. BRILL
1984

MEDICAL DOCTORS

A STUDY OF ROLE CONCEPT AND JOB SATISFACTION
THE EGYPTIAN CASE

BY

THERESA EL-MEHAIRY

LEIDEN
E. J. BRILL
1984

Comité de rédaction—Editorial committee

E. GELLNER (London School of Economics), C. ISSAWI (Princeton University), S. KHALAF (American University of Beirut), M. F. AL-KHATIB (Cairo University), Ş. MARDIN (Boğaziçi University, Istanbul), M. ZGHAL (Université de Tunis).

Rédacteur—Editor

C. A. O. VAN NIEUWENHUIJZE

Le but de la collection est de faciliter la communication entre le grand public international et les spécialistes des sciences sociales étudiant le Moyen-Orient, et notamment ceux qui y résident. Les ouvrages sélectionnés portent sur les phénomènes et problèmes contemporains: sociaux, culturels, économiques et administratifs. Leurs principales orientations relèvent de la théorie générale, de problématiques, plus précises, et de la politologie: aménagement des institutions et administration des affaires publiques.

The series is designed to serve as a link between the international reading public and social scientists studying the contemporary Middle East, notably those living in the area. Works included are characterized by their relevance to actual phenomena and problems: whether social, cultural, economic, political or administrative. They are theory-oriented, problem-oriented or policy-oriented.

ISBN 90 04 07038 9

Copyright 1984 by E. J. Brill, Leiden, Netherlands

All rights reserved. No part of this book may be reproduced or translated in any form, by print, photoprint, microfilm, microfiche or any other means without written permission from the publisher

PRINTED IN THE NETHERLANDS

*To my daughter Noelle
with the hope that
this book may serve
as a reminder of her
responsibility to her
fellow countrymen*

CONTENTS

List of Tables	X
List of Figures	XII
Acknowledgements	XIII
Abstract	XIV

I.	Introduction and Aims of Study	1
	Overview of the Study	2
	Social Policy Background and Government Dilemmas	3
	Social Attitudes of Personnel	7
	References	7
II.	Medicine and Health in the Third World	9
	Contrasting Approaches	9
	Imperialism of Western Medicine	10
	Inescapability of Compromise	15
	The Egyptian Case	18
	The Health Care System	18
	Major Health Care Problems	20
	Economic Constraints	22
	Demographic Considerations	24
	The Culture of Islam	26
	Philosophy of Health	28
	Indigenous Health Practitioners	29
	The Patients' Perspective	31
	References	32
III.	Health Care in its Sociological Framework—The Role of the Physician	37
	Historical Note	37
	Early Parsonian Sick Role Model and the Physician	39
	Post Parsonian Objections to the Model	43
	Limitations for the Egyptian Case	43
	Physician and Patient Relationship in the Third World	48
	Locating the Professions in a Middle Eastern Society	49
	Role Conflict, Role Adaptation and Marginality	53
	References	58
IV.	Medical Education in Egypt	62
	Curriculum Analysis	62

	Student Selection	63
	Student Motivation	63
	The Secondary Socialization of the Medical Student	65
	Ideological Frustrations and Praxis	66
	References	69
V.	Physicians Self Concept and Construction of Role Set	70
	Descriptive Sub Sets of Roles	70
	Therapist, Manager, Educator and Mediator	71
	Approaches to Marginality	72
	Current Issues and Influence on Role Set	73
	The Special Case of Family Planning and Government Policy	73
	Status and Education of Women	79
	References	84
VI.	Research Methodology and Fieldwork Procedure	87
	Pilot Questionnaire	87
	Revised Version	87
	Value Orientation	89
	The Value Scales	90
	Medical Student Questionnaire	92
	Interviews	92
	Credibility of the Data	93
	Translation Linguistics	93
	Criterion Interview	94
	A General Defence of Questionnaires	95
	Research Procedures	97
	The Rural Health Unit	97
	Menoufia Governorate	98
	Minia Governorate	100
	The Urban Health System	102
	Data Collection	102
	References	102
VII.	Some Speculative Interpretations of the Findings	104
	Educational Evaluation	104
	Altruism Submerged	105
	Urban Care Superiority	107
	Theoretical Implications	108
	Sub Sets of Roles and Praxis	109
	Role Performance	111

	Satisfaction as Exchange Theory	116
	Job Satisfaction Overall	118
	Dissatisfactions	118
	Satisfactions	121
	Attempts at Role Integration	127
	Marginality Versus Complementarity	128
	The Illustrating Case of Managerial Experience	152
	References	166
VIII.	Psychological Infrastructure and Job Satisfaction	172
	Personality Variables	172
	Theoretical Discussion	175
	Results of the Value Tests	176
	Job Dissatisfactions as Cognitive Dissonance	182
	References	185
IX.	Summary and Perspectives for the Future	187

Appendix I
Physicians Questionnaire (English Version) 191

Appendix II
Student Questionnaire (English Version) 205

Map of Egypt 209

LIST OF TABLES

Table

1.1	Ranking of the 26 Items (Problems in Delivering Health Services to Rural Egypt Include)	6
1.2	Results by Weighting the Items (Problems in Delivering Health Services to Rural Egypt Include)	7
4.1	Reasons for Originally Entering the Faculty of Medicine (Students Compared with Practising Physicians)	64
7.1	Evaluation of University Education and Desire for Additional Education/Training	104
7.2	Medical Students' View of Mandatory Village Service	106
7.3	Students' Views About Urban/Rural Medical Care	107
7.4	Self Assessed Role Definitions by Two Groups of Rural Physicians and One Group of Urban Physicians	110
7.5	Fulfilling Position According to Ministry of Health Specifications	112
7.6	Analysis of Variance for Mean Scores in Table 7.5	113
7.7	Physicians' Dissatisfactions	119
7.8	Physicians' Satisfactions	122
7.9	Medical Students' Anticipated Disadvantages in Rural Areas Compared with Rural Physicians	124
7.10	Medical Students' Anticipated Advantages in Rural Areas Compared with Rural Physicians	125
7.11	Mean Scores for Satisfactions and Dissatisfactions	126
7.12	Statistical Differences Between Mean Scores for Satisfactions and Dissatisfactions	126
7.13	Variance Analysis of Satisfaction Mean Scores	126
7.14	Variance Analysis of Dissatisfaction Mean Scores	126
7.15	Problems From the Community as Stated by Physicians	131
7.16	Cultural Traditions Stated by Physicians as Impeding Their Work	134
7.17	Cultural Traditions Stated by Physicians as Facilitating Their Work	139
7.18	Problems With Subordinate Staff as Cited by Physicians	144
7.19	Problems Encountered by the Physicians With the Government Supervisors	149
7.20	Problems Encountered by the Physicians With the Ministry of Health Administrators	149

LIST OF TABLES

7.21	Physicians Self Rated Administrative and Supervisory Skills......	153
7.22	Physicians Self Rated Administrative and Supervisory Skills (Sub Group Analysis)...	159
7.23	Professional Competence of Subordinate Staff as Evaluated by Physicians...	164
8.1	Results of the Value Test...	177
8.2	Analysis of Variance of Achievement, Independence, Recognition	177
8.3	Results of Statistical Analysis (t-distribution) of Value Mean Scores	178
8.4	Satisfaction with University Education Versus Values' Mean Scores	179
8.5	Job Fulfillment Mean Scores Versus Values' Mean Scores.........	180
8.6	Job Fulfillment Versus Satisfaction with University Education...	182

LIST OF FIGURES

Figure

7.1	A Position-Centric Model	109
7.2	Distribution of Job Fulfillment Scores	113
7.3	Role Structure of the Egyptian Health Delivery System	130
7.4	Structure of the Rural Health Unit	142
7.5	Physicians' Self Rated Administrative and Supervisory Skills: Group Scores to Question 39	154
7.6	Group Scores to Question 40	155
7.7	Group Scores to Question 41	156
7.8	Group Scores to Question 42	157
7.9	Group Scores to Question 43	158
7.10	Group Scores to Question 44	160
7.11	Group Scores to Question 45	161
7.12	Group Scores to Question 46	162
7.13	Group Scores to Question 47	163
7.14	Group Scores to Question 48	163
7.15	History Taking Competence of Subordinate Staff as Evaluated by Physicians	165
7.16	Counselling Competence of Subordinate Staff as Evaluated by Physicians	166
7.17	Clinical Procedures Competence of Subordinate Staff as Evaluated by Physicians	167
7.18	Follow-up Competence of Subordinate Staff as Evaluated by Physicians	168
8.1	Satisfaction with University Education versus Motivation Value Scores	179
8.2	Job Fulfillment Index Versus Motivation Value Scores	180
8.3	Job Fulfillment Versus Education Satisfaction	181
8.4	Satisfaction Mean Scores Versus Motivation Value Scores	183
8.5	Dissatisfaction Mean Scores Versus Motivation Value Scores	183
8.6	Diagram Illustrating Minia Group	184
8.7	Diagram Illustrating Cairo Group	184
8.8	Diagram Illustrating Menoufia Group	184

ACKNOWLEDGEMENTS

The completion of this study has been a long journey. Many people have guided and helped in diverse ways. To the following I express my deepest gratitude:

To Dr. Robert Ferguson, for his encouragement and guidance throughout this research, in spite of seemingly insurmountable odds.

To Mary Kamenicky, who guided my childhood and developed the potential to learn.

To Dr. Ezzat El-Mehairy, who grew to understand that 'a woman's place' is to serve humanity, for his patient assistance in translating volumes of Arabic into English and his invaluable criticisms on the final text.

To Dr. Mark Kennedy, for his helpful criticisms and especially his faith in my efforts.

To those Professors who laid the foundation for the pursuit of knowledge, Dr. Nicholas Ciaccio, Dr. Cynthia Nelson, and Dr. Frank Blanning.

To Professor Lorraine Baric' for her criticisms and special efforts.

To Dr. Salah El-Sayed and Ms. Soraya Hamdan for prompting me to do the initial pilot study which formed the embryo of this work.

To Dr. Mohi Hussein for his special encouragement and granting me permission to use his value scales.

To Dr. Saad Gadalla special acknowledgement for the role he played.

To my informant who must remain anonymous for providing relevant insights into the problems of rural health service as a young physician sees them.

To the many anonymous respondents who provided the information and insights included herein.

To the Ford Foundation for providing a fellowship to attend Workshop '78, "Planning Management Systems for Programme Coordination and Control" which provided additional knowledge in the management of rural health services.

To the Smithsonian Institution, Washington, D.C., for financial assistance which provided me with a year of study unburdened with financial concerns.

To Dr. Saad Nagi, Dr. Kamel El-Zayat, Dr. E. Valsan, Dr. Amr Mortagi, Ms. Zena Thomas, Ms. Samira Shehata, Dr. Nabil El-Mehairy, and Dr. Nadia Mowaffi, my special acknowledgement.

ABSTRACT

The Egyptian Government is attempting to improve the Health of the Population. One way to do this would be to provide bulk health care services. Official views of weakness in the health care services include the notion that disaffection of medical personnel is a source of service inefficiency.

The present study attempts to document such disaffection by studying the job orientation of four groups of medical personnel.

(a) A group of male and female practising physicians in rural Upper Egypt.
(b) A group of male and female practising physicians in rural Lower Egypt.
(c) A group of male and female practising physicians in the urban setting of Cairo.
(d) A group of male and female medical students in training.

In the light of disaffections uncovered some suggestions are made for improved administrative and professional cooperation in directed activity towards improvement of the health care system.

CHAPTER ONE

INTRODUCTION AND AIMS OF STUDY

"The Conference strongly reaffirms that health, which is a state of complete physical, mental and social well-being, and not merely the absence of disease or infirmity, is a fundamental human right and that the *attainment of the highest possible level of health is a most important world wide social goal* whose realization requires the action of many other social and economic sectors in addition to the health sector." [1]

Since the meeting of the WHO in the optimistic founding years of the United Nations, many cosmic statements about the desirability of good health as a human right have appeared. The above example from a WHO conference in the USSR in 1978 is a typical quotation of those years.

The health status of hundreds of millions of people of the world today is inadequate, especially in developing countries. More than half the population of the world does not have the benefit of proper health care. [2] These problems will not be solved merely by providing additional resources or by repeating existing patterns and types of solutions. For example, urban patterns of health service will not solve rural problems, and ideas derived from a developed country are unlikely to be appropriate for developing countries. Research should make it possible to avoid the expense of proceeding by trial and error and the process of change must be a deliberate one and cannot be left to chance. Therefore, the problems of management of health services should not be viewed in isolation, but as an integral part of the social and political, cultural and economic conditions of the country. [3]

The following text developed out of a pilot study that was executed in Menoufia Governorate, Egypt, at rural health units in which doctors function as Unit Administrators. [4]

Rural Health Units were selected for the original study since these units provide a unique administrative experience. In Menoufia there are 134 health units serving 302 villages and a population of 1.7 million. Administratively, the doctor is in charge of the rural health unit. Because of the pressing need to improve Egypt's health services it was felt that a functional analysis of this group would have relevance not only for this specific group but would also provide indicators for Egypt's Health Services as a whole.

According to 1975 basic statistical information of health services, there were 23,501 physicians on the Medical Registers (1/1/1974), 13,103 are employed by the Ministry of Health. There are 6.51 Ministry of Health physicians per 10,000 population (1536 population per physician). Egypt has 445 beds per 10,000 population in the urban areas and 0.4 beds per 10,000 population in the rural areas. [5] The inequity is scarcely credible.

Most of the Near East and other developing countries have established western type medical schools in which to train their physicians. However, because of the health planners' specialized concern with medicine in the narrow sense and their eagerness to replicate western medical education and health care delivery systems, they tend to overlook the social framework context in which these take place. [6] This study is an attempt to identify some elements of this social framework as they impinge on the physician's functioning in the day to day practice of his occupation.

Overview of the Study

The model for procedure was essentially the classical social science method of asking questions of the population studied. The sampling technique will be described later (see methodology) as well as the construction and administration of the questionnaire. In its own modest way it follows the well beaten track of the established ethnographic studies of the 50's of various occupational groups and highlight certain aspects of their interaction with other facets of the social structure. [7, 8] The methodology varied in the sense that enquiry was by structured questionnaire rather than by case study or participant observation mainly for the reason that the project was encouraged by the Egyptian Administrators in the Ministry of Health and they suggested that the sample should be as large a representation as could be obtained. The writer has previously published a report on some elements of the rural doctor's role and function in Menoufia and the questionnaire used then was taken as a basis for the present investigation. As a result of a problem oriented conference with staff members of the central office of the Ministry of Health and social scientists working at the American University in Cairo, certain other areas of concern were identified and included in the questionnaire (dealt with more fully in Chapter VI) and in particular a section was added on personality factors, mainly social attitudes, which the conference held to be significant, at least putatively. It so happened that there already existed a well validated value orientation scale of Hussein specifically applicable to the Egyptian case (See Chapter VI). [9] The results are presented in Chapter VII and VIII as a series of tables derived from the questionnaires and the discussion follows in Chapter VII. Four factors in particular are considered to be worthy of reasonably extended treatment on account of their prominance.

Chapters I-V are introductory in that they set the broad background against which the present investigation is to be seen. The health of the Third World, judged by widely available morbidity and mortality statistics, is clearly disadvantaged by comparison with the industrialized societies.

Chapter II deals with the special problem of health care in the Third World and in particular the special case in Egypt. Chapter III deals with the operation of the practice of medicine in society generally and here the literature on the subject is mainly in western terms, but in the chapter the credibility of some social explanations of the medical role is questioned, the comparable case of the function of the traditional healers in other developing countries is considered, and subsequently the inter-relation between a western professional ethic and the native healers belief system, and the state of uncertainty that exists. The strain is not unrelated to some different interpretations of the status and functions of the professions in general in the West and in the Third World.

The character of medical education in Egypt is outlined in Chapter IV and the secondary socialization and anticipatory socialization processes that inhere there are seen in Chapter V to contribute significantly to the Egyptian doctor's self concept and his social construction of his role set. It is against this background that the questionnaire's relevance and significance may be understood. This research is offered as a contribution to the social administrative welfare problems of Egypt in particular the social psychological experiences of certain key health professionals.

Social Policy Background and Government Dilemmas

It was my good fortune to be invited to participate in a pre-workshop meeting with the Ministry of Health Administrators in which "Problems in delivering rural health services in Egypt" were defined.

The following group process is being presented here as an example of the "working reality" of the physician administrator. This event evolved as a result of a request to the faculty of the American University in Cairo, Social Science Department, to participate in a meeting with persons involved in the improvement of health delivery services at the Ministry of Health. I was invited to attend because of my ongoing study of the Egyptian physician. The rationale for including social scientists was to provide social science input into the programme, an element which was felt to be lacking by the consultants. There were five Egyptian Administrators present and two American Social Scientists in addition to the writer.

The Chairman and one of the American consultants briefed the American University (AUC) team on the project. The Chairman stated that investigations were currently under way at nine districts including those of Fayum, Beheira, Abnub and Itai el Barud to ascertain the feasibility of the project. If the experiments prove successful, they would be generalized to the Egyptian countryside.

The project is intended to reduce the death rate among children, provide child care in rural areas, curb hazards in the environment and make available ambulance service for rural health units. It is also designed to curb side-effects of childbirth among rural women and facilitate the formation of health groups at each of the project's medical centres. These groups will serve as a nucleus to increase medical awareness among villagers. The scope of this 5 year project would include 4 Governorates, 215 rural health centers, representing ten percent of Egypt's total population and 6,000 nurses.

The meeting commenced with the Chairman introducing the Egyptian participants and the American Consulting team. The three AUC participants were then introduced by the American Consultant who requested a brief self-biography from the AUC group. All meeting interaction was in English.

A John Hopkins University staff member from the American team assumed the role of leader in what was to be a "practice session" for a coming workshop. The participants of the meeting were to act as group leaders of 6-9 persons in the workshop.

The following interaction was identified as a "Nominal Group Process."

Van de Ven [10] states that this process has been used as a means of creative problem solving.[a]

There has been considerable research interest in the comparative effectiveness of individuals versus groups and nominal[b] versus interacting[c] group processes in decision situations which require subjects to generate information concerning a problem. Osborn, a major proponent of "brainstorming" techniques in problem-solving, posited "the average person can think up twice as many ideas when working with a group than when working alone." [11] When comparing the mean number of ideas produced by a group with the mean number of ideas produced by individuals, brainstorming groups were found superior to an equal number of individuals brainstorming independently. [12]

I realized that this would be an opportunity to elicit responses that normally may not be given on a one-to-one basis. This process appeared to releive any threat of being quoted. The atmosphere was tension free, and it was felt that the participants responded fully. The process of "writing down one's thoughts to be *read* back to the group later" may have also been in keeping with assisting those less verbally inclined. The participants were divided into two groups.

---

[a] Creativity in group problem-solving is defined as the reconceptualization of given information on a problem into multiple alternative solution combinations, and bringing a new idea or solution into being which has not existed before.

[b] The nominal group is defined as a group in which individuals work in the presence of others but do not verbally interact. Typically, some written output is obtained from each participant.

[c] The interacting group is defined as a group in which all communication acts take place between members with minimal controls or formal structuring.

Each member of the group was given five 5 × 8 inch size index cards and was instructed to write on the card responses to the statement "Problems in delivering health services to rural Egypt include." This statement was written on the board and the participants were requested to write everything that came to mind. Ten minutes time was given for this process.

Descriptions are the individual's representation of aspects of the real world, and, as such, there are complex relationships between these descriptions and the events they describe. [13]

We find that descriptions are significantly shaped by the individual's experience such as by the status to which he belongs, by the role behaviour engaged in, and that the individual's cognitive representations in turn, determine his behaviour in many ways. [14]

The following is a list provided by the participants. Each person stated one item from his/her card in turn. These items were recorded on a flip chart attached to the board:

Problems in Delivering Health Services to Rural Egypt Include:

1) Village culture and tradition
2) Providing for consumer differences in needs and perceptions
3) Physician dissatisfaction with role and compulsory nature of service
4) Lack of communications systems
5) Poor transportation system
6) Poor environmental sanitation in crowded villages
7) Training inappropriate to rural needs (basic and preservice)
8) Shortage of printed materials
9) Poor quality of supervision
10) Lack of attention to money provided for rural health in relation to other priorities
11) "Outsider" must relate to "insider"
12) Lack of personal motivation for rural areas
13) Poor maintenance
14) Lack of community participation—environmental and behavioural health problems
15) Data system which precludes cybernetic feedback
16) Poor continuous evaluation and feedback
17) Physician maldistribution
18) Under-utilization of services
19) Lack of compliance, especially in endemic diseases
20) Submission of inaccurate reports
21) Poor outreach, especially in small settlements
22) Cumbersome administration hierarchy (Ministry and Local Government)

23) Large population density
24) Inadequate input from the Ministry of Health (MOH) specialized units (i.e. follow-up in field and in-training programme manuals)
25) Inadequate prestige and low income (physicians)
26) Prestige of physician low among peers

After all suggestions had been proposed, participants were requested to discuss and eliminate any duplication of statements. No. 15, data system which precludes cybernetic feedback and No. 16, poor continuous evaluation and feedback were felt repetitive; therefore, No. 16 was eliminated.

It was interesting to note that the Egyptian respondents wanted to join No. 4 item and No. 5 item: lack of communication system and poor transportation system respectively. This was not disputed by the American participants. Perhaps it was felt that "communication" was done by means of "transportation" in view of the totally inadequate telephone communications systems or the feeling of hopelessness involved. Another plausible explanation may be the felt need for tangibles i.e. emergency vehicles. Indeed, it was observed that the Egyptian respondents tended to cite tangibles as priorities.

The participants were then asked to rank the items from 1-5 with the instruction "In your mind, what do you find as the most detrimental—this should be No. 1 priority. Think in terms of *root* cause."

The results appear in Tables 1.1 and 1.2.

Table 1.1

Ranking of the 26 items (Problems in Delevering Health Services to Rural Egypt Include) in order of priority

	1st.	2nd.	3rd.	4th.	5th.
Director of Rural Health Centers Ministry of Health, Dept. Rural Health	7	9	15	21	4
Retired Director of Statistical Dept., Ministry of Health (physician)	2	9	13	6	4
American Resident Consultant (Physician, Ph.D., Public Health)	21	14	6	7	9
Undersecretary of State	4	15	7	24	6
Former Director General of Rural Health	4	14	7	12	24
Director General of Health South Cairo province	4	12	10	15	9
American University Participant (Ph.D. Candidate)	18	24	3	23	14
American University Participant (Professor of Anthropology)	24	14	21	12	7
American Consultant (Short Term Data Analyst)	1	10	12	22	4

Table 1.2

Results by weighting the items (Problems in Delivering Health Services to Rural Egypt Include) as first priority-5 points, second priority-4 points, etc.

Item	Score (Points)	Total
1	5	5
2		0
3	3	3
4	1-1-5-5-5-1	18
5		0
6	2-3-1	6
7	5-2-3-3-1	14
8		0
9	4-4-1-1	10
10	3-4	7
11		0
12	5-2-5-2-3	17
13	3	3
14	4-4-1-4	13
15	3-4-2	9
16		0
17		0
18	5	5
19		0
20		0
21	2-5-3	10
22	2	2
23	2	2
24	2-1-4-5	12
25		0
26		0

SOCIAL ATTITUDES OF PERSONNEL

This item emerged as a prominent force in the views of the participants of the workshop. (See Table 1.2 item 12 "Lack of personal motivation for rural areas".) No discussion of the explanatory power of attitude sampling will be included here (but see page 259); suffice it to say that further items were added to the questionnaire to attempt to evaluate the significance of this proposition from the conference. The items were from Hussein's Value Orientation Scale and its validity and rationale will be discussed later (see Chapter VI). Its particular attraction lay in the fact that it was specifically designed and developed for use in Egypt (i.e. it is not imported from Western psychology).

REFERENCES

[1] Primary Health Care, *Report of the International Conference on Primary Health Care*, Alma-Ata, USSR 6-12 September 1978, World Health Organization, Geneva, 1978, p. 2.
[2] *Ibid.*, p. 2.

[3] El-Mehairy, T. M. 'Medical Doctors: Managerial Abilities and Role Definitions', *Middle East Management Review*, Vol. II, No. 1. 1978, pp. 121-137.
[4] *Ibid.*
[5] Ministry of Health, *Basic Statistical Information of Health Services*, The Medical Packing Co., Press, January, 1975.
[6] Pillsbury, B. L. K., *Traditional Health Care in the Near East* — Unpublished report prepared for the U.S. Agency for International Development, Washington, D.C., March 1978, Mimeograph, Introduction.
[7] Goldthorpe, J. H. 'Attitudes and Behaviour of Car Assembly Workers: A Deviant Case and a Theoretical Critique', *British Journal of Sociology*, Vol. XVII, No. 3, September 1966, pp. 227-240.
[8] Dennis, N., Henriques, F. and Slaughter, C., *Coal is Our Life*, Eyre and Spottiswoode, London, 1956.
[9] Hussein, M. E. A. — *The Specific Values of the Creative Person*, unpublished Ph.D. dissertation, Cairo University, Department of Psychology, 1978, p. 194, (in Arabic).
[10] Van de Ven, A. & Delbecq, A. — *Nominal and Interacting Group Processes for Committee Decision Making*, Unpublished training booklet, 1970.
[11] Osborn, A. F. *Applied Imagination*, (Revised Edition), Scribners, New York, 1957, pp. 228-229.
[12] Osborn, A. F., Hall, E. J., Mouton, J. S., and Blake, R. R., 'Group Problem-Solving Effectiveness Under Conditions of Pooling vs. Interaction', *Journal of Social Psychology* 59, 1963, pp. 147-157.
[13] Biddle, B., and Thomas, E. *Role Theory: Concepts and Research*, John Wiley & Sons, Inc., New York, 1966, pp. 149.
[14] *Ibid.*, p. 150.

CHAPTER TWO

MEDICINE AND HEALTH IN THE THIRD WORLD

Contrasting Approaches

Despite the traditional conservatism of the medical profession, several influential radical leaders such as the writer Frantz Fanon and the activist Che Guevara were physicians. In *The Wretched of the Earth*, Fanon, concludes with this plea:

> "Come, then, comrades; it would be as well to decide at once to change our ways. We must shake off the heavy darkness in which we were plunged and leave it behind ... We must leave our dreams and abandon our old beliefs and friendships of the time before life began. Let us waste no time in sterile litanies and nauseating mimicry ... The European game has finally ended; we must find something different. We today can do everything, so long as we do not imitate Europe, so long as we are not obsessed by the desire to catch up with Europe ... Yet it is very true that we need a model, and that we want blueprints and examples ... European achievements, European techniques and the European style ought no longer to tempt us and to throw us off our balance ... But if we want humanity to advance a step further, if we want to bring it up to a different level than that which Europe has shown it, then we must invent and we must make new discoveries. If we wish to live up to our peoples' expectations, we must seek the response elsewhere than in Europe ... For Europe, for ourselves and for humanity, comrades, we must turn over a new leaf, we must work out new concepts, and try to set afoot a new man." [1]

Fanon's statement makes one wonder if the "Western" model is the right path for the peoples of the Third World. These following pages will discuss medicine and its problems in the developing world.

We will then examine the Egyptian case in relation to the concerns of Egypt in transition, industrializing, growing ... Egypt with the influx of foreigners, foreign goods, foreign ideas which are generating upheavals and strains as she clings to tradition, clothed in the *milaʾyeh*[a] of Islam.

Navarro's extensive analysis of medical systems, claims that underdevelopment, and uneven distribution of resources inside and outside the health sector, is not due to the absence of cultural and technologic diffusion from developed to developing countries, nor the scarcity of capital in poor nations or the presence of dual economies in underdeveloped countries, i.e. the urban-entrepreneurial economy and the rural primitive economy. Underdevelop-

---

[a] *Milaʾyeh* is the traditional black covering worn by many women in lower socioeconomic group.

ment, he states, and the concomitant maldistribution of resources is caused precisely because of the existence of the cultural, technologic, and economic dependency of developing countries, and economic and political control of resources by specific interests and social groups which bring about dual economies in those countries. [2] In his analysis, Navarro is giving prime consideration to Latin America. He finds that there exists a very heavy diffusion of cultural values from developed to developing countries and postulates that this diffusion is more harmful than beneficial to the process of development.

In a study of Western medicine in a Tamil Village, Djurfeldt and Lindberg attempt to demonstrate that the health situation in the village is a consequence of the prevailing economic and political order and the health problems cannot be solved by means of medical technology. They attempt to demonstrate the impotence of Western (or "allopathic") technology by comparing it with the already existing ("indigenous") health services in the village and conclude that both are equally inefficient in dealing with the health situation. They state, "Only a profound transformation of the economic and political structure can give the people of Thaiyur the means to improve their own health." [3]

One is prompted to ask if it is the exchange of ideas, i.e. the diffusion of cultural values from the developed to developing countries, which is harmful or rather the blind submission in toto to this exchange. Another argument advanced by Illich, well known for his misgivings concerning the so called "good life" of contemporary developed industrial societies, has indicated that this technology which is foreign to the climate of underdevelopment, can harm more than benefit the process of development, and that the labour-saving technology of developed society actually creates unemployment in the underdeveloped society. [4] There is therefore a double edged weapon. Do we withhold advanced technology and modern equipment from developing nations and keep them backward or do we *guide* them to "pick and choose" that which seems to be right for them? It appears dangerous to devise solutions encompassing all of the Third world developing nations with a single analysis. Rather, the method should be to search for the historical, political, economic, and religious patterns of *each* nation. This is what will be attempted in the case of Egypt as a background for the physicians practicing medicine within this environment. However, let us review some of the general problems of Third World medicine as well as some of their successes before returning to Egypt.

Imperialism of Western Medicine

There are many obstacles to providing better health care. According to Bryant, some of these obstacles, such as the scarcity of resources, are beyond our influence. He states, "Others might be influenced, but our capability for doing so is often blunted by tradition, professional self-interest, and lack of creativity." [5] What is this "professional self-interest" in terms of the expatriate assisting a developing country? How does it hinder the work: What are his/her motivations—material gain, ethical altruism or some kind of cosmic curiosity about the way others live?

It is important to critically analyze and honestly scrutinize the underlying beliefs and attitudes that determine what we do when we proselytize in advocating change. [6] Historically, the western governments undertook international health work to protect *their* people from exotic diseases. In order to protect international trade it was necessary to contain the spread of epidemic diseases along crowded travel routes. The increased speed of transportation stimulated international commerce and with it epidemic diseases. Massive measures for quarantine at national borders became a high priority. After World War II, the World Health Organization assumed the international quarantine responsibilities of the League of Nations' Health Office which, in turn, had originated in the experience of the office of International Sanitary Conferences and the Pan American Sanitary Bureau. [7]

Less explicit justification than the protection of Western travellers is the hope of political and economic benefit from foreign aid, directly in the sense of 'alignment' and also indirectly as a significant influence on the voting behaviour in the U.N. and not at least, most traditional of all, health care can be viewed as a tempting benefit in the politics of religious expansionism and missionary zeal, in the sense of having the longest history.

In addition, multinational corporations naturally have become involved in developing health services where they have major facilities from the sheer need to maintain a healthy work force. At the personal level, overseas work is viewed as interesting and exciting; tax free benefits and an easy life style are not unwelcome accompaniments. [8] A critical form of exploitation is the brain-drain of Third World physicians which leads to subtle pressures also resulting in the imposition of inappropriate patterns of medical care. [9] These include Western educational systems and modern urban hospitals designed by Western experts which often do not suit the indigenous needs but become "prestige" hospitals. Navarro [10] cites that the medical "aid" to Latin American hospitals has largely been focused on teaching hospitals, perpetuating the pattern of production that benefits the consumption of the donor country and those groups in the recipient country that Frank calls the lumpen-bourgeoisie. (By lumpen-bourgeoisie is meant those domestic social groups in underdeveloped societies that control most of the wealth of their society and who, at the same time, have identical interests to those of foreign industry and commerce. The expression "lumpen" is added to term bourgeoisie because their economic, social, and political power is dependent on the power of the bourgeoisie of the metropolis.) [11]

Disquiet has been expressed concerning the production of large numbers of conventially trained physicians. Basch, for example, writes as follows:

> It is economically impossible to produce enough physicians. The cost of training a doctor to international standards is often higher in poor countries than in wealthier ones; maintenance of faculties and physical facilities is extremely expensive.
>
> After physicians are trained it is often so difficult, if not impossible, to employ them properly in their home countries that large numbers join the "brain drain" and migrate, often permanently, to developed countries. It seems paradoxical that where the proportion of doctors in the population is very low by world standards, there may still be an excess relative to the nation's economic capacity to absorb them. This is true in the major developing countries of origin ("donor countries") of physician migrants: India, Iran, Pakistan, the Philippines, South Korea, and elsewhere, to a greater or lesser extent.
>
> The conventional medical school curriculum in more advanced countries is simply not applicable to the needs of less developed countries. The most telling arguments against the production of more physicians in these settings is their irrelevancy. In recent years a crescendo of criticism has arisen over the common policy in less developed countries of training physicians to provide sophisticated, hospital-based medical care to a population in need of the basic amenities of modern civilization. [12]

Yet another form of exploitation is created by the drug industries who continue to "dump" drugs which have been pulled off the market in developed nations. This is in addition to over-the-counter sale of prescription type medications which sometimes contain noxious substances. The drug industries generally have subsidiaries in developing countries which manufacture the medications; however, profit sharing is usually with Western pharmaceutical companies.[b]

It is not claimed that all persons or governments from "developed nations" are motivated by the above; however, it is imperative that we become aware of these issues facing the exploited Third World. What is needed is social justice and equitable distribution by making access to health care generally available as a human right, implementing the new concept of primary health care to achieve the general goal set by WHO of providing access to "health care for all by the year 2000". [13] This will require changes in many conventional attitudes toward health care provision, not the least in those concerning the education of health professionals. In addition, there are complex interrelationships between health and other socioeconomic factors—its interaction with education, nutrition, and population growth are prime examples. [14]

The notion that the design of health care in the Third World presents new and unique problems for which no ready made solutions exist has been argued

---

[b] The issue of artificial baby milk as the "Third World Poison" could be included in this category.

by King in the following four provisos: That medical care in developing countries differs sharply from medical care in the industrial ones, that its main determinant is poverty of resources than warm climate, that it is a subject of the greatest importance, and that it is possible to gather together a certain body of knowledge as to how this challenge is best met. [15]

That medical care in developing countries differs sharply from medical care in industrial ones is often not appreciated or understood by governments in developing countries in selecting objectives of health expenditures in terms of consumption and investment. The administrative framework for making decisions is usually fragmented, the data base is deficient, and specific measures are seldom evaluated for cost-effectiveness. [16]

These policies are not only inefficient but also inequitable since large numbers of people living in the countryside or city slums often remain beyond the reach of the modern medical sector.

Government expenditures on health in low-income countries seldom exceed 2 percent of GNP. Of the 65 developing countries documented by the World Bank 1975 policy paper, the governments of 17 countries make health outlays that are less than one dollar per capita, and the average outlay for the very poor countries with a per capita income of under 100 dollars is only 87 cents. [17]

Other problems include: Lack of clear national health policies and poor linkage of health service systems with other components of national development, lack of clear priorities and uneven allocation of resources, opposition to changes in the social aspects of health policy, inadequate community involvement in providing health care and inappropriate training of health personnel. [18, 19]

There is abundant evidence that problems of resources including inadequacy and maldistribution of resources for health services in addition to nonutilization of actual and potential resources often reflects such factors as the attitudes of health personnel, disregard of traditional systems and roles, insufficient awareness of the need for community information, physical and social inaccessibility, and poor transport; additional factors to be taken into account are the restricted use of primary health workers for preventive measures, a large number of medical procedures do not require extensive professional training, and the rising cost of health services including education. [20]

Poverty rather than warm climate is a major determinant in health problems of the Third World. [21] Extremely limited resources, poor communications, vast distances, individual and community poverty, and lack of education act and react upon one another in such a way as to maintain the developing countries in a perpetual state of poverty. These are manifested in the low labour productivity, low national product and a low average income per person. Life is beset with problems caused by insufficient or faulty food intake, poor housing conditions, poor health, inadequate public and private provision for medical care, insufficient communication, transport, and educational facilities. [22]

The complexity of these problems is demonstrated in an analysis of a comprehensive nutrition survey of low income families in Calcutta which shows that the nutrition of all age groups improves with rising income. Although the nutrient-income elasticities for young infants are higher than for adults, this does not mean that infant undernutrition is resolved with improvement in income. Rather, the opposite may be true if it is assumed that higher incomes are achieved partly through the mother working with the consequent partial sacrifice of breastfeeding. In fact, the study shows that the marginal propensity of spending on infants diets from additional family income is extremely low, of the order of 5 percent, but calculations about the loss of breastfeeding and the cost of replacing the equivalent nutrients indicates that about 50 percent of the mother's earnings would need to be spent for the maintenance of the infants nutritional health. [23]

Another problem seldom dealt with is that which we will call here negative foreign aid. Some developed nations in their attempt to carry favour with developing nations have created a condition of "aiditis", by literally pouring funds into a country. This phenomenon needs careful examination inasmuch as it exacerbates negative trends within a developing nation. Professionals become over-eager to carry out their favoured research projects, unnecessary to the common good, such as repeating research which has already been done locally or internationally and preparing bibliographies which would only be useful for a few but would provide recognition for the author. An example of repeated research could be the desire of some professionals to "prove the safety" of a birth control device, such as the Copper T with the Silver cord. This intra uterine device has been carefully screened abroad and the pecularities of native women such as liver disease, anemia, or malnutrition would not increase the side effects to any greater degree than any other intra uterine device. However, the use of any steroid would and should require additional research to ascertain its safety as they interact with the above mentioned peculiarities.

As foreign aid flows, so also does greed and those nations "flooding the market" should think twice of the long term effects of any foreign aid. Questions must be asked as to the long term effectiveness of any project, especially in relation to *real aid* to the indigent patient rather than ego-building of local professionals, social scientists and indeed physicians.

Another symptom of "aiditis" is the tendency to reject "aid-in-kind" (sometimes representing millions of dollars), which would assist many to "funds-in-hand" which would aid only a few professionals, providing needless research.

This in turn, creates the status symbol of 'research funds accumulated', petty jealousies, bickering, and the tendency to torpedo a colleague's project. When this situation exists, health projects especially in the field of family planning, will not grow and self-aggrandisement will gnaw away the corners of development.

INESCAPABILITY OF COMPROMISE

That these problems are of the greatest importance, there can be no doubt. The solutions will only be met by gathering together a body of knowledge as to how this challenge is to be met, says King. [24] Hetzel asserts that there is a world-wide movement characterized by community initiatives. These initiatives include basic health care as part of over-all community development. [25]

A series of examples of basic health care has been published in an important monograph edited by V. Djukanovic and E. P. Mach. In this study it was demonstrated that the greater the participation of the community in the development of primary health care services, the greater the motivation to accept and use these services; and with greater acceptance and use of such services, there was less need for expensive curative care. These case studies include the following: [26]

In Bangladesh, where much of the terrain is waterlogged and communications are difficult, a simple system of health care delivery demonstrated in the Savar project provides a good example of a training programme for school and college student volunteers to provide preventive and curative services to rural populations in their own villages. It was shown that adult education and vocational training programmes can be incorporated in a project that both improves health education and helps to increase the per capita income.

For China, the mobilization of the masses has been the main technique for growth and development, and in health care this has meant the broadest involvement of people at every level of society in movements such as the Patriotic Health Campaign, the recruitment of barefoot doctors and the mobilization of the individual to "fight against his own disease".

The basic principle learned from the Chinese experience is emphasis on self-reliance, on brief training and structured part-time use of locally recruited and locally trained people and on the combination of modern and traditional medicine, and on preventive medicine.

Tanzania is one of the 25 countries with the lowest per capita gross national product in the world and a colonial past. In accordance with the 1967 Arusha Declaration, which forms the basis of Tanzania's current health policy, self-reliance was stressed. Village health posts and dispensaries are constructed by the villagers themselves, the Government providing the necessary materials and equipment. Rural health centers are being staffed with primary health workers: medical assistants, rural medical aides and health auxiliaries. The use of the above rural health workers contributes to the equitable distribution of primary health care. In addition, the students in the medical faculty of the University of Dar es Salaam must spend at least 22 weeks in communities doing field work.

Cuba's experience in the health field derives from the transformation of its socioeconomic political structure after the revolution in 1959. Prior to that time there was an absence of a national health system. Today Cuba has a health service system accessible and available to practically 100 percent of the population, with a referral system ensuring the appropriate level of care for each patient. The factors contributing to Cuba's success have been extremely high motivation of the health services, complete literacy, a high proportion of doctors and other health professional staff, good transport facilities, *mass mobilization and full participation of the people.* [27]

The U.S.S.R. has one of the world's highest ratios of physicians to population, however, the training of feldshers continues at a rate equal to that of new doctors. The primary role of the feldshers are to *complement* physicians in both urban and rural practice. There are three levels of feldshers: the general, midwife, and sanitarian feldshers who take a 2" year course; the laborant, nurse, dental technician, and pharmacist feldshers with 1 year and 10 months of training; and the "dental doctor" with 2 years and 10 months training. Their functions and training have been documented by Storey. [28]

Most of the causes of morbidity and mortality in less developed countries can be recognized and managed at the local community level by personnel with one to two years' training based on a completed primary education. [29]

A series of examples of community involvement in basic health care is presently being studied to try to determine what factors are responsible for community motivation and organization. These case studies include the following as cited in the WHO Chronicle for March 1977. [30] The examples, taken from all corners of the world, give hope for improvements in health in developing nations.

In Botswana, the case study was concerned with community participation, which began with the building of a primary school at Mochudi in the early 1920's; since then a pattern of community involvement in education, communications, and agriculture, has continued.

In Costa Rica, the case study was about community participation in development projects (including primary health care) in the canton of San Carlos.

In Indonesia, it was concerned with community participation through 'gotongroyong' (the practice of mutual self-help) in developmental activities in two villages, Balongmasin (in East Java) and Nglebak (in Central Java).

In Mexico, the case study was about a programme for stimulating and coordinating socioeconomic and health development in the Chiapas highlands, where road building, bringing piped water, and promoting primary health care are being carried out by the use of local volunteers.

In Senegal, the case study was concerned with activities in the region of Thies, where the people have constructed and are operating (on a self-help basis) rural maternity centres, village dispensaries, and nutrition rehabilitation centres.

In the Socialist Republic of Vietnam, the case study was concerned with the solution of health problems by community participation, as illustrated by descriptions of three villages, Quang An, Dong Tien, and Tan Ly.

In Sri Lanka, the case study was concerned with the Sarvodaya (universal awakening) Shramadana (sharing of one's time, thought and energy for the benefit of all) movement which was initiated during the 1950s and has promoted a variety of activities (e.g. in agriculture and irrigation, preventive health work, co-operative farms, young settlement schemes, etc.) at village level throughout the country.

In Samoa, the case study was about the women's committees, which for more than 50 years in villages throughout the country have played an active role in providing health care.

In Yugoslavia, the case study was about the remarkable progress made in Ivanjica in improving the health services and other developmental activities with the help of the local community.

Another example is Niger where they have established village health workers with their village pharmacies chosen by the community and trained traditional birth attendants whose role was previously limited to burying the placenta and giving elementary care to the child and mother. The cost of training each attendant is about U.S. dollars 21 for 15 days including supplies and equipment. [31]

The illustrations mentioned fall into two major categories. On the one hand, there are nationally adopted programmes such as in the U.S.S.R., China, Cuba, and Tanzania; on the other, there are schemes covering more limited areas such as Bangladesh and Niger. What has characterized these successful national programmes is a strong political will that transformed a practical methodology into a national endeavour, and a fundamental decision to accept substantial changes and initiate new procedures rather than looking for solutions within existing systems elsewhere i.e. the West.

Interpretations of successful patterns frequently reveals the significance of the emergence of an enthusiastic leader with local knowledge in association with local communities and organizations, such as has been the case in Ernakulan. [32]

The foregoing cases also illustrate the major shift from a curative to a curative-preventive approach from urban to rural populations and from the privileged to the underprivileged. Most of the cases have utilized King's general rule for employing the various members of the medical care team: "Push tasks down the pyramid to the humblest and cheapest cadre capable of doing (them) satisfactorily," [33] illustrating that a "deprofessionalization" of technology goes hand in hand with the use of primary health workers with limited task oriented training.

Having reviewed the problems and successes of other Third World countries, we now turn to the Egyptian case.

THE EGYPTIAN Case

The Health Care System

The Ministry of Health system has been selected for this study because it is the nominal provider of health care services to the roughly 32 million Egyptians who have annual per capita incomes of less than L.E. 150.[c] The government structure is relevant to administration of the Ministry of Health system. Egypt is divided into 25 governorates, each with a governor appointed by the President and an elected Governorate Council. The governorates are divided into 132 districts that are subdivided into 755 official villages. There are a total of about 4,000 separate village communities in Egypt. Twenty-one of the twenty-five Governorates are classified as rural and four as urban (Cairo, Alexandria, Port Said, and Suez). Within each rural governorate, communities are designated as urban or rural. In November 1976, the 36.5 million resident citizens of Egypt were classified as 44 percent urban and 56 percent rural. [34]

There are separate health care systems within the Egyptian health delivery system. The minister of health, appointed by the president of Egypt, serves a term which rarely exceeds three years because of the demands of the post and obligations which ultimately require that he restricts his private practice. The seven major departments of the Ministry which include Administrative and Financial Affairs, Pharmaceutical Affairs, Dental Affairs, Specialized (Hospital) and Emergency Medical Care, Control of Endemic Diseases and Basic Health Services, Preventive Affairs, Central Ministry Service, are each headed by a physician considered a tenured civil servant holding the title of Under Secretary. This central organization is essentially replicated at the governorate level. A director general for health is jointly appointed by the governor and the minister of health, but is held accountable to the Minister.

---

[c] 1.50 Egyptian Pounds = 1.00 Pound Sterling.

The government, in an attempt to assure that the people of Egypt have access to comprehensive health care services, operates a national health care system that provides services to the population for a nominal registration fee per contact. The seeds for this expansive health service network were planted during the Nasser regime following the 1952 Egyptian Revolution which entitled all Egyptians to both free education and health services.

The Ministry of Health in Cairo today supervises the operation of a system which includes: [35]

1. Almost 2,300 rural health facilities, about 1,700 of which are ambulatory care units, the rest are centers and small hospitals with 10 to 40 beds, as well as outpatient clinics;
2. In urban areas, about 220 maternal and child health centers, 300 health offices (usually responsible only for birth registration, food inspection, and immunizations), 200 school health units and hospitals, and over 100 general ambulatory care health centers and multi-speciality clinics;
3. Over 350 general and speciality hospitals, usually with large outpatient facilities, located in major cities.

The Ministry of Education has teaching hospitals within nine medical schools which provide a full range of secondary and tertiary care services, and outpatient care. These hospitals are under the administration of the medical school deans, the universities, and the Ministry of Education. The research institutes of the Ministry of Health also provide limited inpatient and outpatient health care services on a referral basis. However, throughout the rest of the system, there are no referral requirements; and an Egyptian can request health care at any government facility he chooses.

Another health care system, a health maintenance type of organization regulated by the Ministry of Health, The Egyptian Health Insurance Organization, provides comprehensive health services to about 1,200,000 employed Egyptians. This organization operates an ambulatory care clinic system and ten hospitals with inpatient care only. It has a strict well-defined referral system which excludes spouses and children. [36] There are also separate health care systems for military personnel, police, and employees of the Ministry of Transportation.

Private health care facilities, not included in this system are used primarily by upper and middle income urban Egyptians. An estimated 75 to 80 percent of the active physicians in urban areas devote late afternoons and evenings to private, fee-for-service practice after their government job obligations in the Ministry of Health or Ministry of Education are met. Ministry of Health physicians assigned to rural areas are permitted to make home visits to patients for which they can charge tax-free fees. Small proprietary hospitals under a variety of ownership arrangements account for less than 5 percent of hospital beds in Egypt which serve the upper and middle class. The Cairo

Curative Organization and Alexandria Curative Organization operate eleven and five hospitals, respectively. These serve primarily as facilities for private patients but must also retain a number of beds for the indigent patient. This varied and complex system forms the backbone of Egypt's health care services.

Major Health Care Problems

Inasmuch as a major function of the rural physician is preventive medicine a brief review of the health status and problems in Egypt will now be presented. However, an in-depth discussion of these problems is considered beyond the scope of this thesis and is therefore, not provided here.

The crude death rate in Egypt in 1975 was reported to be about 12 per 1,000 persons, near the worldwide average. [37] Average life expectancy at birth in 1975 was about 55 years for females and 52 years for males. [38] Maternal mortality is about one death for every 1,000 births, roughly 15 times the rate in the United States. [39] The reported infant mortality of 116 per 1,000 live births, compared to the worldwide rate of 85, is believed to be lower than the actual rate, because of registration practices. The actual rate in some areas may be 180 or higher per 1,000 live births. [40]

Diseases of the digestive system are the leading cause of death, followed by diseases of the respiratory and circulatory systems. [41] Agespecific mortality rates suggest that more than half of infant deaths are from diarrheal illnesses. [42] Illnesses associated with the reproductive and related systems, digestive system, and accidents, poisoning and violence, in that order, account for almost two-thirds of the admissions to the Cairo University hospital system. [43]

Deaths from neoplastic and degenerative diseases are not as important as other causes of mortality. Deaths from heart disease were about 169 per 100,000 population in 1972, [44] as compared with 337 in the United States in 1976. [45] Cancer is reported to have accounted for about 22 deaths per 100,000 population in 1972, [46] compared with 176 in the United States in 1976. [47] However, because of the cultural reluctance to accept cancer this is most probably an underreported figure.

Infection and toxemia are reported to be among the leading causes of maternal deaths. Complications associated with childbirth are common in Egypt and at times leave residual damage to kidneys or reproductive organs. Anemia is also a frequent complication. [48]

Results of dietary studies showed that the average diet of low-income, nutritionally vulnerable groups—children under five and pregnant and lactating women—provided only 76 percent of recommended caloric allowances, [49] and that the average amount of protein in the diet of those groups was below the recommended allowances, and that only 11 percent of their protein was from animal sources. [50] Except for anemia among women, specific nutrient deficits among adults are not conspicuous. Although about half of rural farm labourers apparently suffer from secondary anemia as a result of heavy iron losses associated with schistosomiasis and hookworm infections, vitamin deficiency syndromes have not been recently reported. [51] Preliminary results from a 1978 nationwide survey of preschool nutritional status conducted by the Egyptian Nutrition Institute and the U.S. Center for Disease Control indicate that nearly half of surveyed children from low-income families exhibit mild and moderate forms of protein-calorie malnutrition as measured by weight-for-age, [52] while height-for-age data for the same group showed that about 20 percent have signs of chronic undernutrition. [53] Approximately sixteen percent of children under age two weigh less than 75 percent of American reference group medians. [54] A major factor in infant and preschool mortality and a leading cause of illness in the adult population are due to infectious diseases and their complications.

The estimated annual incidence of typhoid and paratyphoid fevers in 50 per 100,000 population; in Alexandria the incidence is estimated to be 150 per 100,000. [55] The incidence of cerebrospinal fever is estimated to be about 3 per 100,000 population yearly. [56] Streptococcal disease and rheumatic fever occur with an apparent frequency of five to six cases per 1,000 children yearly between the ages of 6 to 15 years. This is about three times the rate for the same age group in England and Europe. [57] Tuberculosis is a major problem in Egypt. There is a reported mortality rate of between 7 and 8 per 100,000 population. [58]

Leprosy has been known in Egypt for several thousand years. It is estimated to affect more than two persons per thousand population, or over 70,000 persons for the nation as a whole. [59] All types of hepatitis, A, B, non-A, non-B are reported to be present. The total annual occurence is estimated to be greater than 150 cases per 100,000 population. [60] Rabies is a persistent problem in Egypt. There are an estimated 2,000 cases per year in the country, all of which are fatal. [61] According to a recent study, trachoma and acute eye infections have left major visual disability in nearly five percent of the inhabitants of rural villages and between one and two percent of those in urban areas. [62] Poliomyelitis remains a problem in Egypt. Between 1971 and 1976, there were about 1,700 cases of paralytic polio per year in Egypt. [63] A study in early 1976 revealed that nearly one-half of paralytic polio patients had received no vaccine. [64] An epidemic of Rift Valley Fever occurred in the south east section of the Nile Delta in the fall of 1977. [65] It is feared that it may become endemic or enzootic in the country. [66] A major contributor to infant and preschool mortality in Egypt is measles. It has been identified as a cause of nearly two-thirds of deaths reported to be due to infectious and parasitic diseases in the one-to-four age group. [67]

The most important parasitosis in Egypt is schistosomiasis (bilharziasis). Present since the days of the Pharaohs, there are increasing numbers of Egyptians infected because of Egypt's population growth rate. It is reported that 80 percent of primary school children in some areas in Luxor are infected. [68] In some villages in the Nile Delta, S. Mansoni prevalance rates of up to 55 percent have been reported. [69] Eradication of schistosomiasis in Egypt does not seem possible with available technologies. Preventive measures such as immunization or massive behavioural change as was the case in China accompanied by widespread availability of potable water systems for the disposal of excreta, seem to be in the distant future. [70] Other parasitic diseases endemic in Egypt include Amebiasis and Giardia lamblia. Although malaria was once endemic, with several major epidemics prior to 1972, only 960 cases were reported during 1977. [71]

About 9,500,000 of Egypt's 38 million people are in its work force. [72] The reported national total of occupational accidents is 45,000 yearly. [73] Pesticide poisoning remains a problem. In a recent sample survey of agricultural workers results indicated that almost all had some evidence of chronic pesticide poisoning. [74]

Protection of the workers' health is a recognized responsibility of the Egyptian government. This is evidenced by the comprehensive laws and regulations and mechanisms for compensating workers who are injured. However, because of poor coordination the laws and regulations are not strictly enforced. In an effort to rectify these problems in 1977 a Ministry of Health Plan includes both short-term (1977-1978) and long-term (1978-1981) goals. [75]

Economic Constraints

In order to better understand the Egyptian case, a brief review of Egypt's current economic development status and prospects for the future will be presented. The per capita gross annual domestic product was about 228 dollars in Egypt in 1977. [76] A household expenditure survey executed in 1974-75 showed that the rural population had a per capita income about one-half that of the urban population (93 dollars versus 183 dollars). [77] Since the cost of living in rural areas is lower, the difference in real income is somewhat less. The lowest 40 percent of the people in the rural areas, in terms of per capita income, accounted for about 25 percent of the total income in those areas, whereas, the lowest 40 percent in the urban areas accounted for about 21 percent of the total income in those areas. However, this GNP might not be realistic since it is not broken down into classes and sections.[d] The current

---

[d] An interesting discussion on this issue appears in the 'A Discussion on Ray H. Elling's Paper', Raporter: Margaret MacKenzie, *Social Science and Medicine*, Vol. 12, Pergamon Press, Ltd., Great Britain, 1978, pp. 117-120.

five-year (1978-1982) Economic and Social Development Plan projects an increase in per capita gross domestic product to about 357 dollars in 1982. Counting assistance from foreign sources, about 28 percent of Egypt's gross national product over the five-year period is planned for investment, requiring substantial capital investments in both the industrial and agricultural sectors. [78]

In 1973 the open-door policy or *infitah* was developed. *Infitah* means much more than just liberalizing trade or restructuring the international economic relations of the country, although liberalizing trade in Egypt's case involves relinquishing import restrictions with no matching measures to help the country's exports, thus making the country more dependent on the outside world. It also means that Egypt seems to be heading towards a free enterprise system, dominated by world capitalism. [79]

Intensive efforts to build up industry began in the first part of the 19th century, but foreign powers forced Egypt to dismantle the state capitalist system of that period. In the second half of the 19th century this was completed. With the second half of the 20th century, Egypt was back again for almost two decades investing and developing state capitalism. However, now the current policy is to dismantle state capitalism. [80, 81]

Criticising Egypt's open-door policy, an Egyptian political scientist states:

> It seems that the declared rationale of *infitah* is at fault. The basic logic is that domestic savings are deficient and production techniques are backward, and hence that Egypt has to attract foreign capital which will bring in both financial resources and advanced technology. But that is not a very convincing case to make for *infitah*. There is widespread official complaint that many of the loans the country has received are not being used. Also, the foreign investment projects of *infitah* are mainly in peripheral fields of activity, with very little linkage. *Furthermore, the control of whatever technology is brought in remains in foreign hands. What Egypt seems to be getting is some secondary productive activities, and not advanced technology*. [82] (Emphasis added.)

Contributing to the complexity of the situation, Egypt has an unemployment rate of only 2 percent. [83] However, this is perhaps an inaccurate figure because there is much disguised unemployment and underemployment as a result of government policy of assuring employment for graduates of universities and high technical institutes.

The demand for skilled labour in neighbouring Arab countries has resulted in large numbers of educated and trained Egyptians being employed outside Egypt. The 1976 census showed that about 1.43 million Egyptians or 14 percent of the labour force, were abroad that year. [84] However, remittances from citizens working abroad were estimated to be about 286 million dollars in 1977. [85] This vast emigration of trained manpower creates a policy dilemma for Egypt. How can Egypt meet this challenge? According to one physician-educator, reduction of students entering the faculty of medicine would produce "trained physicians" rather than semi-training due to large numbers. He also suggests that yearly "cost evaluations" of training physicians be made and physicians should be required to serve the people in rural or indigent areas for periods longer than the present mandatory year or repay the government for their cost of training. He also stated that they should also repay the government if they emigrate.[e]

The brain drain, according to one Egyptian woman social scientist, can be a solution of a kind. She states:

> "Immigration can be *solution to a problem existing in the receiving country*, such as the filling of essential positions, such as that of physicians in the United States. It can also be a solution for the problem of the person emigrating because he is seeking a better position for himself and fulfilling his professional identity. By providing himself among the other scholars of the world, he will render a service to his country by honoring its name. (Emphasis added) [86]

Clearly, there are many contrasting views to Egypt's problems, but the Egyptian government has its own solutions. The Egyptian five-year (1978-1982) plan calls for a number of reforms. [87] For example:

> Government jobs are to be changed from permanent "welfare" positions to positions in which satisfactory performance can be rewarded by reappointment and unsatisfactory performance punished by firing;
> The wage structure is to be re-evaluated and the system of tying wages to academic certificates is to be abolished in favor of wages geared to job requirements and productivity;
> Present education policies are to be re-evaluated to base academic offerings on the needs of the society, university enrollment is to be limited, and vocational training is to be promoted; and
> Public sector enterprises are to be given greater freedom to manage their own affairs and to retain more of the "profits" for improving the quality and efficiency of their operations without government interference; they are to be judged by results.

Thus, if such reforms are carried out, a major increase in productivity in all sectors, including health, is likely to be possible, *if the population increase is checked* and it is to this problem that we now turn.

Demographic Considerations

Egypt, like so many of the Third World societies has widespread pronatalist sentiment. This is based on a history of high infant mortality, and a religious view that procreation is an act of God. Reinforced by prior colonialization, some developing nations see fertility control as a means of the Western world

---

[e] Conversation with Dr. E. Ekiabi, professor of surgical medicine, El-Azhar University, March 10, 1980.

to emasculate the ex-colonial world in addition to the fact that children are seen as an additional labour force. This is aggravated by the problems of age structure where the "population pyramid" of expanding younger age cohorts creates a burden to the economy. Riesman, writing in *The Lonely Crowd* illustrates the pronatalist sentiments of some societies thus:

> "Indeed, the individual in some primitive societies is far more appreciated and respected than in some sectors of modern society. For the individual in a society dependent on tradition-direction has a well-defined functional relationship to other members of the group. If he is not killed off, he "belongs"—he is not "surplus", as the modern unemployed are surplus, nor is he expendable as the unskilled are expendable in modern society." [88]

In spite of the present regime's policy of educating all children from 6-12 years, the expanding population problem makes it difficult to keep pace and although the adult illiteracy rate has been reduced from 95 to 70 percent in the last 60 years, the absolute number of illiterates in Egypt has increased. [89]

The economic balance and the population growth has left the country with the debatable issues that perhaps fertility control and family planning is a waste of time and money and some policy makers see rapid economic growth, accompanied by regional integration and population redistribution, as the only viable approaches to "solving" the population problem of the forcasted population of 60 million inhabitants by the year 2000. [90]

It had been anticipated that the migrant workers and landless peasants were to be absorbed into the industrial sector. These aspirations have not totally materialized and the debates of heavy vs. light-industries, private vs. public sector, foreign vs. domestic investments continue. In addition, the migrant worker is displaced in the metropolis. Today about 44 percent of the Egyptian population lives in cities with more than 20,000 compared with 37.4 percent in 1960. [91]

In the past thirty years, the Egyptian population has doubled from approximately 19 million people in 1947 to over 38 million people in 1976. [92, 93] Although fertility rates have declined only modestly during the same period, general mortality rates were halved, primarily as a consequence of declines in infant and child mortality. [94] The population rose steadily until 1960 at an annual average rate of 2.38 percent per year and the rate remained relatively high (2.54) between the 1960 and 1966 census. [95] Preliminary results of the 1976 census indicate that the annual average rate of increased slowed to 2.31 between 1966 and 1976. [96]

Some of the factors which appear to be primarily responsible for continuing high fertility in Egypt include female illiteracy. About 71 percent of adult females are illiterate. [97] This restricts their participation in the country's cultural, political, and economic activities. The Egyptian social customs, and practices tend to encourage early and universal marriage and to be suspicious of the use of contraceptives. Because of the high rate of infant mortality, which has declined slowly in the last twenty years, a desire to replace the lost child remains a strong disincentive to limiting fertility.

Birth control, fertility rates and the management of population growth are obviously significant components of overall health policy. The physicians in rural health units as well as public hospitals play an important role in the family planning programme. It is with this important aspect of the physicians functions in mind that the present field study encompassed the self evaluation of the physicians role.

The crucial question of Islamic beliefs as well as traditional beliefs held by the physician plays an important influence in the manner in which he delivers health services. Does he/she believe family planning to be beyond the dominion of man and in God's hands?

The Culture of Islam

Undoubtedly Islam plays a dominant role in health; but what are the views of the developing professional male or female as they appear to be reasserting the values of traditionalism and fundamentalist views of religion, especially in the faculty of medicine where staircases and classrooms were segregated by the students (according to old Islamic traditions which segregated the sexes). We can view this phenomen as a revitalistic movement as they have occurred throughout history or we could view this movement as a search for identity in an otherwise rapidly changing society toward industrialization which the open-door policy and peace have helped to develop. But crucial questions to be answered in this study are their views and how they affect the development of the professional.

Mead emphasizing the need for a "careful knowledge of the culturally determined character structure of a given people includes religion as well as a knowledge of local region, class, occupational and ethnic origin, and politics." [98] Here we will examine the role of Islam in health. This relationship has long been recognized in the Middle East. For example, in Saudia Arabia the radio and telephone were made acceptable by first having verses of the Koran spoken over them. [99] In Lebanon the installation of a village pump for uncontaminated water was sanctioned in quotations from the Koran that "cleanliness was required from every faithful Moslem." [100] The Koran has been used to provide sanction for cooperation and land improvement [101] and in Egypt it is frequently cited in family planning programmes.

A century ago, Egypt as many other Muslim countries relied largely on therapies of Arabian medical traditions which was neither elitist nor alien to its environment. Avicenna, Rhazes Haly Abbas, Albacasis, and others learned from folk medicine and passed on to the less learned herbalists, midwives, apothecaries and barber surgeons lessons from their own experience as well as the theory and practice of the Greek and Indian systems.

The dialectical picture of human growth is a reflection of Koranic wisdom. The principle of fission is symbolized in the Koran in the emergence of the human pair from a 'Single Self' [102] and of fusion in the mixing of male and female fluids in the zygote. [103] Both strivings serve toward survival. Yet the instinct for 'balance' [104] and 'proportion' [105] given to man demands avoidance of excess, either in separation or in merger. The balance is upset by the 'covetous self' (nafs al-ammara). It seeks to expand by absorbing the necessary non-self, thus destroying the roots of its existence. The 'censuring self' (nafs al-lawamma) harshly rebukes the 'covetous self' and confines it to narrow and rigid boundaries. The 'tranquil self' (nafs al-mutmainna) makes peace by creating a different set of demands and new means of satisfaction, thus starting a new cycle in the spiral of growth. [106]

Sterility is not viewed as a personal failure in Islam and the Koran has specific advice in accepting the sterile state. "He leaves some barren as he wills, for Him belongs knowledge and power". [107] However, Muslim divorce law maintains sterility as grounds for divorce.

Breast feeding is regarded as the child's right according to the Koran and rural women as well as a great majority of urban women breast feed the "recommended" two years. In view of the above practice, research on steroid contraception use during lactation has been a major concern. This included trial use of Depo Medroxy Progestone Acetate (DPMA). It is for this reason that practices in contraception in more developed countries where breast feeding practices are of shorter duration can not be adopted without proper trials to find out if hormonal metabolites transmitted through breast milk have an adverse effect on the health and growth of the child. It is important that this tradition be reinforced rather than adopting methods of artificial feeding in programmes related to lowering the infant mortality rate.

Care of the aged, orphans, diet and burial regulations are all carefully expounded upon in the Koran. Koranic teachings provide patterns for physical as well as mental well being, from conception until death.

God must not be tempted and the proper observations of His rules must be kept as exemplified in the practices of an Egyptian surgeon who, according to his wife, "will not answer the phone regarding an ill patient if he has not showered or performed the proper absolutions following intercourse, eating pork, or having had an alcoholic drink. Nor will he visit the hospital prior to these absolutions, and surgery is prefaced with the prayer "In the name of God the merciful." In citing this example, it is felt that this is not a unique situation and that many physicians respond with a fear of God as well as the evil eye. Because of Islam's emphasis upon conduct, ritual and order, it provides a form of psychological security as well as an acceptance of the will of God. There is here no clear sighted uncomplicated devotion to the task in hand, no Benjamin Franklin like inner directedness, no hitching of the wagon to a single star, no whiff of the Protestant ethic. The Egyptian doctor's praxis is vitiated ab-orgine by ideological clashes which can never go away.

Philosophy of Health

The following is a brief overview and general description of folk beliefs and indigenous practitioners. This will assist the reader in better understanding of the cultural milieu and actually existing life philosophy as pertaining to the notion and practice of health and disease. Many studies describe these and other beliefs in great detail, some of which are listed in the following references. An excellent survey of these sources has been documented by Barbara Pillsbury in her report on Traditional Health Care in the Near East which has been a major source of information. [108]

Robert Redfield's concepts of little and great traditions which he used to describe the relationship between peasant culture and that of the larger society of which it is a subordinate part, can be useful in describing the relationship between peasant belief systems and Islamic theology.
Redfield states:

> In a civilization there is a great tradition of the reflective few, and there is a little tradition of the largely unreflective many. The great tradition is cultivated in schools or temples; the little tradition works itself out and keeps itself going in the lives of the unlettered in their village communities. The tradition of the philosopher, theologian and literary man is a tradition consciously cultivated and handed down; that of the little people is for the most part taken for granted and not submitted to much scrutiny or considered refinement and improvement. [109]

Perhaps the most essential philosophy underlying illness in Egypt is the belief that all things, good and bad are controlled by Allah. The ethos of predestination underlies these beliefs. Folk religious beliefs play an important role in the philosophical system underlying many health practices. Often, beliefs and acts referred to as "the religion" meaning formal religion, are in reality, not the precepts of formal Islam. Some of these beliefs are attributed to the hadith, or prophetic traditions, which are considered part of the formal structure. Perhaps the two most misconceptually accepted beliefs attributed to religion are the opposition to family planning practices and female circumcision.[f] The positive values placed on children, the care of the mother in old age

---

[f] Infibulation and clitoridectomy predates both Islam and Christianity. Many Moslems believe it is *Haram* (against the religion) not to have it performed. However, it is not prescribed in the Koran. In addition to the psychological traumas inflicted upon the "victims" of this procedure, urinary infections and birth traumas, are only a few of the many complications which may result.

and help on the farm, are positive motivators for increased fertility, rather than just religious beliefs.

Just as the beliefs in folk religion play an important role in health practices, the belief in supernatural non-human spirits usually referred to as *jinn* are believed to populate the world. Mentioned in the Koran, they are believed to possess the same characteristics as humans. These spirits may be good or evil, male or female and must be treated according to their demands. A *jinn* may cause its victim to become ill. The placation of these spirits is through the Zar ceremony. Women and children are thought to be most susceptible and individuals passing through a major life crisis such as childbirth.

Perhaps the most common belief held by both rural and urban Egyptian, the rich and the poor, the illiterate as well as the most educated and even long time foreign residents of Egypt is the evil eye called ʾ*ain il-hasud* or ʾ*ain il-wihshah*.

> The evil eye is a non-material, non-individualized power that can cause illness, accidents, debility, disability, and death as well as other misfortune. Its main characteristics have to do with anxieties over social relationships and with fear of envy. The evil eye is sometimes said to be an independent evil power that acts through certain people and in certain situations. It is also said that there are simply certain people whose look is evil. [110]

A major means of defence is wearing the color blue or a verse from the Koran (usually Ayet el Korsi). Gifts for the new born infant are often earrings of blue turquoise or a gold *moshaf* (charm with a Koranic verse), which is believed to protect the person against illness and misfortune caused by the evil eye. Often, census collectors find difficulty in collecting data because the rural people fear envy, a cause of the evil eye. It is also a reason for leaving a child unwashed with the hope of diverting envy. Little boys are sometimes dressed as girls or an ear lobe may be cut on the boy child in an attempt to avert the evil eye.

Other beliefs include *Musharara*, a pre-Islamic concept referring to an abnormal state of supernaturally caused harm. Some of the symptoms include: sterility, lactation failure, illness, wounds that refuse to heal, eye disease, and blindness. [111]

Rabt, a loss of sexual potency, is believed to be caused by sorcery. Cures are sought through traditional healers.

Indigenous Health Practitioners

The "village barber" (Halag Siha) historically played an important role as a traditional health official. [112, 113, 114, 115, 116, 117] He previously had the responsibility for registering births and deaths. His "professional" knowledge was passed down from father to son. Today the "village barber" is disappearing from the village scene as many of the villagers turn to more conventional treatment by antibiotics. However, they prescribe and administer herbal "folk cures" (*wasfāt baladiyya*), provide first aid treatment, give injections, and perform minor surgical procedures. They are sought for treatment of jaundice (hepatitis) in which case they iron (burn) the patient, usually on the arm. They also perform male circumcisions on both Muslim and Coptic boys. This is done amidst ritual and regarded as a religious event. [118, 119, 120] Islamic tradition dictates circumcision for all males.

The "village midwife" (Daya) is traditionally the woman who attend births in rural communities. As the health barber "inherits" his role from his father, likewise, the *daya* inherits her profession through the female line in her family. The *daya* provide prenatal care and supervise the labor and delivery. [121] A symbiotic relationship exists with the rural health units and the *daya* who refers difficult cases to the doctor. Efforts are currently being made to co-opt this "traditional healer" as an aid in family planning and to better train her to eliminate neonatal tetanus, a complication reported by several physicians. She also supervises the *sebou*, a celebration which takes place on the seventh day after childbirth.

Another important service is the "deflowering" of the new bride, a culturally important event in the villages. She is reported to "assist" the new bride if an "accident" has occurred by scratching the vaginal canal so that proof of the maiden's virginity may be secured.

Muslim Sheikhs and Coptic Saints are specialists in "supernaturally caused" illnesses. They may be male or female, and are respected by the rural peasant and urban poor for their religiosity and ability to diagnose (divine), treat and cure illness through knowledge and use of the Book. They are sometimes called upon in the villages for the dissolution of sorcery. This is what is often referred to as "witchcraft beliefs" by the physician. Women who are either sterile or neurotic generally seek out their services.

Another service performed by the *sheikhs* and saints is the making of amulets and charms to be worn, displayed at home, in an automobile, or on a donkey cart as a protection against the evil eye and other misfortunes such as accidents. [122, 123, 124]

Holy men or holy women's tombs are visited on Fridays (the Moslem holy day), by those seeking cures from sacred places believed to possess healing powers for female sterility or *afrit* 'possession'. The weekly Friday service (hadra) includes a religious trance ritual, a *zikr* in which much animated physical activity is permitted in an otherwise traditional society. [125, 126, 127]

The herbalist ('Atar') prescribes folk cures (wasfāt baladiyya). He is usually consulted for first resort treatment since his herbs and spices are used primarilly by women, many of whom are reluctant to expose themselves to a physician.

Elderly women (Sittat Kebar or Sittat Kibira) are often consulted for health advice and frequently act as a liaison between existing health facilities and the local women. The family planning services are beginning to use these women for bringing in candidates for family planning. Although *Sittat Kebar* usually does not ask for renumeration, the family planning programme does renumerate these people.

Bonesetters, "gipsy" Practitioners of Clitoridectomy and Zar Organizers are other indigenous health practitioners.

But a crucial question is how the patients view the government health service.

The Patients' Perspective

In a study on the attitudes of public opinion about health services in Egypt a number of complaints were voiced.[128] These complaints are presented here to provide insight into the actual conditions in the field as seen by the patient.

The following complaints concerning the governmental hospitals were mentioned:

1. The behaviour of the hospitals' staff is criticised by many persons. A repeated kind of complaint that pointed to the attitude of physicians, nurses and other para-medical personnel towards the patient was given.
2. A frequent complaint was the absence of physicians on call during working hours, a case taken by many people as an evidence to the carelessness of some physicians. This situation is more evident in reception rooms. In some cases the physicians are not available at the outpatient clinics, so the patients wait a long time till the arrival of the doctor.
3. Complaints mentioning the improper quantity and/or quality of the meals offered to the patients in hospitals were given.
4. Some complaints touched upon the situation of some hospital buildings, lodging facilities, sanitation and other service needs. Also the lack of beds in hospitals leads to the discontent of many patients with long waiting lists. This may lead to the discharge of some patients before they achieve complete cure.
5. There were a few complaints about the visit charges which should be paid by visitors to some hospitals in order to be allowed to visit. These fees are minimal and are used as an extra income to the service budgets in hospitals. This measure also serves to regulate the large number of visitors for each patient.
6. It was mentioned in some complaints that some physicians refer their private cases from their private clinics to the public hospitals and that they pay more attention to these patients than those admitted from the out-patient clinics.

The following complaints concerning the rural health services were mentioned:

1. Some beds in rural centres are not used.
2. Practitioners working at rural health units are not performing their work with complete competence. This may be due in some cases to their recent employment or lack of equipment and other facilities.

3. Some of the practioners are not found in their units during working hours. In some cases, also where the physician is absent, he is not replacd by another one within a reasonable period.
4. According to a recent permission, physicians are allowed to make benefit of home visits during the afternoon period. This led some people to have the belief that physicians have become careless about their essential free service, being attracted by the paid visits or afternoon clinics.
5. Some patients are not convinced in the validity or effectiveness given to them free in rual units.

The following were complaints about environmental health:

1. The problem of deficient sanitation, especially in large towns is a matter of common complaint. Many dangers may threaten the community as a result or a complication of lacking sanitation. For example the blowing-up of sewers may result in the dissimination of contageous diseases.
2. The increased incidence of flies and mosquitoes due to the accumulation of garbage and stagnant water in streets is a topic of repeated complaints.
3. Some foods and food stuffs are exposed in streets under no hygenic regulations. Besides being a source of infection, they form an optimal environment for the multiplication of flies.
4. Many foodhandlers do not follow the rules declared by the Ministry of Health to regulate and control food handling.
5. Sanitarians and other personnel assigned to inspect shops and factories are not sufficiently strict in their observations, thus many factories and shops can escape the health regulations.

The preceeding comments serve to illustrate some of the complex problems inherent within government service projects. These issues are examined sociologically in the following chapters.

REFERENCES

[1] Fanon, F. *The Wretched of the Earth*, Grove Press, Inc., New York, 1966, pp. 252-255. Quoted in Landy, D. *Culture Disease and Healing*, Macmillan Publishing Co., Inc., New York, 1977, p. 265.
[2] Navarro, V. *Medicine Under Capitalism*, Prodist, New York, 1976, pp. 3-32.
[3] Djurfeldt, G., Lindberg, S., *Pills Against Poverty*, Curzen Press, Sweeden, 1976, p. 17
[4] Illich, I. Outwitting the "developed" Nations, in Elling, R. H. (ed.) *National Health Care*, Aldine Atherton, Inc., Chicago, 1971, pp. 263-276.
[5] Bryant, J. *Health and the Developing World*, Cornell University Press, London, 1969, p. 311.
[6] Taylor, C. E. Changing Patterns in International Health: Motivation and Relationships, *American Journal of Public Health*, August 1979, Vol. 69, Number 8, pp. 803.
[7] Howard, J. N. *The Scientific Background of the International Sanitary Conference, 1851-1938*, Geneva WHO, 1975.
[8] Taylor, *op. cit.* pp. 805.
[9] Frankenberg, R. and Leeson, J. The Sociology of Health Dilemnas in the Post-Colonial World: Intermediate Technology and Medical Care in Zambia, Zaire, and China in De Kadt, E. and Williams, G. (ed.) *Sociology and Development*, Travistock Publications, London, 1974, p. 273.

[10] Navarro, *op. cit.* p. 13.
[11] Frank, A. G. 'Lumpen bourgeoisie and Lumpendevelopment: Dependence, Class, and Politics in Latin America', *Monthly Review Press*, New York and London, 1973, p. 5 cited by Navarro, *op. cit.* p. 13.
[12] Basch, P. F. *International Health*, Oxford University Press, New York, 1978, pp. 302-303.
[13] WHO/UNICEF, Report of World Conference on Primary Health Care at Alma Ata, Soviet Kazakhstan, September 1978.
[14] Bryant, *op. cit.* p. 312.
[15] King, M. (ed.) *Medical Care in Developing Countries*, Oxford University Press, London, 1966, pp. 1-7.
[16] World Bank Sector Policy Paper, Health, Washington, D.C., March 1975, p. 32-33.
[17] *Ibid.*, pp. 32-33.
[18] Djukanovic, V. and Mach, E. P. *Alternative Approaches to Meeting Basic Health Needs in Developing Countries*, WHO, Geneva, 1975, pp. 13-17.
[19] U.S. Department of Health, Education, and Welfare, Health: United States 1975, p. 120, 136. Cited in *The Organisation for Economic Co-operation and Development (OECD) Studies in Resource Allocation*, DePenses Publiques De Sante, Paris, July 1977, p. 46.
[20] Djukanovic, *op. cit.* pp. 13-17.
[21] King, *op. cit.* pp. 1-7.
[22] Djukanovic, *op. cit.* p. 10.
[23] Reutlinger, S. and Selowsky, M., *Malnutrition and Poverty*, Published for the World Bank, The John Hopkins University Press, Baltimore, No. 23, 1976, p. 4-5.
[24] King, *op. cit.*
[25] Hetzel, B. S. (ed.) *Basic Health Care in Developing Countries*, Oxford, Oxford University Press, New York, 1978, p. 9.
[26] Djukanovic, *op. cit.*
[27] Fernandez, A. F., 'The National Health System in Cuba in Newell, K. W. (ed.) *Health By the People*, World Health Organization, Geneva, 1975, pp. 13-29.
[28] Storey, S. B., 'The Soviet Feldsher as a Physician's Assistant', U.S. Department of Health Education, and Welfare, Public Health Service, National Institute of Health, DHEW Publication No. (NIH), pp. 42-58.
[29] Hetzel, *op. cit.* pp. 150-151.
[30] WHO Chronicle, March 1977, cited by Hetzel, *op. cit.* pp. 4-5.
[31] Fournier, G. and Djermakoye, I. A., 'Village Health Teams in Niger (Marad Department)', in Newell, *op. cit.* pp. 128-144.
[32] Valsan, E. H., 'Successes and Problems in Family Planning Administration: Experience in Two Districts of Kerala, India', *Studies in Family Planning*, The Population Council, New York, June, 1977, pp. 148-156.
[33] King, M., 'The Auxiliary—His Role and Training', *Journal of Tropical Medicine and Hygiene*, 73, 1970, pp. 336-346.
[34] Central Agency for Public Mobilization and Statistics, Arab Republic of Egypt: *Preliminary Results of 1976 Census*, Cairo, Table 4.
[35] Health in Egypt: Recommendations for U.S. Assistance Report, Institute of Medicine, National Academy of Sciences, Washington, D.C., January 1979.
[36] *Ibid.*
[37] Ministry of Health, Arab Republic of Egypt: *Basic Statistical Information of Health Services*, Cairo, July 1977, p. 3
[38] *Ibid.*
[39] Health in Egypt: Recommendations for U.S. Assistance Report, *op. cit.*
[40] Health in Egypt: Recommendations for U.S. Assistance Report, *op. cit.*
[41] Ministry of Health, *Basic Statistical Information of Health Services*, GOARE, July 1977.
[42] *Ibid.*
[43] Ministry of Health, GOARE, March 1978.
[44] World Health Organization: *World Health Statistics Annual*, Vol. I, *Vital Statistics and Causes of Death*, Geneva, 1976, p. 191.

[45] Health in Egypt: Recommendations for U.S. Assistance Report, *op. cit.*
[46] *World Health Statistics Annual, op. cit.*, Vol. I, p. 189.
[47] Health in Egypt: Recommendations for U.S. Assistance Report, *op. cit.*
[48] Ministry of Health, Arab Republic of Egypt: *A Proposal for a Community Based Integrated Family Planning and Maternal and Child Health Project*, Cairo, December 1977, Table 26, p. 103.
[49] Aly, H. 'Nutritional Problems in Egypt'. Paper presented at the Conference of the International Union of Nutrition Scientists, Cairo, Arab Republic of Egypt, May 1977, pp. 1-2.
[50] Shabander, S. and Mobarak, E. M., *et al. Malnutrition and the Health Care Delivery System in Egypt*, Ministry of Health, Arab Republic of Egypt and Cairo University, Cairo, 1977, p. 7.
[51] *A Proposal for a Community Based Integrated Family Planning and Maternal and Child Health Project, op. cit.* p. 34.
[52] Brink, E. 'Arab Republic of Egypt Nutrition Status Survey' (in draft), U.S. Center for Disease Control, Atlanta, Georgia, July 1978, p. 46.
[53] Ministry of Health, Arab Republic of Egypt: *Basic Statistical Information of Health Services, op. cit.* pp. 19-44.
[54] Ministry of Health, Arab Republic of Egypt: *Basic Statistical Information of Health Services, op. cit.* p. 46
[55] Akkad, A. M. 'Statistics and Epidemiology of Typhoid Fever', *Journal of the Egyptian Public Health Association*, Vol. XLV, No. 1 and 2, 1970.
[56] Health in Egypt: Recommendations for U.S. Assistance Report, *op. cit.*
[57] Health in Egypt: Recommendations for U.S. Assistance Report, *op. cit.*
[58] Wahdan, M. H., *et al.*, 'A Surveillance Study on Poliomyelitis in Alexandria', *The Journal of the Egyptian Public Health Association*, Vol. III, No. 5, 1977, pp. 305-316.
[59] Health in Egypt: Recommendations for U.S. Assistance Report, *op. cit.*
[60] Health in Egypt: Recommendations for U.S. Assistance Report, *op. cit.*
[61] Health in Egypt: Recommendations for U.S. Assistance Report, *op. cit.*
[62] University of Alexandria and University of California at San Francisco, *Endemic Trachoma in Egypt, a Persistant Public Health Problem*, Alexandria, undated.
[63] Virus Research, Training, and Production Center: *Annual Report for 1976*, Cairo, 1977.
[64] Health in Egypt: Recommendations for U.S. Assistance Report, *op. cit.*
[65] Health in Egypt: Recommendations for U.S. Assistance Report, *op. cit.*
[66] Abdel-Wahab, K. S., *et al.*, 'Rift Valley Fever in Egypt, 1978', *The Lancet*, 30 Sept., 1978, p. 745.
[67] Health in Egypt: Recommendations for U.S. Assistance Report, *op. cit.*
[68] Miller, F. 'Prevalence and Distribution of Schistosomiasis in Egypt: Part I. A Review', University of Michigan School of Public Health, Ann Arbor, March 1978.
[69] Alamy, M. A. and Cline, B., 'Prevalence and Intensity of Schistosoma Haematobium and S. Mansoni Infection in Qualyub, Egypt', *American Journal of Tropical Medicine and Hygiene*, Vol. 26, No. 3, May 1977, pp. 470-472.
[70] Warren, K. S. and Mahmoud, A. 'Targeted Mass Treatment: A New Approach to the Control of Schistosomiasis', *Transactions of the Association of American Physicians*, Vol. LXXXIX, 1976, pp. 195-204.
[71] Health in Egypt: Recommendations for U.S. Assistance Report, *op. cit.*
[72] World Bank: *Arab Republic of Egypt: Economic Management in a Period of Transition*, Washington, November 1977, Vol. II, Section 728.
[73] Health in Egypt: Recommendations for U.S. Assistance Report, *op. cit.*
[74] Health in Egypt: Recommendations for U.S. Assistance Report, *op. cit.*
[75] Ministry of Health, Arab Republic of Egypt: *Work Environment and the Health of the Working Class in Egypt*, Cairo, August 1977.
[76] Ministry of Planning, Arab Republic of Egypt: *Five-Year Plan (1978-1982), Vol. I, The General Strategy for Economic and Social Development*, Cairo, August 1977, p. 51.
[77] World Bank, *Arab Republic of Egypt: Economic Management in a Period of Transition*, Vol. 1, (Report No. 1815), Washington, D.C. November 1977, Annex 1.1

[78] Ministry of Planning, Arab Republic of Egypt: *Five-Year Plan, op. cit.*
[79] Khalek, G., 'The Open Door Policy in Egypt: A Search for Meaning, Interpretation and Implications' in Thompson, H. M. (ed.) *Cairo Papers in Social Science*, American University in Cairo Press, Cairo, Volume Two, Monograph Three, March 1979, pp. 74-97.
[80] Mustafa, A. A., 'The Breakdown in the Monopoly System in Egypt After 1840', in Holt, P. M. (ed.) *Political and Social Change in Modern Egypt*, London, Oxford University Press, 1968.
[81] Owen, R., 'Egypt and Europe: From French Expedition to British Occupation' in Owen, R. and Sutcliffe, (ed.) *Studies in the Theory of Imperialism*, London: Longman, Ltd., 1971.
[82] Khalek, *op. cit.* pp. 96-97.
[83] World Bank: *Arab Republic of Egypt: Economic Management in a Period of Transition, op. cit.* Section 4.74.
[84] Central Agency for Public Mobilization and Statistics, Arab Republic of Egypt, *Preliminary Results 1976 Census*, Cairo, November 1977, p. 5.
[85] Ministry of Planning, Arab Republic of Egypt: *Five-Year Plan, op. cit.* Table 5.
[86] Saleh. S. A. W., 'Brain Drain in Egypt', in *Cairo Papers in Social Science*, American University in Cairo Press, Cairo, Volume Two, Monograph 5, May 1979.
[87] Ministry of Planning, Arab Republic of Egypt: *Five-Year Plan, op. cit.* Vol. I, pp. 37-38.
[88] Riesman, E., *The Lonely Crowd*, Doubleday Anchor Books, New York, 1954, p. 26.
[89] Waterbury, J. *Egypt, Burdens of the Past Options for the Future*, Indiana University Press, American Universities Field Staff, Bloomington and London, 1978, pp. 45-48.
[90] *Ibid.*, pp. 45-48.
[91] Central Agency for Public Mobilization and Statistics, *Preliminary Results of 1976 Census, op. cit.* pp. 8-12.
[92] Omran, A. R. *Egypt: Population Problems and Prospects*, Carolina Population Center, Chapel Hill, 1973, p. 15.
[93] Central Agency for Public Mobilization and Statistics, *Preliminary Results of 1976 Census, op. cit* p. 5
[94] Omran, *op. cit.* p. 15.
[95] Central Agency for Public Mobilization and Statistics, Arab Republic of Egypt, *Statistical Year Book*, Cairo, October 1975, p. 4.
[96] Central Agency for Public Mobilization and Statistics. *Preliminary Results of 1976 Census, op. cit.* p. 6.
[97] Central Agency for Public Mobilization and Statistics. *Preliminary Results of 1976 Census, op. cit.* p. 13.
[98] Mead, M., 'Determinants of Health Beliefs and Behaviour', *American Journal of Public Health*, Volume 51, 1961, pp. 1552-1554.
[99] Taylor, C., and others, 'Experience with Human Factors in Agricultural Areas of the World', United States Department of Agriculture, Extension Service, No. 1018, 1949, (Multilithed) p. 19 in Mead, M. (ed.) *Cultural Patterns and Technical Change*, United Nations Educational and Scientific and Cultural Organization, Mentor, 1955, p. 260.
[100] Brunner, E. and others, 'Farmers of the World', Columbia, University Press, New York, p. 99, in Mead, *ibid.*, p. 260.
[101] Afif, I. T., Land Ownership in the Middle East' Foreign Agriculture, Vol. 14, No. 12, pp. 269, in Mead, *ibid.*, p. 269.
[102] Holy Koran, 4:1.
[103] Holy Koran, 76:2.
[104] Holy Koran, 80:7.
[105] Holy Koran, 80:19.
[106] Al-Azhar University, *op. cit.* p. 11.
[107] Holy Koran, 42:50.
[108] Pillsbury, Barbara, Traditional Health Care in the Near East (mimiograph). A Report Prepared for the U.S. Agency for International Development, Washington, D.C., March, 1978, Contract no. AID/NE-C-1395.

[109] Redfield, Robert, Peasant Society and Culture. Chicago, Ill.: University of Chicago Press, 1958, p. 70.
[110] Pillsbury, *op. cit.* p. 20.
[111] Pillsbury, *op. cit.* p. 46.
[112] Ayrout, Habib, *The Egyptian Peasant*, Boston: Beacon., 1963.
[113] Blackmann, Winifred S., "Sacred Trees in Modern Egypt." *Journal of Egyptian Archeology* 11: p. 56-57, 1926.
[114] El-Hamamsy, Laila, *"Belief Systems and Family Planning in Peasant Societies."* in *Are Our Descendants Doomed? Technological Change and Population Growth.* Harrison Brown and Edward Hutchings, eds. pp. 335-357. New York: Viking Press, 1972.
[115] Fakhouri, Hani, Kafr El-Elow: An Egyptian Village in Transition. New York: Holt, Rinehart, Winston., 1972.
[116] Kennedy, John "Circumcision and Excision in Egyptian Nubia." *Man* (New Series) 5 (2): p. 175-191, 1970.
[117] Gadalla, Fawzy, "Some Cultural Implications in Medical and Public Health Practice in Egypt." *Journal of the Egyptian Public Health Association* 37 (3): p. 63-74, 1962.
[118] Kennedy, *op. cit.* p. 175-191.
[119] Lane, Edward William, 1842 *The Manners and Customs of the Modern Egyptians.* Reprint. New York: E. P. Dutton, 1966.
[120] Ammar, Hamed, *Growing Up in An Egyptian Village.* Reprint New York: Octagon, 1966, 1954.
[121] El-Hamamsy, Laila, *op. cit.*, pp. 335-357.
[122] Blackmann, Winifred S., *The Fellahin of Upper Egypt: Their Religious, Social and Industrial Life Today with Special Reference to Survivals from Ancient Times.* Reprint. New York: Barnes and Noble, 1968.
[123] Fakhouri, *op. cit.*, p. 71.
[124] Messiri, Nawal, "The Sheikh Cult in Dahmit Life." In a Symposium on Contemporary Nubia. Robert Fernea, ed., pp. 219-237. New Haven, Connecticut: HRAF Press.
[125] Pillsbury, *op. cit.* p. 33.
[126] Barclay, Harold, "Study of an Egyptian Village Community." *Studies in Islam* (New Delhi) July pp. 143-166. October pp. 201-226.
[127] El-Islam, M. Fakhr, "The Psychotherapeutic Basis of Some Arab Rituals." *International Journal of Social Psychiatry* 13: 265-268.
[128] Ministry of Health, Arab Republic of Egypt, *Health Profile of Egypt, Public Opinion Towards Health Services*, Memo Number 2, May, 1978.

CHAPTER THREE

HEALTH CARE IN ITS SOCIOLOGICAL FRAMEWORK
THE ROLE OF THE PHYSICIAN

HISTORICAL NOTE

As early as 1929 Henry E. Sigerist, historian-physician wrote the pioneering statement on status and role of the patient.[1] Published originally in German, it predates Talcott Parsons [2, 3, 4] series of papers and books which attempt to formulate a theoretical model that would account for the physician-patient relationship and explain their status and role in society. Whether Parsons read Sigerist's paper is debatable. Their contributions, regardless of the shortcomings are important to medical sociology, not only as theoretical models but also in the historical context of that discipline. It is, therefore, relevant to examine these issues as they relate to this study.

Sigerist is perhaps best known as an outstanding medical historian for his two volume work *History of Medicine*. His paper written in 1929, "The Special Position of the Sick", is probably the first full theoretical treatise on the status and role of the ill person in society. Sigerist provides us with a sociological model as well as a historical analysis. He has pointed out that the place of medicine in a society is determined by the current societal and economic structure, the valuation that society places on health and disease, the tasks assigned to its physicians, and the technology of medicine available to doctors at the time.[5] He understood the cross-cultural as well as the urban-rural differences notably absent in Parsons analysis.

> "The custom of a weekly day of rest, which we derive from the East, has brought a definite pattern into our lives. The beginning and the end of daily work, the hours of meals, all these make up the rhythm of our lives, which vibrates in a different tempo for city dweller, for farmer, for factory worker, for white-collar worker. (The pervasive influence of daily employment in producing a rhythm in life is a modern phenomenon of Western culture, which, for example, is unknown in the East; as a consequence, pathology takes a somewhat different form.)
>
> An undisturbed rhythm means health. A change in the rhythm, perhaps when a farmer moves into the city and starts a city job, means a risk to health and produces altered conditions of illness and treatment." [6]

He discusses the primitive attitude as well as the underlying religious ethic of 'helplessness and helpfulness' as is evidenced in the following:

> "The view of disease as a punishment for sin, which is contained in Babylonian literature, is also the dominant judgment voiced in the Old Testament. God has revealed his law. Whoever follows it piously will be blessed in this world. Whoever

breaks the law will be punished. Every disease is a punishment. Every suffering is a suffering for sins of the individual himself, for those of his parents, or for those of his relatives. This is a thought of brazen consequence, of clearest simplicity. This attitude is that which sets in such tragic relief the situation of Job, who suffered though he was a just and perfect man.

Nevertheless, sickness is not only punishment. It also serves to expiate sin. If a man becomes ill, he can thereby atone for his wrongdoings and find purification." [7]

He goes on to analyze the privileged position the sick man enjoys:

"Illness releases. It releases from many of the obligations of society, first, from school attendance, and generally from work duties. The sick person is relieved from many important concerns with which society demands that the healthy busy themselves. Yes, the sick man even becomes the object of duties, the recipient of special attention. Illness frees a man also from the performance of many occupations. It also lessens the degree of responsibility or removes it entirely, a viewpoint which has revolutionized the penal law from its foundations. [8]

Perhaps the most important observation in Sigerist's work is the fact that medical care is often rationed by ability to pay. In 1960 he wrote ideas which were considered radical at that time:

"One thing is certain, that the laissez faire system has failed in the distribution of medical care as it has failed in other fields. This is evidenced by the fact that even in the wealthiest countries large sections of the population remain without adequate medical care, and that billions are wasted through unnecessary illness. There is no escape ... medical services must be organized. All health work must be planned. A highly differentiated organism cannot function unless all parts cooperate planfully. Competition must be replaced by cooperation. Rugged individualism under such a plan becomes anarchy. Organization is not identical with regimentation, as some conservatives would make us believe." [9]

The following paragraph, from a 1975 policy paper of the World Bank, may be compared in its essentials with the statement of Sigerist.

"The private market cannot be expected to allocate to health either the amount or the composition of resources that is best from a social perspective. The most critical failure of the market derives from the inability of consumers of health services to choose rationally. This inability is in part a consequence of the extraordinary complexity of medical problems and the consumer's lack of experience as a patient. Market failure also results from the presence of externalities. For example, procedures which held the spread of communicable diseases yield benefits to entire communities and, therefore cannot be chosen properly by individuals acting in their own interest. The health care system possesses many of the characteristics of public utilities. Often the unit producing services (health station, clinic or hospital) must be large relative to the local service area so that effective competition is not possible. For these and other reasons, governments have found it necessary to intervene in the health sector." [10]

The above illustrates that the practice of public health involves the political process and the challenging of some powerful interests in society, which will not readily yield their influence. [11]

Sigerist's assertion that health care is primarily a social relationship bears special significance to this study. Patient-practitioner relationships are best viewed in the framework of social roles. Sigerist points out a different relationship in the culture of the Kubu of Sumatra in which the Kubu native does not seek a cause for illness. "He simply cuts off from society any person whom disease strikes." [12] In other words, rather than a spontaneous event, it is viewed as a well-rehearsed confrontation in which the participants have learned to expect specific ways. What is the implication for this study of construing health care as a social role relationship? This interaction between helping agent and person requiring help is patterned in socially established ways and shows predictable regularities. Assuming that the patient-practitioner relations are a patterned sector of culture, they are transmitted from those who know about them to others. These roles, therefore, are learned patterns of behaviour.

Parsons presented his analysis of medical practice as part of a general theoretical treatise on the nature of social systems. [13] Illness, according to Parsons, must be viewed as a social phenomenon rather than just a pathophysiological process. According to Parsons, when people become ill, they assume a social role, which is characterized by the following role-expectations: [14]

(1) Sick persons are not held "responsible" for their incapacity.
(2) They are exempted from their usual role and task obligations.
(3) They must want to leave the role and "get well".
(4) They are obliged to seek and comply with technically competent medical advice.

Early Parsonian Sick Role Model and the Physician

According to Parsons, the first aspect of this model, the nonresponsibility of the patient and the view that something more than rational will is necessary to return to the non ill state, paves the way to the patient's entering a therapeutic course. Nonresponsibility places the ill person in a position of deviance from his society, and consequently must be viewed as a problem of social control. Parsons states: [15]

1. The conformity-deviance "dimension", or functional problem, is inherent in socially structured systems of social action in a context of cultural values.
2. The relevance of tendencies to deviance, and the corresponding relevance of mechanisms of social control, goes back to the beginning of the socialization process and continues throughout the life cycle.

3. Except in a highly qualified sense at the very beginning of life the tendencies to deviance are not random relative to the structure of the cultural norms and the social action-system, but are positively structured.
   a. The need-dispositions of personality structure are a resultant of interaction in the socially structured role system from birth on, and whether conformative or involving an alienative component relative to role-expectations, are structured relative to the role system of the society. This structure of need dispositions may be taken at any moment in time as one of the components determining the behaviour of the individual.
   b. Whatever the "fit" or lack of it between structure of need-dispositions and role-expectations, individuals in social situations are exposed to a whole series of "structured strains" which may further accentuate the difficulty of conformity. Such strains tend to be reacted to in terms of a special set of psychological propensities and mechanisms, the mechanisms of defense and of adjustment. This set of circumstances further structures the tendencies to deviance.
4. The tendency to deviance is finally also conditioned by the objective opportunities provided in the social system, in the structuring of which the "loopholes" in the system of social control are particularly important.
5. Every social system has, in addition to the obvious rewards for conformative and punishments for deviant behaviour, a complex system of unplanned and largely unconscious mechanisms which serve to counteract deviant tendencies. Very broadly these may be divided into the three classes of a) those which tend to "nip in the bud" tendencies to development of compulsively deviant motivation before they reach the vicious circle stage, b) those which insulate the bearers of such motivation from influence on others, and c) the "secondary defenses" which are able, to varying degrees, to reverse the vicious circle processes.
6. Structured deviant behaviour tendencies, which are not successfully coped with by the control mechanisms of the social system, constitute one of the principal sources of change in the structure of the social system.

It must be kept in mind that Parsons analysis was based upon middle class American society. He acknowledges that the roles which individuals occupy in modern society and gives primary consideration to strains which arise in the occupational system and the nuclear family.[a] These roles can lead to dissatisfaction and frustration. The consequence of these strains can be seen within sociological ideology as revolutionary action. "... this in itself is highly important from the point of view of the social system since it prevents the relevant motivations from spreading through either group formation or positive legitimations." [16] Therefore, the sick role permits one means of temporary deviance from usual role-expectations for oppressive qualities of the social

---

[a] The Parsonian model is both culture and class bound and would have to be radically modified to be applicable to other cultures even to various class and ethnic grouping. See Zola's Study of Symptomatology among American Ethnic Groups in Zola, I. K., 1966, Culture and Symptoms: An Analysis of Patients' Presenting Complaints, *American Sociological Review*, 3: 615-630.

roles which individuals must live. These were viewed by Parsons as familial, or occupational. Let us briefly consider this aspect within its historical perspective for Egypt. F. M. Sandwith,[b] writing about ankylostomiasis (hookworm disease) in "The Medical Diseases of Egypt" in 1905 stated: [17]

> "It is impossible to know what amount of the population is affected, but the returns of the recruiting commissioners for the Egyptian Army throw some light upon the number of young adult male peasants, liable for conscription, who are attacked by ankylostomiasis. Their figures show that 3.3 percent in Upper Egypt and 6.2 percent in Lower Egypt are rejected for obvious anaemia. Among the diseases for which conscripts are rejected, ankylostomiasis is certainly the most common. Every province furnishes rejections for this cause, Menoufia being the highest with 13.9 percent, but this is only a rough clinical test, *for the English recruiting officer only rejects those who are obviously too anaemic to serve in the army*, and to these figures must be added several soldiers who are later invalided from the service for anaemia. The seaport towns seem to enjoy some immunity. The disease does not seem to be indigenous in the Sudan, but is common amongst the Egyptian soldiers there. It will probably spread in Upper Egypt when perennial irrigation extends further south. *I have never heard of any case occurring in the English troops in Egypt.*" (emphasis added)

The sick role, isolating the deviant, prevents group formation. The writer, a physician, failed to acknowledge the greater implications of his statement. Sigerist on the other hand states: [18]

> "Labor power spent in the process of production must be restored. Periods of work must be followed by periods of rest, and this rest should in certain cases be under medical supervision. In handling our automobiles we have learned that it is cheaper to have them overhauled periodically and to have minor repairs made before the car breaks down. A program of human conservation would make use of the same principle. *The promotion of health moreover requires the provision of a decent standard of living with the best possible living and labor conditions. The promotion of the people's health is undoubtedly an eminently social task that calls for the coordinated efforts of large groups, of the statesman, labor, industry, of the educator, and of the physician who, as an expert in matters of health, must define norms and set standards*. (Emphasis added)

In Parsons' framework, he stresses individual adjustment within the sick role allowing adaptation rather than change in the social system. The physician can be viewed as an agent of social control where he provides "legitimation" of illness which exempts the client from his/her usual obligations (familial, military, occupational). Parsons, however, does not consider in depth the strains which make patients seek such legitimation originally.

---

[b] Sandwith's titles on the frontcover included: Consulting physician to H. M. the Khedive and to Kasr-el-Aini Hospital, Cairo; Lecturer at the London School of Tropical Medicine; Knight of Grace of the Order of St. John of Jerusalem; Member De L'institut of medicine, Constantinople; and of the American climatological association; formerly Vice Director of the sanitary department of Egypt; Professor of medicine and examiner at the Egyptian government school of medicine; physician to Kasr-el-Eini Hospital, etc.

Socialization and therapeutics (as a technology) have similar characteristics as processes of social control.

> "... that deliberate psychotherapy is, even within the role of the physician, not an isolated phenomenon, but may be regarded as the specialization of features of that role which are present in what has sometimes been called the "art of medicine." All good medical practice therefore, we have maintained, has been and is to some degree psychotherapy. Psychotherapy as a mechanism of social control, therefore, builds on and extends what must be regarded as an "automatic" or latent set of meachanisms which have been built into the role of physician independent of an application of theories as to what psychotherapy, or social control processes, should be." [19]

The comparison of this relationship with that of parent and child are elaborated by Parsons. Four major features of the relationship are presented. These features have the activity of parent or therapist as their point of reference. They are: support, permissiveness, manipulation of reward and denial of reciprocity. [20] Although the patient and child are not the same thing and the doctor and parent are different in the magnitude of their involvement with the dependent person, the process of returning the ill person to society and socializating the child have important similarities. The patient being as a child is the result of the physical and emotional traumas of illness and the physician assuming the role of parent is linked to his having superior knowledge and experience in health.

On the whole, however, Parsons' analysis of the doctor-patient relationship stresses formality and distance rather than closeness and trust. For example, in his pattern-variables he describes those features which create distance. [21] In his later work Parsons appears to elaborate this theme in terms of what he calls the "competence gap" between professionals. This stratified relationship grants the professional a superordinate position and clients occupy a subordinate one. He states:

> Relative to its relevant "laity," the professional relation is by its nature asymmetrical and thereby drastically different from the democratic associational relationship among "peers." In one essential aspect, the primary axis of this asymmetry lies in the superior competence of the professional ... Seeking the services of a competent physician or lawyer is different from peers "agreeing" about what should be done in a distressing situation ... In all ... these basic respects, there exists a "competence gap" between professionals and lay persons. [22]

This position is maintained by the physician and carries with it the problem of potential exploitation when the physician can take advantage of the patients' technical incompetence. "Such a competence gap must be bridged by something like what we call trust." [23]

Is the competence gap (and stratification) a necessary feature of professional-client relationship or is it merely a description of professional dominance? Freidson's critique of the medical profession provides an analysis within the broader theory of professions. We will focus on some of his conclusions and their more problematic aspects.

Post Parsonian Objections to the Model

Freidson doubts the profession's ability to regulate itself through broad normative patterns and doubts Parsons' acceptance that a continuity exists between the normative patterns which he describes and actual performance of practicing physicians. He argues that normative expectations must be distinguished from actual performance.

> "Parsons does not specify performance at all, but only expectations. Furthermore, those expectations are part of the broad institutional norms connected with professions as officially organized occupations. They are, in fact, the normative segment of the formal organization of professions, expressed by codes of ethics, public statements of spokesmen for the profession, and the like. they are quite distinct, analytically and empirically, from the actual norms of individual professionals ... Furthermore, even if they can explain adequate performance by reference to the effectiveness with which the performer was "socialized," they cannot explain the particular kind of deviant performance into which an "undersocialized" worker is led. And finally, it should be noted that the norms or values are themselves so broad and general as to be difficult to relate to even so critical and issue of performance as the process of self-regulation. More concrete norms seem necessary for the analysis of medical work." [24]

According to Freidson the model (collectivity-orientation) describes the publicly held norms of the profession but not necessarily the orientation of individual members of the profession.

> "The 'collectivity or service orientation' usually refers to the orientation of *individual* members of an occupation rather than to organizations. But clearly, the attitudes of individuals constitute an entirely different kind of criterion than the attributes of occupational institutions. Unlike the latter, which can be determined empirically by the examination of legislation, administrative regulations, and other formal documents including prescribed curricula, the attitudes of individuals must be determined by the direct study of individuals." [25]

Freidson finds the collectivity-orientation incompatible with some aspects of medical care where physicians charge excessive fees and refuse to work in rural or slum areas.

Limitations for the Egyptian Case

It is here we should compare Freidson's and Parsons' model for the Egyptian case. We shall examine this issue within the Egyptian context in the study of individual physicians ruling out the ... "preoccupation with the type of medical man and medical work to be found in the highly visible prestigious teaching and research institutions of medicine and concentrate instead on the vast majority of medical men who work in the obscurity of a full-time everyday practice. The former are spokesmen, the leaders, and sometimes the models of the profession. The latter *are the profession.*" [26] In this case the obscurity is *real*—the urban ministry of health hospital—the village health unit.

Freidson doubts the medical profession's[c] ability to regulate itself and consequently discounts the physicians' autonomy in controlling the conditions of practice. He asserts that all occupations seek this autonomy but only the professions justify it by virtue of their elaborate training and technical knowledge which implies that only other physicians are capable of determining who may practice medicine but in effect *do not* have much influence over quality control of medical care which is often determined by administrators, patients and politicians.

In Egypt we have a unique situation where the majority[d] of administrators in the Ministry of Health are physicians, the patients (in public facilities) have little if any control over the quality of medical care other than the refusal of services. It is, however, because of the socialized nature of "public medicine" in Egypt that the politician has the *power to control* medical care.

Freidson believes that autonomy should not be left to the physicians and attempts to provide guidelines to evaluate the question of professional autonomy as it directly affects the public interest.

> "... it follows that in the latter dimensions of the profession's work autonomy is not justified, that those dimensions do not represent a truly esoteric matter which only members of the profession, with their special training, can properly control. It is a question of public, not only professional, policy to determine what diseases should be recognized as illness in the public interest and what not; whether or not a given state or activity is deviant; whether it is illness, crime, or sin, or whatever; whether it is minor or serious, illegitimate; and whether medicine or any profession should have jurisdiction over it. In the determination of such moral issues the profession is but one of a number of publics." [27]

It would seem from the above that Freidson wants to see some degree of control eroding professional autonomy yet his attitude toward mobilization of patients as a whole is uneasy.

> "The ... mobilization of patients themselves into organized action groups is, to my mind, a last resort, appropriate only when all other devices have failed and when services remain nonetheless rigidly unresponsive to patient needs. When patients are organized into such groups, issues become undesirably stereotyped and negotiation takes place in terms that are not likely to serve the mutual benefit of

---

[c] This is all seen within the context of the American Medical Practice.

[d] According to in informed source, approximately 90% of the administrators in the Ministry of Health are physicians.

all parties. It would be a tragedy if medical (and, for that matter, educational and welfare) services were so deeply resistant to accommodation of client needs that confrontation politics become the rule of the day. I think it can be avoided by a properly designed system of care." [28]

Frankenberg criticizing the above statement has this to say:

"His criticism of society here deserts him. First of all he assumes there *is* a solution acceptable to *all* parties. Second, he fails to learn the lesson of the path trodden by sociologists of race relations, significantly now called black studies. Third, he shows a liberal fear of confrontation. Finally he assumes that a system of care can be designed independently of concrete group interests, falling into the same kind of fallacy as he rightly ridicules in those sociologists who see the solution to the problems of medicine simply in the reform of the medical school." [29]

As was previously mentioned, Parsons discusses the stratification between patient and physician and states that the competence gap which places the physician in a superordinate position is minimized by the element of trust. Freidson argues that the competence gap is in actuality too great because of the specialized technical knowledge the physician possesses.

"So long as the goal of therapy is maintained and physicians are held to know how to achieve it, physicians will maintain a place of privilege and "authority" by virtue of their expertise quite independently of bureaucratic office, and patients will hold a place of subordination by virtue of their helplessness and ignorance." [30]

Thus the physician is able to maintain his power. This is evidenced in the practice of requiring the patient to sign a blanket permission upon admission to most U.S. hospitals.

In Egypt, the "public practice" patient is more often than not illiterate which places the patient in an exaggeratedly subordinate position; however, the patient clings to traditional beliefs that the physician does not understand and feals insecure about. In turn, the physician may then doubt his own competence. However, one can easily observe the physicians maintaining power by withholding information regarding diagnosis and therapy from the patient as well as from the family. Although this practice has its roots in the cultural traditions of reluctantly disclosing *any* bad news, it is most probable that in view of the great cultural gap between patient and physician, the competence gap is broadened. Briefly, Parsons believes in the professions' capacity for self-regulation and that trust acts as a mechanism to modify the competence gap, whereas, for Freidson, professional autonomy and dominance have become crucial factors in the delivery of health services.

Because of the differential distribution of technical knowledge, a tendency toward stratification in client-professional relations, conflict and change follow. Freidson does not develop this thesis. However the conflict is evidenced by the growing womens groups some of whom recommend that women even treat themselves,[e] and the nurse practitioner may be a response to this conflict. It is interesting to note that some states were reluctant to license nurse practitioners, perhaps in an effort to retain power in the hands of the physician.

Freidson claims that the private practice, based on fee for service should remain. He states that it provides the patient with the freedom to choose. Compare his statement with that of the sociologist Zola who reaches a different conclusion on the basis of an extensive study of the presented complaints of members of several ethnic groups in the city of Boston.

> "Symptoms, or physical aberrations, are so widespread that perhaps relatively few, and a biased selection at best, come to the attention of treatment agencies ... There may even be a sense in which they are part and parcel of the human condition ... The empirical reality may be that illness, defined as the presence of clinically serious signs, is the statistical norm."[31]

Freidson, on the other hand, states:

> "Only a system that provides the individual patient himself with the opportunities and resources to exercise his own choice of practitioner and service is likely to sustain such human standards. In evaluating that problem in the light of paying the physician, it seems to me that the most flexible and direct method of supplying individual patients with such choice as individuals (rather than as members of some organized group negotiating contracts) is the fee-for-service method. By the nature of the method, one patient's decision to use a physician's services is directly and immediately translated into a financial benefit to the practitioner chosen. This does not mean that a capitation or salary basis of payment cannot be set up in a way that allows fairly flexible patient choice, but only that fee-for-service provides the most direct and *immediately consequential* means of doing so. Furthermore, it is most easily refined as a flexible method of control by the insurer or the insured: they may refuse to pay a fee for any single unacceptable service rendered, and are thereby able to exert sanctions over every *single* unacceptable action on the part of the practitioner." [32]

Freidson looks at this aspect with rose coloured glasses. Does the patient *really* have the *choice* to withhold payment? Not so, with most physicians using credit bureaus to collect late payments. Nasty, intimidating letters (from the bureau) suggesting a poor credit rating and possible legal action if payment is not promptly made is the rule of today. In addition, to what extent does a poor urban or rural patient have in *selecting* who will provide the service in emergency rooms or outpatient clinics. Freidson goes on to say that low-income patients should have some type of insurance. Let us again review Sigerists' reflection of the insurance game.

---

[e] See Boston Women's Health Book Collective, *Our Bodies, Our Selves*, New York: Simon and Schuster, 1973 and Leeson, J. and Gray, J., *Women and Medicine*, Tavistock Publications, London, 1978.

"... the position of the sick worker must inevitably be a little dubious. His place does not really exist, in the sense that the sick man through becoming ill becomes an outsider to the economic order. The state enjoins upon its individual members who are economic liabilities that they put aside a part of their pay during their times of health as insurance against times of sickness. With this institution, the worker acquires a right to help and care. He cannot work, but he will, nevertheless, be paid—with money that he himself has earned. He is not more at the mercy of society, no longer a recipient of charity ..." [33]

In Egypt, what choice can the poor patient execute? The patient may opt to refrain from visiting the free clinic or hospital and tolerate his/her illness or may visit a "private physician", as a preliminary report [34] has indicated. Twenty-three percent (23%) preschool children with health problems visited a "private doctor" whereas only 13.5% reportedly visited the Central Health Unit, 13.5% visited the pharmacist and 3.8% visited the health barber (traditional healer). However, the "private doctor" most probably is the physician from the Central Health Unit Clinic. Many patients believe that the physicians free services are inadequate and that they get better care if a sum of money is paid. The above mentioned study failed to indicate this distinction.

Freidson's solutions for control over professional dominance and autonomy are incomplete. He recommends a review board made up of other professionals (sociologists, lawyers?) to evaluate professional performance according to some *unspecified* criteria. [35] This would only result in a shift of power to the review board composed of professionals. The decision making processes of American hospitals are usually controlled by non-medical boards, whereas, in Egypt, the board is generally composed of physicians.

Freidson's beliefs in the fee-for-service practice and control through formal review bodies of medical and non-medical professionals are weak control mechanisms. Even his suggestion that patients could express their feelings through votes of confidence remains doubtful in view of the freedom which professionals may move from one area to another and opt not to work in the rural or poor segments of the society. Consequently he fails to state the political implications of controlling professional autonomy. These controls are only possible under socialistic government control, in which Egypt tentatively fits. However, the dichotomy of socialistic versus the fee-for-service remains and will probably continue to remain to be the Egyptian case.

Freidson remains detached throughout his observations and refers to himself as writing a "sociology of medicine"; however, this detachment does not permit him to see the pain and sufferings nor the poverty in the life and death situations which the physicians must deal with which require him to assume the "veneer" of the superordinate in order to cope with an otherwise intolerable situation. He remains detached from the experience of suffering and builds on Parsons theory of deviance in which deviance is viewed in categories of minor deviance (colds) and major deviance (cancer). He does not develop his critique to include the helpless position of the sick, their vulnerability for exploitation nor their poverty. Perhaps more important, both Parsons and Freidson fail to recognize the patient who rejects his/her illness; such as the devoted wife and mother who has no time to be sick, or the machismo male who refuses to accept illness as a threat to his masculinity, the masochistic business man of professional who must get the project finished as well as the student who will suffer intolerable pain rather take medication which might cloud thought processes. Nor do they consider the basic issues such as the life view and conditions of the rural villager. For instance, in Egypt, where the peasant woman might not visit the clinic where family planning assistance is given because of fear of her neighbours' opinions, the influence of the evil eye, lack of education, the tendency for the bread winner or male child to have their medical needs taken care of first, etc.

But perhaps most important, both Parsons and Freidson fail to consider the Third World at all.

Physician and Patient Relationship in the Third World

The professions have presented the social scientist with two profiles: [36] they are seen to provide a structural basis for a free and independent citizenry in a world threatened by bureaucratic tyranny, and at the same time are viewed as harbouring a threat to freedom. Altruistic motivation and a collectivity-orientation have been attributed to the professional and yet it is claimed by others that he suffers from a trained incapacity for social responsibility. [37]

In addition to Parsons and Freidson, the literature of the Professions has been extensively documented for example, Carr-Saunders and Wilson, [38] Greenwood, [39] and Hughes. [40] Major ideas have evolved from these studies. The first thesis holds that the professional role can be conceptualized by a series of traits each with a continuum of professionalism at one end and non-professionalism at the other. [41] A continuation of this theme holds that a variety of occupations have progressed only so far on one continuum and may continue to do so until they become professionalized. [42, 43]

The second theoretical approach is seen in the functionalist models which are limited to those elements which have functional relevance for society as a whole or for the professional-client relationship. [44, 45]

In order to understand these inconsistencies we must seek to understand how these views relate to different professions at different points of time by examining the theoretical concept of professionalisation. Since it can be argued that not all occupations are equally professionalised and some are not highly advanced in the process of professionalisation while others are at the endstate of professionalism, we will seek to understand the medical 'profession' in Egypt within this perspective.

Occupations which are associated with peculiarly acute tensions have given rise to a number of institutionalized forms of control, 'professionalism' being one. Professionalism becomes redefined as a type of occupational control rather than an expression of the inherent nature of occupations. Therefore, a profession is not an occupation, but a means of controlling an occupation. [46]

Most theorists have written about developed industrialized nations and have failed to consider the significance of their theories for the developing Third World nations, many of which have a colonial past. This idea is taken up by Johnson who argues that the present theories can not adequately explain the character of those occupations referred to as professions, as they have developed in emerging new countries. Many of the professions in the Third World have undergone a process of historical development which vastly differs from that experienced by similar occupations in the industrialized world. Also, the developing countries emerged from and are embedded in social structures and power relations which differ from the metropolitan country. [47] He believes that these differences are due to the nature of the relationship of the professions to the colonial administration and the post-colonial state where different forms of institutionalized occupational control were generated.

We will examine Johnson's thesis in detail here as it applies to Egypt, a post-colonial country.

Locating the Professions in a Middle Eastern Society

The colonialist-physician, Sandwith, writing in 1905 on the medical history of Egypt had this to say: [48]

> "During the French occupation, in 1799, Kasr el Ainy palace was turned into a military hospital, and Baron Larrey studied various diseases there and lectured to the midwives. Bonaparte also ordered a commission to prepare a plan for organizing a civil hospital for the sick of Cairo, and a hospital of 300 beds was opened in the Ezbekia quarter. Both these hospitals were disused when the French left Egypt, Kasr el Ainy was turned into barracks, became a ruin, was rebuilt by Muhammad Ali in 1812, and then became a preparatory school till 1837, when Clot Bey succeeded in getting leave to transfer to it the hospital and medical school which he had started in 1827 at Abu Zaʾbel. The medical school is thus the earliest of all the government schools in Egypt, and was called into existence by the ravages of plague and cholera in Egypt between 1824 and 1840. The names of the European professors that deserve mention are: Clot Bey, who besides vaccination, introduced into modern Egypt hospitals, schools of medicine, pharmacy and midwivery, sanitary and quarantine departments, all of which, in an improved form still exist; Pruner, Griesinger, Bilharz, and Reyer. Kasr el Ainy hospital and school

after 1858 were left chiefly in the hands of Egyptian professors educated in Europe, and were not productive of any scientific work. The Board of Health, except the army, having been separated in 1881 from the Quarantine department, which became responsible at the different seaports for preventing the introduction of human and animal diseases from abroad, proved to be so incompetent during the 1883 epidemic of cholera, that it was swept away among the earliest British reforms in 1884.

Since then a new era has begun of new hospitals all over Egypt extending into the Sudan, a Sanitary Department famous even outside Egypt for its practical methods of stamping out epidemic diseases, a Veterinary school, a model Oriental hospital at Kasr el Ainy, and a completely new School of Medicine, which has necessitated the creation of various scientific departments, *which never existed until the occupation of the country by England.* (emphasis added)

Interestingly enough he concludes this chapter with the following:

The varied history of Egypt must never be forgotten by the investigator who wishes to study the modern habits and customs of the people.[49]

Under the yoke of colonialism, various forms of institutionalized occupational control evolved, the most significant of which was corporate patronage. Johnson views corporate patronage as the reverse of professionalism in the sense that "it is the client—a powerful corporate client—which regulates the profession rather than the members of the occupation itself. Where corporate patronage prevailed professionalism, with all the cultural and organizational attributes we have come to associate with this form of colleague authority, never developed." [50]

Complementing the outflow of British professionals to the colonies, perhaps an even greater number of developing professionals travelled to continue their education abroad, as was the case in Egypt. This commenced with linkages to the code of ethics, examinations, etc. in the colonialized nation. In spite of these influences, Johnson argues that the culture of professionalism was always in tension with the realities of the colonial power structure, fundamentally in opposition to the development of professionalism as a form of occupational control. Instead, what was transmitted was an ideology which masked the reality of occupational subservience to client control, especially where colonial administration was a major source of the demand for professional services. [51] In Egypt, this demand was not as great because of Egypt's colonial ties until 1914 to the Turkish empire during the British imperialist era. However, Hourani, writing of Egyptian Nationalism during that era says:

"For twenty-three years (1884-1907) Egypt was ruled in effect by the British Agent and Consul-General, Sir Evelyn Baring, later Lord Cromer. Cromer's rule gave Egypt financial stability, a better and more extensive system of canals, a better administration of justice; but it also meant the restoration of the authority of the Khedive, only restrained by British control, of the financial privileges of the foreign bondholders, and of the economic and legal privileges of the foreign communities. As Lutfi al-Sayyid said, the fragile self-confidence of the nation, or at least of its small educated class, was shattered. Those who realized, after Tall al-Kabir, the disunity of the nation, the incompetence of its leader, and the absolute helplessness of Egypt in the face of a European Power, either retired into silence or drew, like 'Abduh himself, the moral that since Egypt could not drive out the British she must try to profit from their presence." [52]

The British recruitment services stressed the General Medical Council registration in England as the main criterion for registration in the colonies. The residuals of this policy remain evident in Egypt today where degrees from Europe or America had not been acceptable until recent years, in addition to the fact that non-academic degrees, for example, the MRCP and FRCS[f] are still considered qualifications for teaching in the majority of the universities.[g] This policy led to tensions between the demands of professionalism, on the one hand, and a developing system of corporate patronage of professional occupations on the other. This resulted in the professional occupations being subjected to the patronage of the colonial administration and dependent on its distribution of social and economic rewards. Johnson clarifies this point: [53]

> "In a number of colonial territories a fully developed system of corporate patronage of the professions emerged; that is, where the government as the major consumer of professional services had the power to define its own needs and the manner in which they were to be catered for. In most colonies there was, of course, some diversity of demand for professional services. In imperial India, for example, professionals catered for the needs of both large-scale metropolitan business firms and an indigenous commercial class. In general, however, a large, heterogeneous class with the economic power to effectively compete for the services of a homogeneous professional group has not existed. In other words, there was no viable basis for independent professional practice nor was there a secure foundation for the emergence of professionalism as a form of occupational control. Under these conditions the technically-based authority of the professions was subordinated to extra-professional sources of power. The professions were so placed that they enjoyed neither exclusive nor final responsibility for their services; ultimate authority lay with the corporate patron.

Under corporate patronage the professional shares the values and status of the patrons. The past situation in Egypt bares this out, where the high fees charged for medical education guaranteed that the recruits to the professionion were of a certain 'type' and from a specific status.

Johnson further supports his argument with the following tenets: [54]

1. Conditions of war reduce the potentiality of professional autonomy.
2. Under patronage, where the patron and client are one, there is always pressure to reduce client uncertainty at the expense of occupational autonomy which in general professional attitudes conducive to experimentation and research are suppressed.

---

[f] Member Royal College of Physicians and Fellow of the Royal College of Surgeons.
[g] An exception to this is Cairo University which changed this regulation recently.

3. Corporate patronage favoured particularism in so far as professional knowledge was developed in accordance with the special needs of the patron as was the case in the development of social anthropology.
4. The 'local' orientation of the professional was associated with the ethic of limited responsibility in so far as the professional was concerned with the consequences of his occupational activities only as to their relation to the patron's needs.
5. In corporate patronage, professionals take up an apolitical stance in so far as the expression of political views may embarrass the patron.
6. Patronage has affected power relations within professions but also between professions.
7. As professions remain dependent on the corporate patronage of the state, they retain many of the characteristics of the professions under colonialism.

This is indeed true of Egypt where the State dominates policy and education. Although the shared view that 'Western education' and 'metropolitan links' have been a source of strength among professionals in developing countries in providing both the conditions of organisational autonomy and independence of mind, [55] the political situation in Egypt after the exit of colonialist powers did not foster organisational autonomy. In fact, it served only to disillusion those professionals who were 'Western educated' and continues to do so today, as was the case in a recent nation-wide study of Engineers. [56]

Jeffery writing about India supports these arguments in stating that: [57]

> "State involvement in allopathic medicine in India has prevented and will continue to prevent the growth of a medical 'profession'. If anything, recent trends show a movement further away from the ideals of 'professionalism'. Similar trends in advanced industrial countries have been related to changes in the division of labour, rising levels of general education and increasing bureaucratisation. In China, there has been a conscious policy to make experts 'red'. The Indian pattern is different. The State structure has subverted medical autonomy in complex ways, and is unlikely to permit the establishment of a medical monopoly. Doctors have used international links and the legacy of professional symbolism to protect some areas from intrusion, but they remain on weak ground."

To sum up one can say in this review that Johnson's thesis provides us with a unique background for the study of professions in the Third World. Johnson's typology is an attempt to outline a framework which focuses upon the client-professional relationship and stresses not only variations in the potentiality for autonomy of an occupation, but also variations in the social characteristics of the consumer as a fundamental condition giving rise to variations in institutionalized forms of control.

Against a background of Johnson's thesis, what can be said of Egypts' medical 'profession'? In reality, the development of syndicates or professional societies in Egypt requires the blessing of the government. Recent developments in the political situation from a colonial past through a period of 'socialized control' during the Nasser regime followed by a more 'democratic' form of government lead one to expect a growth in the middle class. However, state control and involvement in the distribution of medical care and education will continue to act as a stop-gap, away from the ideals of 'professionalism'.

ROLE CONFLICT, ROLE ADAPTATION AND MARGINALITY

Definitions of health and illness vary in different sociocultural milieu. Illness involves a pathophysiologic process whereas medicine is a social institution. For example, Egyptian definitions of illness may differ from those of other cultures. This may contribute to conflicts when Western medicine is introduced in competition with established indigenous traditions. [58, 59]

Societies have developed a number of roles, such as the role of doctor, patient, nurse, etc., related to health and illness. The ways in which people who occupy these roles are expected to act are referred to as role expectations. These expectations associated with medical roles pattern the behaviour of both healers and the sick in predictable ways. The institution of medicine is the totality of roles and role-expectations related to health and illness, and includes a large number of collectivities which are systems of "concretely interactive specific roles". [60]

These collectivities within the institution include the doctor/doctor, doctor/patient, doctor/nurse relationships as well as professional organizations of physicians. [61] In indigenous systems this would include the traditional healer/patient relationship or clinic orderly/patient relationship. Other patterns within the institution of medicine include: parent/sick child and in a more traditional setting would include mother-in-law/daugher-in-law or grandmother/grandchild.

The foregoing is a simplified introduction which does not include the philosophical issues concealed within 'role'. A brief review will be presented here in addition to some of the controversies regarding 'role theory'.

Banton, in the text 'Roles', states that it is necessary to assume in the examination of particular roles that there is agreement among all the parties affected as to the definition of the role in question. [62] In his definition of role, he points out that a psychological approach is likely to concentrate upon how these ideas are held by individuals. The structural approach traces the way the sharing of norms and expectations creates networks of rights and obligations. [63] Gross and others define role in terms of problems of 'role complexes', 'role-sets', 'role-clusters', 'role conflict', and have placed importance upon the relationship of subjective role definition to reference group theory. [64]

Certainly the assertion that 'the concept of role is at present still rather vague, nebulous and non-definitive' clearly states the paradox as Neiman and Hughes write:

> "Frequently the concept is used without any attempt on the part of the writer to define or delimit the concept, the assumption being that both writer and reader will achieve an immediate compatible consensus. Concomitantly, the concept is found frequently in popular usage which adds further confusion." [65]

Banton making the same criticism, states:

> "What Linton and Newcombe define as role would, in Kingsley Davis' terminology be a status; what Davis defines as a role, Newcombe calls role behaviour, and T. R. Sarbin role enactment." [66]

Goffman commenting on the sometime use of role as applied to a social position and sometime use to the behaviour associated with a position states: "It is a position that can be entered, filled and left, not a role, for a role can only be performed; but no student seems to hold to these consistencies nor will I." [67] Role is sometimes used to denote individual behaviour and sometimes typical behaviour, but Banton concludes that "yet there has been a growing tendency for divergent definitions to be dropped, and a genuine consensus has been achieved which still permits a range of slight variations allowing scope to the interests of writers with different approaches." [68] Allowing for the problems of definition, we turn to Sarbin who writing about role theory states:

> "Role theory attempts to conceptualize human conduct at a relatively complex level. In a sense it is an interdisciplinary theory in that its variables are drawn from studies of culture, society, and personality. The broad conceptual units of the theory are *role*, the unit of culture, *position*, the unit of society, and *self*, the unit of personality. We define position as a system of role expectations.
>
> Coordinate with role is the concept of the self. Its origins and its dimensions are described in cognitive terms. The ultimate units of the self are inferred qualities, the conceptualization of which is aided by the use of qualifying terms such as adjectives." [69]

The most significant debate surrounding the concept was in response to Dahrendorf's now famous publication of 'Homo Sociologicus' or the history, significance, and limits of the category of social role.

Dahrendorf discusses the unreality and dangers of a model of man as a role conformer. However, he states that sociologists are concerned here with an artificial construct which has value for sociological theory but not a philosphical statement about man. [70]

Role theory, therefore, elaborates two main themes. The first is concerned with structure and with specifying positions within social structure which persist beyond the incumbency of any single person. The second is focused on face-to-face interaction and the many ways, both obvious and subtle, in which it is defined and managed by the persons involved. [71]

This tradition in role theory derives from the thesis that the self arises out of social interaction such as Cooley's idea, "Each to each a looking-glass reflects the other that doth pass", [72] and Mead's 'taking the role of the other', [73] to the social psychology of Theodore Newcomb [74] and Biddle and Thomas. [75]

One concept of role defines the doctor's role as the way he regularly behaves toward his patients, yet another concept finds it in the norms that society has generally adopted and laid down for doctors.

Merton [76] develops his thesis upon role 'set'. The expectations of various others often conflict, therefore, social mechanisms exist to cope with a situation which would otherwise make the role-set inefficient. There are certain social mechanisms for coping with the above conflict. Merton identifies these as follows:

First, a person's job is recognized as more important than membership in a voluntary organization so he will not be penalized for putting his job first.

Second, differences in power among members of the role-set will set priorities.

Third, a person may not be seen in action by members of his role-set.

Fourth, any member of a role-set may not know that his demand conflicts with that of another member.

Fifth, occupants of similar statuses may support each other against threats from members of a role-set.

Sixth, a person may abridge his role-set so as to make the remaining set more workable.

Merton regards the last as a limiting case because it is not so much a social mechanism as an individual action which alters the social structure to some extent. He gives priority to the social structure when he states that the composition of a role-set is ordinarily not a matter of personal choice, and also 'typically, the individual goes, and the social structure remains'.

Typically the individual does not change the social structure and it is here that we find the physician in isolation, for example in the rural areas, unable to alter the structure. Merton's treatment of the 'social mechanisms' as a means of resolving conflict within a role-set especially that which states 'a person may not be seen in action by members of his role-set' is relevant. The physicians' supervisors are usually not in the rural clinic; however, the parents, mother-in-law, husband, and cousin are usually seen in the action of the examination and treatment in Egypt. The case of the "elite' physician, unaware of the indigent patient's societal codes, beliefs, and traditions, treating the patient in 'Parsonian' fashion is more often than not a manifestation of Merton's 'social mechanism' that 'any member of a role-set may not know that his demands conflict with that of another member.'

So we turn to the self/other role theorists. Mead, famous for his attempt to explain the emergence of the human self, conceptualizes the self as socially created that develops out of man's capacities to read significant gestures and to play. Commenting in a discussion of role theory, Heading, in answer to the question "... does role theory have any possible place for the individual?", states: [77]

"... Certainly role-theory has a place for the individual personality. Both George Simmel and G. H. Mead recognized that modern man can be examined in terms of all the roles associated with social positions presently occupied, along with some precipitates of positions occupied in the past and, possibly, some aspects of positions with which the individual identifies without actually occupying them, the last being non-membership reference-models. The diversity of these roles for the different individuals is surely a major source of individuality."

The concept of reference groups, then, reduces the determinism of earlier role theory. However, Levinson [78] cautions the sociologist against maintaining a unitary concept of role. He points to three aspects of the concept; there are the structurally given demands, the person's own conception of his role and the concrete actions of the role incumbent. He states:

"Just as social structure presents massive forces which influence the individual from without toward certain forms of adaptation, so does personality present massive forces from within which lead him to select, create, and synthesize certain forms of adaptation rather than others. Role definition may be seen from one perspective as an aspect of personality. It represents the individual's attempt to structure his social reality, to define his place within it, and to guide his search for meaning and gratification." [79]

Erving Goffman [80] has stated that all social relationships are governed in part by the physical settings in which they occur. The stages where the therapeutic drama takes place vary and likewise the whole social psychological aspects of the encounter. Let us consider the "modern" medical private practice in Cairo. Parsons' version of the sick role and asymmetrical relations are in evidence where the practitioner has control over the terms of relationship in which he can arrange the furnishings, timing, and assistants to suit himself. A different pattern emerges in the public hospital, the rural health center and the patient's home. More people are involved in the drama and the physician is subject to many cultural as well as organizational constraints. As a result, he might not be able to exert the same kind of leverage on the patient's behaviour. As the settings shift, the relationships also shift, with consequential conflicts and strain. The question here is how the physician adapts to role strain in the different physical settings of rural and urban Egypt.

Role Adaptation and Marginality

In spite of frequent attention to the healer's role by anthropologists, only recently have attempts been made to conceptualize the role in order to build models for more systematic analysis. [81] Landy has examined the effects on the curer's role in the contest between indigenous systems of medicine and

Western medical systems. He uses the concept of role adaptation from a model of role strain suggested by sociologist Goode. [82] The notion is related to the concepts of cultural broker and role ambiguity.

Role Adaptation is defined as the process of attaining an operational sociopsychological steady-state by the occupant of a status, or status set through sequence of "role bargains" or transactions among alternative role behaviours. [83] Referring to the traditional curers' possibilities for role adaptation, insofar as the elements of ideology and behaviour patterns of the impinging culture are adopted to enhance therapeutic efficacy and status, he states:

> "Some curers may resemble marginal men caught in an insoluble dilemma between the drag of the culture of orientation on the one hand, and the pull of the culture of reference—that is scientific Western medicine—on the other. But frequently the curer maintains his position strongly in his membership group while borrowing liberally from Western medicine, without necessarily identifying with the reference group, in which realistically he accepts the fact that the doors to membership are closed, and without losing his psychological and social stability, through fruitless floundering between the two cultures." [84]

The above is seen in the context of rapid culture change. Alternative behaviour possibilities as well as expectations, rewards and obligations, originate both within and without the indigenous social system. Likewise, the physician practitioner "displaced" into another cultural milieu confronted with "over demanding" total role obligations will equilibrate role relationships and role sets through continual bargaining and consensus with other actors in the system and consequently will reduce role strain. [85]

Seen in the context of the cultural broker the traditional curer is viewed by Landy as having a crucial stake in the maintenance of the indigenous culture. "... for the more closely it begins to approximate the donor culture, the more vulnerable his role becomes. *Adaptation for role preservation consists of selecting only those changes that will preserve his role while at the same time minimally disturbing his already intruded culture.*" [86] Likewise we may view the physician as part of the same process in the rural health unit.

Therefore, on the psychological level, Landy concludes that it may be assumed that if role adaptation to cultural stress is to be achieved, it must be accompanied by cognitive change or by what Wallace [87] terms "mazeway resynthesis".

> "There is first of all a considerable reluctance (drag) to changing the old way, because of its symbolic satisfying value. As the old way, however, leads to less and less reward, and as frustrations and disappointments accumulate, there are set in motion various regressive tendencies, which conflict with the established way and are inappropriate to the existing maze. The individual can act to reduce his discomfort by several means: by learning a new way to derive satisfaction from the maze; by encapsulating the regressive strivings in a fantasy system; and by reifying

to himself his current way and maze, regarding a major portion of it as dead, and selecting (from either traditional or foreign regions, or both) part of the existing maze-way as vital, meanwhile mourning the abandoned (or abandoning) portion."

The curer may have to undergo continual adaptation, dependent upon the pace of cultural change, "... not only socially in seeking constant realignment of interpersonal relationships, but also psychologically in assimilating or redirecting the ever-increasing flow of new ideas, values, and technology, in learning rewarding paths in the changing external maze, and in repressing some paths in his internal mazeway while adding on others. His personality inventory would include a tolerance of cognitive dissonance, a capacity to "compartmentalize" dissonant values and role requirements. [88]

Therefore, the physician in distant rural areas like the traditional curer similarly achieves viable role adaptations. He is like the "Marginal Man" as Press suggests with the cultural broker role of a teacher in Yucatan, whose role-set is strengthened as it embodies larger numbers of mutually dependent roles from both cultures. In the physician's case the rural environment and Western education renders his "total configuration" "the more ambiguous" [89] In such a case rule viability, and by implication role adaptability, are strengthened by the incumbent taking on visible, essential, and needed roles or role characteristics of both the host and the contacted culture. [90] Press points out that "As the bicultural passes from one behavioural complex or role-set to another ... it is possible that he is clearly identified at one time or place, and viewed ambiguously at another, and that this very ambiguity increases role adaptability." [91]

REFERENCES

[1] Sigerist, Henry E. '*Die Sonderstellung des Kranken*', Kyklos, Jahrbuch des Institute für Geschichte der Medezin in der Universität Leipzig, 2: 11-20, 1929. (translated by Rowena Connell and later reprinted in Henry E. Sigerist on the Sociology of Medicine, (ed.) Milton I. Roemer.)
[2] Parsons, T., *Essays in Sociological Theory, Pure and Applied*. New York, The Free Press, 1949.
[3] Parsons, T., *The Social System*, New York, The Free Press, 1951.
[4] Parsons, T., 'Illness and the Role of the Physician' in Kluckhohn, and Murray, H. (ed.) *Personality in Nature, Society and Culture*, Second Edition, New York, Alfred A. Knopf, Inc., 1953.
[5] Sigerist, Henry E., 'Place of the Physician in Modern Society', *Proceedings of the American Philosophical Society*, Vol. 90, 1946, pp. 275-279. Cited by Suchman, E. A. in Sociology and the Field of Public Health, Russel Sage Foundation, New York, 1963, p. 58.
[6] Roemer, M. I. (ed.) *Henry E. Sigerist on the Sociology of Medicine*, MD Publications, Inc., New York, 1960.
[7] *Ibid*.
[8] *Ibid*.

[9] *Ibid.* pp. 9-22.
[10] World Bank Policy Paper, 1975, cited by Basch, P. F. *International Health*, Oxford University Press, New York, 1978, pp. 262-263.
[11] Beuchamp, D. E. 'Public Health as Social Justice', *Inquiry*, Volume 13, pp. 3-14.
[12] Roemer, *op. cit.* pp. 9-22.
[13] Parsons, T., *The Social System*, New York, The Free Press, 1951, pp. 428-479.
[14] *Ibid.*, pp. 436-437.
[15] *Ibid.*, pp. 320-321.
[16] *Ibid.*, pp. 312.
[17] Sandwith, F. M., *The Medical Diseases of Egypt*, Part I, Henry Kimpton, London, 1905, p. 245.
[18] Roemer, *op. cit.* pp. 9-22.
[19] Parsons, T., and Fox, R., 'Illness, Therapy, and the Modern Urban Family,' *Journal of Social Issues*, Volume 8, 1952, pp. 31-44.
[20] *Ibid.*, pp. 31-44.
[21] Parsons, T., *The Social System*, New York, The Free Press, 1951, pp. 454-455.
[22] Parsons, T., 'Research with Human Subjects and the Professional Complex', *Daedalus*, 98 1969, pp. 325-360.
[23] *Ibid.*, pp. 336.
[24] Freidson, E., *Profession of Medicine*, New York, Dodd, Mead and Company, 1970, p. 160.
[25] *Ibid.*, pp. 80-81.
[26] *Ibid.*, p. 160.
[27] *Ibid*.
[28] Freidson, E., *Professional Dominance, The Social Structure of Medical Care*, Aldine Publishing Company, Chicago, 1970, pp. 226-227.
[29] Frankenberg, R. 'Functionalism and After? Theory and Developments in Social Science Applied to the Health Field', *International Journal of Health Services*, 4 (3): 1974, pp. 411-427.
[30] Freidson, *op. cit.* pp. 176.
[31] Zola, I. K., 'Culture and Symptoms: An Analysis of Patients Presenting Complaints', *American Sociological Review*, Volume 3, pp. 615-630.
[32] Freidson, *op. cit.* pp. 218-219.
[33] Roemer, *op. cit.*
[34] Preliminary Survey of Health Facilities and Households in Lower Egypt, Oct. 1979, Mimiograph, (no author).
[35] Freidson, *op. cit.*
[36] Johnson, T., *Professions and Power*, Macmillan Press, Ltd., London, 1972, p. 17.
[37] Merton, R. K., 'The Machine, the Worker and the Engineer', *Science*, January 1947, pp. 79-81.
[38] Carr-Saunders, A. M. and Wilson, P. A., 'The Emergence of the Professions', *Encyclopedia of Social Science*, Macmillan, New York, 1944.
[39] Greenwood, E., 'Attributes of a Profession', in Noscow, S. and Form W., *Man, Work and Society*, Basic Books, New York, 1962.
[40] Hughes, E. C., *Men and Their Work*, The Free Press, New York, 1958.
[41] Moore, W. E., *The Professional: Rules and Roles*, Russell Sage Foundation, New York, 1970.
[42] Goode, W. J., 'The Theoretical Limits of Professionalization', in Etzioni, A. (ed.) *The Semi-Professions and Their Organizations*, The Free Press, New York, 1969.
[43] Etzioni, A., *The Semi-Professions and Their Organizations*, The Free Press, New York, 1969.
[44] Barber, B., 'Some Problems in the Sociology of the Professions', *Daedalus*, 92, 4 (fall), 1963, pp. 669-688.
[45] Parsons, *op. cit.*
[46] Johnson, *op. cit.*
[47] Johnson, T., 'Imperialism and the Professions' in Halmos, P. (ed.) *The Sociological*

Review Monograph, *Professionalization and Social Change*, Keele University, Volume 20, Dec. 1973, pp. 281-389.
[48] Sandwith, F. M., *The Medical Diseases of Egypt*, Henry Kimpton, London, 1905, pp. 10-11.
[49] *Ibid.*
[50] Johnson, *op. cit.*
[51] *Ibid.*
[52] Hourani, A., *Arabic Thought in the Liberal Age, 1798-1939*, Oxford University Press, London, 1970, p. 197.
[53] Johnson, *op. cit.* p. 289.
[54] *Ibid.*, pp. 281-389.
[55] Shils, E., 'Demagogues and Cadres in the Political Development of New States, in Pye, L. W., *Communications and Political Development*, Princeton, New Jersey, pp. 64-77, 1963, cited by Johnson, *op. cit.*
[56] El-Mehairy, T. M., El-Raghy, S. M., El-Mehairy, A. E., 'Egyptian Metallurgical Engineers: Is Education Meeting the Changing Situation in Energy and Materials?', Paper presented at the International Materials Congress, Sponsored by the National Academy of Sciences, Washington, D.C., March 26-29, 1979.
[57] Jeffery, R., 'Allopathic Medicine in India: A Case of Deprofessionalization.' *Social Science and Medicine*, 11, 10, July 1977, pp. 561-573.
[58] Parsons, T., 'Definitions of Health and Illness in the Light of American Values and Social Structure', in E. Gartly Jaco (ed.) *Patients, Physicians and Illness*, New York, Free Press, 1958.
[59] Shiloh, A., 'The Interaction Between the Middle Eastern and Western Systems of Medicine', *Social Science and Medicine* Volume 2, 1968, pp. 235-248.
[60] Parsons, T., *The Social System*, New York, The Free Press, 1951.
[61] Parsons, T., *Social Structure and Personality*, New York, Free press, 1970.
[62] Banton, M., *Roles: An Introduction to the Study of Social Relations*, London, 1965, p. 36.
[63] *Ibid.*, p. 29.
[64] Gross, N., Mason, W. and McEachern, L., *Explorations in Role Analysis: Studies of the School Superintendency Role*, New York, John Wiley and Sons, Inc., 1958.
[65] Neimann, L. and Hughes, J., 'The Problem of the Concept of Role—A Re-Survey of the Literature', *Social Forces*, 30, 1951, pp. 141-149.
[66] Banton, *op. cit.* p. 28.
[67] Goffman, E. *Where the Action Is*, Doubleday, New York, 1969, p. 39.
[68] Banton, *op. cit.* p. 28.
[69] Sarbin, T. R., 'Role Theory' in Lindzey, G. (ed.), *Handbook of Social Psychology*, Addison Wesley, Reading, U.S.A., 1954, p. 223.
[70] Dahrendorf, R., *Homo Sociologicus*, Routledge and Kegan Paul, London, 1973.
[71] Holland, R., *Self and Social Context*, The Macmillan Press, Ltd., London, 1977, pp. 81-190.
[72] Cooley, C. H., *Human Nature and the Social Order*, New York, 1902.
[73] Mead, G. H., *Mind, Self and Society*, The University of Chicago Press, Chicago, 1934.
[74] Newcomb, T., *Social Psychology*, New York, 1950.
[75] Biddle, J. J. and Thomas, E. J. (eds), *Role Theory: Concepts and Research*, New York, 1966.
[76] Merton, *op. cit.*
[77] Bradbury, M., Heading, B. and Hollis, M., 'The Man and the Mask: A Discussion of Role Theory' in Jackson, J. A. (ed.), *Role*, Cambridge University Press, London, 1972, pp. 41-64.
[78] Levinson, D. J., 'Role, Personality and Social Structure', in Coser, L. and Rosenberg, B. (ed.), *Sociological Theory*, Collier-Macmillan, New York and London, 1969, p. 305.
[79] *Ibid.*
[80] Goffman, E., *The Presentation of Self in Everyday Life*, Edinburgh, University of Edinburgh Social Science Research Center, 1958.

[81] Landy, D., 'Role Adaptation: Traditional Curers Under the Impact of Western Medicine', *American Ethnologist*, Volume 1, 1974, pp. 103-127.
[82] Goode, *op. cit.* pp. 483-496.
[83] Landy, *op. cit.*
[84] *Ibid.*
[85] Goode, *op. cit.* p. 485.
[86] Landy, *op. cit.*
[87] Wallace, A. 'Mazeway Disintegration: The Individual's Perception of Sociocultural Disorganization', *Human Organization* Volume 16, p. 26. cited by Landy, *op. cit.*
[88] Goode, *op. cit.* p. 478.
[89] Press, I. 'Ambiguity and Innovation: Implications for the Genesis of the Cultural Broker', *American Anthropologist*, Volume 71, pp. 205-217.
[90] Landy, *op. cit.*
[91] Press, *op. cit.*

CHAPTER FOUR

MEDICAL EDUCATION IN EGYPT

The central concern of this study is the Egyptian Doctor's experience of practising his profession. The background and training expectations he brings to his work inevitably entail tensions between anticipations and reality. Therefore, the field study involved practicing physicians as well as medical students. Although the methodology and analysis will be dealt with in detail in Chapter VI and VII, it was felt appropriate to refer to certain aspects of the results obtained in this section which will be mainly concerned with the analysis of the nature of these tensions.

Curriculum Analysis

The student enters medical school after attending the "science section" in high school. His first year at the university, called the preparatory year, is at the faculty of science and he/she studies the basic science courses of physics, chemistry, biology (zoology and botany) and mathematics. Subsequent years, at the faculty of medicine, begin with two-year courses including anatomy and physiology, biochemistry and histology with one examination at the conclusion of the second year. During the following year, pathology, bacteriology, parasitology and pharmacology are given. The last 2½ years of the curicula are devoted to general medicine, general surgery, pediatrics, gynecology, obstetrics, opthalmology, ear, nose and throat, hygiene (encompassing epidemiology, social and industrial medicine), special medicine (neurology, cardiology and chest), special surgery (urology, orthopaedics and neurosurgery), and forensic medicine.

The student graduates with a M.B., B.Ch. after approximately six and one half years of education. Clinical rounds are daily in the last 2½ years. Rounds like the classrooms are crowded. As many as 50 medical students attend "rounds" together. However, as a recently graduated physician informed me, "You may return as much or as often as you want on your own to examine the patients."

The physician after the above 6½ years preparation may not practice until completion of a one year internship which comprises of six months at a university hospital and six months at a Ministry of Health hospital. The course of study is subdivided into the following:

    2 months — General Medicine
    2 months — General Surgery
    2 months — Pediatrics

2 months — Gynecology, Obstetrics
2 months — Student choice of specialization (however, entry into his/her "chosen" specialization is determined by his/her final grade)
1 month — Emergency
1 month — Anesthesia

This is followed by one year (or possibly more) of mandatory service, mostly in the villages.

How does the medical student view his forthcoming service? How do these views concur with older colleagues "in the field"? Is there a consensus of opinion?

Student Selection

A portion of this study enquires about how the physician retrospectively perceives his education while fulfilling his role in the circumstances of practice.

Education in Egypt follows a "weeding-out process." National examinations begin when a child is in the sixth grade, followed by examinations in the ninth and twelfth grades. The ability to carry on to higher level and/or scientific studies is determined by success in the National Examinations. All education is free from primary to the Ph.D. level; therefore, there is extreme competition and familial pressure. During exam time, the country becomes mobilized, parents may not go to work in order to assist their children in preparing for the exams. Mothers prepare special foods. Little or no social life transpires during exam period. This applies to the university professor as well as to the house servant. It is through this 'carnet de passage' that the medical student enters the medical schools of Egypt. He or she has made the highest grades on the Thanawaia Amaa[a] in the country, thus permitting him to enter the hallowed halls of medicine. Although entrance is non-discriminatory as to sex or background, by virtue of this process, essential in dealing with thousands of students, the elite are generally the ones who succeed through privileged physiological and psychological amenities.

Student Motivation

Students were asked to rate on a scale of 1-5 why they originally entered the faculty of medicine. Table 4.1 ranks their reasons and the opinions of the "in-field" physicians and presents them for comparison. It clearly indicates that there is a marked consensus of opinion with the exception of one item namely the high Thanawaia Amaa grade. Students rated it at forty-three percent (43%) whereas the older professionals rated it with only twenty-eight percent

[a] Thanawaia Amaa is the name for the final national examination given at the end of the twelfth year of education.

(28%). This may be due to the yearly increasing numbers of students aspiring to enter this prestigious faculty. In addition, as was previously stated, the student is extremely "grade conscious" at this point of his career. The choice to specialize, the opportunity to join the university teaching faculty and even the distance of placement from Cairo for rural service depends on higher final grades.

Table 4.1

Reasons for Originally Entering the Faculty of Medicine
(Students compared with practising Physicians)

Reason	Students n=105	Physicians Combined sample n=136
Fascination with the Subject of Medicine	61%	56%
Prestige	41%	38%
Financial Reward	16%	18%
Family Encouragement	39%	35%
Desire to Help Others	65%	58%
High Thanawaia Amaa grade	43%	28%

Other reasons cited by practising physicians were "No doctor in the family." (Age 23), "Medicine is a noble profession." (Age 24), "Desire of father, I personally wanted engineering." (Age 52), "To know the secret behind the human presence in the world." (Age 27), "It is an honest job to satisfy God on the condition that you do it properly and honestly." (Age 26).

The trend toward religiosity exemplified in the statements above is an indication of the new religious movement in Egypt toward traditionalism. Islam is a way of life and today's Egyptian youth are seeking to identify with religious movements. This is especially true in the faculty of medicine where many female students are wearing traditional long dresses and covering their heads. This is not due to familial pressures.

As illustrated in Table 4.1 the "Desire to help others" was a major influencing factor for entering medicine, whereas "Financial reward" ranked lowest.

The questionnaire distributed to 105 fourth year and fifth (final) year medical students[b] sought to obtain their projected views of village service in terms of anticipatory socialization and their clinical and psychological preparation for the village (Appendix II).

The socialization process in medical education has been extensively studied. [1, 2, 3] Elliot Freidson argues that "education is a less important variable

---

[b] For the purpose of analysis, both years were considered as one group since it was found that no significant difference was demonstrated between both groups.

than the work environment. There is some very persuasive evidence that 'socialization' does not explain some important elements of professional performance half so well as does the organization of the immediate work environment". [4]

> If medical education molds the medical man, the exigencies of practice are likely to be the proof of the mold. It is for performing his role in the circumstances of practice that medical education prepares the physician. And it is in the realities of practice rather than in the class-room that we find the empirical materials for clarifying and articulating the actual rather than the imputed or hoped for nature of the professional role. [5]

THE SECONDARY SOCIALIZATION OF THE MEDICAL STUDENT

"To become a part of society and a subject of sociological analysis, man must be socialized, chained to the fact of society and made its creature. By observation, imitation, indoctrination, and conscious learning, he must grow into the forms that society holds in readiness for him as an incumbent of positions. His parents, friends, teachers, priests, and superiors are important to society above all as agents who cut into his *tabula rasa* the plan of his life in society. ... Scientifically it may be plausible and useful to interpret the educational process as the socialization of the individual, but morally it is crucial that the individual be capable of holding his own against the claims of society. ... For society and sociology, socialization invariably means depersonalization, the yeilding up of man's absolute individuality and liberty to the constraint and generality of social roles. Man become *Homo sociologicus* is exposed without protection to the laws of society and the hypotheses of sociology. If the assumption of role conformity has proved extraordinarily fruitful in scientific terms, in moral terms the assumption of a permanent protest against the demands of society is much more fruitful." [6]

Dahrendorf postulates that roles leave their incumbents a range of individual choice [7] and also accepts the existence of the phenomenon of successful deviance from expectations, a phenomenon Merton called "rebellion" because it leads to changes in the social structure. [8]

Therefore, it would seem important to view the socialization process of the medical student with the above in mind as a historical perspective. When indeed does the socialization process begin and when, if ever, does it end as the student proceeds from pre-clinical student to practising physician in the hospital clinic and rural health unit. When also, does he cease to see himself as a student?

Post-dating Mead's account of how the social-self is created, [9] Merton and Kit [10] and Sherif [11] confirm that people relate not so much to a 'generalized other' but to 'significant others'. People identify with groups of which they are not actually members such as would be the case of the young medical student who displays 'anticipatory socialization' by behaving in the manner of his superiors and instructors, thus the concept of 'reference groups' which eases the determinism of earlier role theory is relevant here.

The choice of reference groups has been suggested to rest upon the personal loyalty to significant others in their social world. For Sullivan, "significant others" are those persons directly responsible for the internalization of norms. Socialization is a product of gradual accumulation of experiences with certain people, especially those with whom we stand in primary relations, and significant others are those who are involved in the cultivation of abilities, values, and outlook. [12] What is crucial, according to Shibutani, [13] is the character of one's emotional ties with them. Those who think the significant others have treated them with affection and consideration have a sense of personal obligation that is binding under all circumstances and they will be loyal even at great personal sacrifice. This is generally the accepted belief held with regard to the socialization process of medical students in Egypt. Admittedly professors are regarded with great esteem and looked upon as demi-gods, especially in the medical profession; however, not all primary relations are necessarily satisfactory, and responses may be negative. This negativity could be indicated by the analysis of the physicians education. Research by Tadros [14] at Kasr-el-Aini hospital, in which thirteen respondents were followed, indicated that many feelings of hostility, resentment, etc. were expressed by the medical student in all stages of training toward their instructors and supervising physicians. It has been cited [15] that a person may go out of his way to reject the known expectations of significant others. This may account for the type of orientation where some remain loyal to the parental culture (in this case the culture of the educators) while others seek desperately to become assimilated into the larger world (the village culture).

It is interesting here, however, that the medical student in his final years "anticipated" the problems in the rural health units closely related to those already in the field. To what extent has this "awareness" been part of the socialization process? It might be argued that it is at this stage, based on the forementioned results, that perhaps the student begins to view his world within the confines of his parental culture—is indeed socialized—and has begun to *become* a physician in his two final years of training. More research at this level of the educational process would be necessary to see if indeed this is the case.

Ideological Frustrations and Praxis

How do these professionals view their university education? Questions were asked relating to the adequacy of their education and if they felt additional education or training would benefit them to execute their work more effectively or to improve his/her position in the medical profession. Knowledge as to why they originally entered the faculty of medicine was obtained by asking the respondents to rank the following on a scale of 1-5:

a. Fascination with the subject of medicine
b. Prestige
c. Financial reward
d. Family encouragement
e. Desire to help others
f. High Thanawaia Amaa grade
g. Other (specify)

Referring to American medical students, Funkenstein makes the following comment:

> Across the nation medical students are restless, unhappy and markedly dissatisfied with the education they are receiving. They feel that medical school is a poor learning experience and that their personal development is being impeded. These future physicians are disenchanted with medical school policies which they blame for the inadequacy of the health care delivery system. The majority of students complain that they experience constant anxiety and stress. A "dehumanizing experience" is their most frequent characterization of medical school. [16]

The number of complaints of the Egyptian physician did not differ exceedingly from those voiced by their colleagues in a developed nation. However, they did differ somewhat in kind.

In general, reservations were held with respect to the adequacy of their education. Several cited that their education was sufficient for general practice, indicating that for any specialization additional education would be necessary. Many respondents complained of the lack of practical experience due to the insufficient facilities and the large number of students. "It is not unusual for 50 students to work on one cadaver." [c]

Some physicians felt the professors were of low standard and indicated that the faculty were not interested. It should be stated here that lecturers who progress academically to become professors at Egyptian universities are selected by virtue of their final grade i.e. academic achievement and are actually "the cream of the crop" scholastically. However, academic salaries for university professors are low. A full professor at a national university earns a monthly teaching salary of LE 150.[d] Therefore, in order to supplement this earning, practice concerns may interfere with teaching objectives.

Classrooms are indeed crowded and may have as many as 1000 students. It is not unusual for a student to leave his/her home three hours prior to a lecture to "secure a place." Some respondents stated: "Medical education requires continuous education" and that "a degree is not enough to practice successfully." One physician complained about the concentration on dictating information. This statement was verified by my informant who complained

---

[c] This statement was made by a recently graduated physician during a conversation in January, 1979.
[d] Egyptian pounds 1.50 = Pound Sterling 1.00.

that because of the emphasis on rote learning and essay exams they had difficulty passing qualifying exams in Britain and the United States. Historically, emphasis on rote memory is part of the educational system in Egypt. This may be a residual of Koranic recitation. Even the Arab desert bedouin is known for his ability to recite the genealogy of his camels, poetry and astrology.

Other comments stressed that medicine was a profession which required continuing education. Some examples were:

"I consider myself still beginning."
"A doctor needs specialization and needs to constantly renew his knowledge and keep up with recent developments."
"Medicine is a life and experience—not only an education."
"Books are one thing, practice is something else which comes in time."
"Experience gives one a chance to perform surgery without fear."

Overwhelmingly the complaints of inadequate practical experience, facilities and the large numbers of students may indicate that perhaps Egypt is training untrained physicians, if their evaluation of the educational system is correct.

It is important to note here that the majority of the respondents (85%) were under 40. Those respondents over 40 were more positive in their evaluations. As a group 85% felt that their university education had adequately prepared them for their profession. However, 95% of those respondents over 40 also stated that they needed additional education and/or training to carry out their present work more effectively.

One respondent, aged 49 stated: "At my time we had less students and the teachers were more serious and punctual."

One male doctor in viewing his education adequately summed it up as: "Because I am a successful doctor and most of my cases are cured with the will of God; I always feel like working except for the administrative complications."

Respondents were asked "Would you like to receive additional education or training to carry out your work more effectively?" Eighty-eight percent of the total sample indicated a desire for additional education and/or training.

In citing the type of training they would need to improve his/her position in the medical profession, a vast number of suggestions were made. Some examples were:

1. Practical training with specialization in large equipped hospitals
2. Laboratory investigation
3. Most recent clinical developments
4. New techniques
5. Training for confidence and experience
6. Training for skill improvement

7. New equipment
8. Duties of the Rural Health Unit and General Practioner
9. Specialization in a good general hospital
10. Training abroad

In reply to the kind of education they would need there was a consensual desire for higher degrees. Perhaps this indicates the realization that to get ahead, specialization is important, in addition to the Egyptian societies' ascription applied to higher degrees as a high status symbol.

REFERENCES

[1] Becker, H., Greer, B., and Hughes, E., and Strauss, A. L., *Boys in White: Student Culture in Medical School*, University of Chicago Press, Chicago, 1961.
[2] Merton, R. K., Reader, G. G., and Kendall, P. L. (ed.), *The Student Physician*, Harvard University Press, Cambridge, Mass., 1957.
[3] Bloom, S. W., 'The Sociology of Medical Education: Some Comments on the State of a Field', *The Milbank Memorial Fund Quarterly*, Vol. 43, April 1965, pp. 143-184.
[4] Freidson, E., *Profession of Medicine*, Dodd, Mead and Company, Inc., New York, 1970, p. 89.
[5] Freidson, E., *Professional Dominance: The Social Structure of Medical Care*, Aldine-Atherton Press, New York, 1970, p. 18.
[6] Dahrendorf, R. *Homo Sociologicus*, Routledge and Kegan Paul, London, 1973, pp. 38, 39, 83.
[7] *Ibid.*, p. 84.
[8] Merton, R. *Social Theory and Social Structure*, Chicago, Ill. Free Press, 1957, cited by Dahrendorf, *op cit.* p. 84.
[9] Mead, G. H., *Mind, Self and Society*, University of Chicago Press, Chicago and London, (1934), p. 134.
[10] Merton, R. K. and Kitt, A. S., *Continuities in Social Research, Studies in the Scope and Method of 'The American Soldier'*, (ed.) Merton, R. K. and Lazarsfeld, P. F. Free Press, New York, 1950.
[11] Sherif, M., 'Reference groups in Human Relations' in (ed.) Sherif, M. and Wilson, M., *Group Relations at the Crossroads*, Harper and Row, New York, 1953.
[12] Sullivan, H. S., *Conceptions of Modern Psychiatry*, W. H. White Psychiatric Foundation, Washington, D.C., 1947, pp. 18-22.
[13] Shibutani, T., 'Reference Groups as Perspectives' *American Journal of Sociology*, Volume 60, May 1955, pp. 562-569.
[14] Tadros, F., 'A View from Within: Student Perspectives on Medical Education and Medical Practice in Egypt', M. A. Thesis, Department of Anthropology, The American University in Cairo, July 1979.
[15] Grinker, R. R. and Spiedel, J. P., *Men Under Stress*, Blakiston Co., Philadelphia, Pennsylvania, 1945, pp. 122-26.
[16] Funkenstein, D. H., 'The Learning and Personal Development of Medical Students Reconsidered', *The New Physician*, Vol. 19, pp. 741, Sept. 1970, as quoted by Hughes, E. et al., *Education for Professions of Medicine, Law, Theology and Social Welfare*, McGraw Hill Book Co., New York, 1973, p. 94.

CHAPTER FIVE

PHYSICIANS SELF CONCEPT AND CONSTRUCTION OF ROLE SET

Descriptive Sub Sets of Roles

This section concentrates on the physician's role. However, since much of the performance of health clinic is determined by lower echelons, those aspects are discussed in Chapter VII.

The question here is whether the physician's professional identity is an individual product arrived at via the process of adult socialization (medical education) or whether the physician's behaviour is primarily dominated by the structural components of his/her working situations while *practising* medicine.

Rather than a general rule for the professional doctor in Egypt, we find the medical professional role is determined by the anticipatory socialization, cultural and geographical determinants. Parsons [1] has provided a model of the medical professional role in terms of attributes. The attribute which assumes that the professional role is "functionally specific" states that the physician, as a specialist in health and disease, is expected to restrict his professional concerns to the areas of promotion of health and problems of illness.

An important paradigm for the analysis of structures of role relations was developed by Merton in his paper "The Role Set", originally published in 1957. [2] His major discussion was Linton's distinction between the status persons occupy in a social system and the role they perform as incumbents of this status and Linton's observation that each person occupies multiple statuses and hence has multiple roles, one for each status. [3] Merton, however, emphasizes that a social status does not entail a single role

> but an array of associated roles. This is a basic characteristic of social structure. This fact of structure can be registered by a distinctive term, role-set, by which I mean that complement of role relationships which persons have by virtue of occupying a particular social status. As one example: the single status of medical student entails not only the role of a student in relation to his teachers, but also an array of other roles relating the occupant of that status to other students, nurses, physicians, social workers, medical technicians, etc. [4]

Role-set so defined differs from Merton's description of status-set which refers to the various roles of an individual associated with different statuses he or she occupies, such as medical student, daughter, catholic, etc.

However, let us view the physician as a nonexclusive multispecialist [5] with a number of roles such as: physician healer, administrator, and teacher within a single status. In this capacity he/she interacts with the villager, staff, or people from the community.

> "An analysis of the phenomena referred to when the term "specialization" is employed discloses that two different things govern its use: first the amount of behavior engaged in by an individual, relative to others; and second, the number of differentiated behaviors engaged in for a given domain of behavior. The differences between the part-time and full-time teacher involves the amount of teaching, whereas the differences between neurosurgeon and the general practitioner involves the amount and the number of differentiated behaviors, called "medical practice", customarily performed by each." [6]

Specialization is a term which refers to the amount and numbers of types of particular differentiated behaviours engaged in by a person. [7] A physician who is engaged in some combination of teaching and service, supervision and administration or some other limited combination, who has colleagues also engaged in some of the same behaviours, would be considered a nonexclusive multispecialist in this context. It is this role multiplicity that we will consider.

Benne and Sheats, [8] who are primarily concerned with conversational behaviour of members in discussion groups, have described and recorded a number of role stereotypes. Some examples are: the encourager, the hostile critic, etc. These roles, however, do not have the institutional support of the traditional roles such as doctor or mother; they do nevertheless emerge in the interaction process. The number-of-roles dimension is also utilized in the application of the role-taking approach to psychopathology indicated in the widely accepted postulate that the more roles in a person's behaviour repertory, the "better" his social adjustment—other things being equal. [9]

Rather than observe the number-of-roles in situ, respondents in the present study were asked to check their MAJOR function in performing their work. Listed were administration, supervision, teaching (staff and patients), medical care, and other. Would the physician's definition of the multiplicity of roles correlate with his adjustment pattern? Is there a consensus of opinion as to the role definitions between the rural and urban categories of the study?

Therapist, Manager, Educator and Mediator

According to Goode, a "professional community" can be identified by the fact that:

> "(1) Its members are bound by a sense of identity.
> (2) Once in it, few leave, so that it is a terminal or continuing status for the most part.
> (3) Its members share values in common.
> (4) Its role definitions vis-a-vis both members and non-members are agreed upon and are the same for all members.
> (5) Within the areas of communal action there is a common language, which is understood only partially by outsiders.

(6) The community has power over its members.
(7) Its limits are reasonably clear, though they are not physical and geographical, but social.
(8) Though it does not produce the next generation biologically, it does so socially. Through its control over the selection of professional trainees and through its training processes it sends these recruits through an adult socialization process." [10]

The "agreed upon" role definitions as mentioned in statement number four will be briefly outlined in anticipation of the results obtained from the questionnaires in Chapter VII.

The term "number of roles" will be used to mean the roles of therapist, manager (administrator, supervisor), educator, mediator, etc. Naturally, one would expect consensus among physicians viewing their role as primarily therapist or healer. However, the role of manager or supervisor should eventually force itself as a major role with the emergence of a complex and extended medical system. Along with this role one would anticipate the usual dissatisfactions inherent with administrative procedures. It would also appear that such problems would differ markedly between rural an urban segments of the same community as well as between developing and developed countries.

In a developing country the rural physician is expected to assume also the role of a teacher providing health guidance, health seminars, showing health films, promoting health awareness, instructing and lecturing in general health, etc.

Another role for the physician working in traditional societies is the mediator. This would be evident particularly where resolution of conflicts stems from culture residuals where the clan plays an important role. Vendetta in the Egyptian southern traditional society is not uncommon. Cole [11] and Evans-Pritchard [12] have studied the Arab clan in the "Empty Quarter" of Saudi Arabia and the Sanusi of Cyrnaica. Bedouin tradition stresses "an eye for an eye, a tooth for a tooth." [13]

In view of the above it is not surprising that the physician immersed in such traditional societies accepts such a role as mediator which carries with it considerable prestige, leadership, and acknowledged possession of correct judgement.

Approaches to Marginality

Before considering the rural physician as a marginal man, the concept requires clarification. It was first discussed in the literature by Park [14] and later developed by Stonequist. [15] A marginal man has been defined as an "individual who through migration, education, marriage, or some other influence leaves one social group or culture without making a satisfactory adjustment to another and finds himself on the margin of each but a member of neither." [16]

Wardwell argued in his study of the chiropractor that occupational marginality need not involve an intermediate position between two different groups, roles or cultures: "... there can be marginality to a single well-defined social role ... A marginal role is an imperfectly institutionalized one, which means that there is some ambiguity in the pattern of behavior legitimately expected of a person fulfilling a role ..." [17]

This concept will be used in Chapter VII when we discuss the rural physician in Egypt.

Current Issues and Influence on Role Set

The Special Case of Family Planning and Government Policy

Egypt has a population increase of about 2.5% per annum. The crude birth rate is estimated as almost 38 per 1000 persons. Since 1962, with President Nasser's declaration, the government has tried to reduce the population increase. [18] Also, the distribution of population in Egypt is incompatible with optimal social and economic development. This is indicated by the striking phenomenon of the congestion of 99% of the population on about 3.5 percent of the whole area of the country, as quoted in the "Egyptian Gazette". [19]

The above article further states:

> "The Minister said that the performances of the Governors and heads of the local government bodies would be evaluated in view of the extent of their success in implementing social and economic development plans.
>
> "Since the Governors", he said, "were chosen from among the natives of each respective governorate and since they were invested with presidential powers in their governorates we expect much of them in the sphere of development."
>
> In January, President Sadat issued a republican decree delegating presidential powers to the governors, in an attempt to decentralise the government system and deepen the democratic practice.
>
> Moreover, the President, in a speech during his tour of the Qena, Assuit and Suhag governorates last week, declared wider authority to the governors to boost the development of their governorates.
>
> The Minister of State for Cabinet Affairs (Mr. Soliman Metwalli) also affirmed that the chiefs of village councils and local executive committees would be assigned certain tasks including planning and follow-up of development projects, within the framework of the master plan for development.
>
> Mr. Metwalli urged the leaders of the National Democratic Party in the governorates to contribute to the achievement of the goals of the national action in the fields of production and services.
>
> He, moreover, invited the Egyptian experts and scientists in the field of family planning to promote the new conception of the small family and to orientate people to minimize their births to avoid the population explosion." [20]

It is interesting to note that in this study only a small number of physicians mentioned family planning as "other roles or functions."

This is rather surprising considering that a million dollar research-training programme was completed last year and currently a multi-million dollar house-to-house distribution of contraceptives research-training programme is being carried out. Such a programme was undertaken in an attempt to discover the most advantageous way of establishing a unique family planning contraceptive service. The undertaking consists of: 1) Giving a service i.e. making supplies of contraceptives available and distributing them, 2) Monitoring their use, 3) Training personnel in the necessary skills.

Perhaps, rather than research based upon the physicians' knowledge of contraceptive use and training programmes utilizing the above approach, more research is needed to understand the physician's *attitudes* toward contraception and *his beliefs* about contraception and Islam.

The attitude of Islam in family planning is worth brief consideration here. Dudley Kirk, in discussing Moslem natality states:

> Empirically Islam has been a more effective barrier to the diffusion of family planning than Catholicism. The monolithic character of Islam in this regard is overlooked because of its enormous territory, its linguistic diversity, its political atomization and the absence of a central religious hierarchy. [21]

However, he further asserts:

> Moslem countries are all in the category of developing nations, and all have low indices of material development. These are usually lower than those of non-Moslem neighbors. High levels of education, industrialization and other aspects of modernization associated with declines in the birth rate have not made strong headway as yet in Moslem countries. In fact, class differentials in natality in the UAR, for example, suggest that a general rise in the level of living might at first tend to raise the birth rate, because of better nutrition, health, and other factors. [22]

The "official" stance of Islam is summed up by Dr. Muhammad Sallam Madkour, head of the Department of Islamic Law at Cairo University. He has made a thorough survey of Islamic pronouncements on the subject of birth control and concludes:

> There has been no Koranic text or definitive statement in the Hadith (prophetic tradition) that constitutes proof or evidence (on which to base a precise opinion). There has been only individual reports which were somewhat contradictory and the scholars have come out with different opinions. [23]

He also concludes that the majority of the Moslem jurists have declared the use of contraceptives to be lawful, and only a few scholars have come out against it.

What is evident from the above statements is that other factors in Moslem societies account for high fertility, such as high infant mortality, the importance of sons, security in old age, etc.

In the present study, when only nine physicians out of a sample of 50 (18%) feel that their role encompasses family planning, one must question the efficacy of such on-going training research programmes. Clearly a new approach is needed.

Family planning is currently being taught in medical schools within a course called General Health. When questioned about the course in family planning, my informant stated: "We hate it (The General Health Course), not many students go to attend. We call it the W.C."[a]

It is worth noting here that the group of medical students mentioned previously in this study, were questioned about family planning education. The majority (over 80%) indicated that family planning was treated very briefly (and rather superficially) in their General Health Course (social medicine). They expressed a desire to learn more about such an important sociomedical subject, and an awareness of its impact on development in Egypt.

Official policies in the last fifteen years to reduce the population growth rate have evolved slowly toward a national commitment to reduce fertility. The Egyptian Family Planning Board is extremely cautious and rightfully so about using contraceptives from developed nations without proper trial considering the specific diseases and problems of the Egyptian woman, such as anemia and liver disease due to the high incidence of bilharziasis.

Between 1962 and 1973, emphasis was on increasing the availability of family planning services to decrease the birth rate. A shift in emphasis occurred between 1973 and 1975, when government policy stressed the reduction of population growth through the improvement of socioeconomic conditions. Reflecting this change, the Supreme Council became the Supreme Council for Population and Family Planning and the Executive Board became the Population and Family Planning Board, now responsible for planning and coordination. However, the current policy seems to embrace both positions as exemplified by a recent visit arranged by the afore-mentioned board to Fayum.[b]

It was the Arab bedouin who perhaps "discovered" the first intrauterine device by insert a fruit pip into the female camel during the long migratory marches. Historically contraception existed in primitive societies, although fertility was primarily controlled by abortion, infanticide or prolonged lactation. In contemporary developed nations, contraception is widely used. For

---

[a] He is using water closet (WC) as a derogatory term indicating that these studies are viewed in a very negative way.

[b] The visit had been arranged to a PDP (population and development) village by the Population and Family Planning Board for the present writer.

example, in the United States the 1965 National Fertility Study reported that 97 percent of fecund women had used, or expected to use contraception. [24] However, the proportion of users in the developing countries is considerably smaller with wide variations, not only from country to country but between rural and urban populations. This is evidenced in Mauldins data from sample surveys in Mysore, Egypt, India, Korea, Pakistan, and Turkey indicating that the proportions which practiced family planning varied from 1 to 36 percent. [25]

There are many controversies surrounding the issues of implementing widespread use of contraception in the developing countries through family planning programmes. Gadalla writing about fertility and family planning in a rural Egyptian Community summarizes these issues as follows: [26]

First, there is the view that it is wasteful to attempt any family planning program in a traditional society before it has "modernized". Without such development it is argued that people will continually be motivated to have large families. This view is severely criticized by family planning advocates.

The second view maintains that certain aspects of social and economic development must be present in the society before family planning can be successfully implemented.

The Third view is that under the present conditions of most developing societies, family planning can be successfully implemented through a strong and well designed motivation, communication and information program focused toward appropriate targets in the population. This method is based upon surveys which indicate that in most developing countries a significant proportion of the society desires less children.

The final view assumes that the use of contraceptives can be spread in developing societies through a "marketing" approach. Based on survey findings, supporters of this view have argued that the major need in family planning is not motivation and persuasion, but the provision of information and services to the masses.

In additions, there are those who debate whether contraceptive use in developing countries will result in a significant decline in societal fertility levels. It is argued by family planning advocated that couples who had more children than they desired, did so because they lacked contraceptive services and information and not because they wanted more children. According to Gadalla, those who believe family planning in developing countries will not result in a significant societal fertility decline reject one or more of the following assumptions which are implicit in the proponents' point of view: [27]

> (1) that the stated desired family size is a "true" expression of a "real" conviction about the number of children that people in the developing countries want to have; (2) that there are no personal, familial, social, economic, or cultural factors other than the unavailability of contraception that would prevent people in the

developing countries from achieving and not exceeding the desired family size; and (3) that the desired number of children in the developing countries is low enough that is, the goal is achieved, a considerable decline in societal fertility levels will result.

The above serves to illustrate the endless arguments among social scientists and demographers about the real causes of fertility decline in developing countries.

The legitimacy of organized support for family planning is almost universally accepted. However, the efficacy of government programmes for accelerating a decline in fertility prior to or concomitantly with social and economic development is still a debatable topic. The reliability of data in terms of fertility reduction arouses skepticism when they concern the larger developing countries where modernization is generally limited to urban areas. However, there is indication in world fertility surveys of a fertility decline in special situations such as Hong Kong, Singapore, The Republic of Korea, and Some Caribbean Islands all notable for their relative homogeneity and the efficiency of internal communication. A recent review of fertility decline in developing countries since World War II indicates that the fastest declines occurred in such cases. [28]

A reduction is also evident in China, Indonesia, Malaysia, The Philippines, Thailand, and Turkey in Asia; Egypt and Tunisia in Africa; and Brazil, Colombia, The Dominican Republic, Mexico, and Venezuela in Latin America, illustrating that prior rigid reproductive patterns are now yielding to the impact of a variety of modernizing influences. In Thailand the 1974-75 survey conducted as part of the World Fertility Survey found that births had dropped 17 percent in a decade among women aged 25-29, 26 percent among women aged 30-34, and 32 percent among women aged 35-39. [29]

Most of the countries cited have antinatalist policies and government family planning programmes. However, other factors can alter the level of the birth rate other than family planning within marriage such as a rise in the age at marriage; also changes in the age structure of the population will also affect the crude birth rate, increasing it if women of reproductive age become a larger component, decreasing it if they constitute a smaller segment. Coital frequency, changes in nutritional status and breastfeeding practices also affect fertility and, consequently, the crude birth rate.

The most recent projections prepared by the United Nations already incorporate declines in both fertility and mortality. Unless some catastrophe intervenes, population growth is assured not only until but well beyond the year 2000 because of the young age structure of today's population. In the developing world, where 72 percent of all people live, 40 percent of the females are under age 15, over 25 percent are currently in the young reproductive age group 15-29. [30]

In spite of most developing nations having this age structure, government perceptions of the problems vary greatly as evidenced at the consultations organized in 1975 by the United Nations Population Division to consider government response to the World Population Plan of Action. [31] Asia and the Pacific country delegates affirmed support of quantified and dated target for reduced population growth in order to promote human welfare. Latin American delegates emphasized the need to distinguish between two types of action: one directed at studying the relations among socioeconomic, political, and demographic structures; the other directed at examining the demand generated by population growth for different types of services such as housing, health, and education. The African delegates, emphasized questions of international equity and economic cooperation, the position on population growth being that high rates could be an economic liability in some places but a benefit in others. West African delegates did not view rapid population growth as an impediment to the development in their area.

A common theme emerged in the following propositions:

> (a) Population policies and programmes are an integral part of national development planning;
>
> (b) Although development factors influence demographic behaviour, the latter also affects the former;
>
> (c) The interrelations between population and development factors are imperfectly understood, and consequently, the effects of indirect action in the field of population (through programmes directed towards affecting specific population variables) cannot be foreseen with any precision;
>
> (d) Research on the interrelationships must be undertaken or intensified to ensure that governments shall have a better base for: (1) formulating policies, implementing them, evaluating them; (2) for integrating them in planning for development. [32]

It can be seen that there is not so much a disagreement on fundamental issues with regards to the social benefits of family planning services, but this conference serves to illustrate the role of the differences in culture, political and economic systems, and stages of demographic and economic transition.

What is the fate of Egypt's population problem? The future for Egypt has hope, according to Gadalla: [33]

> With the promising prospects of accelerating developmental aspects that create conditions conducive to low fertility, improving and intensifying existing family planning services, and implementing innovative approaches for making contraceptive supplies and information directly available to the people, there is hope that Egypt's birth rate will decline much faster than has been the case to date.

But is there hope for that segment of society born female? How does this core problem of population control, clearly a massive concern of central governments, influence the lives of the producers—the individual women locked in the traditions and culture of their own societies? This issue is examined in the following section.

Status and Education of Women

The women in Egypt, as in other parts of the world, walk the line between the demands of society, often the other sex, and realities of herself.

The future for Egypt's "masses" of females is not optimistic. According to the International Labour Organization (ILO) Labour Force Projection for Egypt, the 1985 Population (in millions) projection is 50.2. The labour force projection is 13.4 for male and 1.6 for female. [34] This renders a particularly bleak future for women as victims of sexual and educational biases which begin at birth for many Egyptian females.

Although the Koran speaks angrily about the father "whose face darkens" when he is told of the birth of a daughter and the prophet having repeatedly stressed the importance of giving equal affection and care to children of both sexes, death rates of female infants are nearly 20 percent higher than rates for male infants in Egypt. [35] This pheonomenon is currently being studied and preliminary findings indicate the following:

1. As long as breastmilk was sufficient to meet the child's nutritional needs no sex difference in development was observed, but during the period when the child required supplemental feeding the incidence of malnutrition among girls increased by 40 percent over the incidence among boys.
2. Most mothers (73 percent) of newborn girls believed that they had caused unhappiness to their husbands by given birth to a female child. Therefore, it should be emphasized here that Islamic and traditional cultures are not necessarily the same. Analysts of woman's status in the Middle East have blamed Islamic traditions. According to one female social scientist:

> "... putting these teachings into practice is not a matter of correcting individual abuses of Islamic Law. The basic problem lies in the condition of conflict between these laws and those of European origin. What accounts for the low status of women in public and increasingly private sectors of social life is hardly the religious tradition but is ironically enough, the civil and penal laws of Europe, and especially France, which has been superimposed on Middle Eastern people." [36]

In the following brief description, we will refer to some historical Islamic roots of Feminism through the eyes of the Islamic philosopher Amin as the background to the study of Women in Egypt.

As early as 1899 Quasim Amin (1865-1908) published a book on the emancipation of women. His starting point was for that period a familiar one, the decay of Islam seen in the perspective of Darwinism. He felt that the Islamic community was too weak to face the pressures on it from all sides, and if weak it cannot survive in a world ruled by the laws of natural selection. [37] He cites the decay not due to Islam but rather the disappearance of the social virtues of "moral strength", and the cause of that was said to be ignorance—ignorance of the true sciences from which alone can be derived the laws of human happiness. This ignorance, according to Amin begins in the family.[c] The relations of man and woman, of mother and child, are the basis of society; the virtues which exist in the family will exist in the nation. The work of women in society is to form the morals of the nation. [38] Amin goes on to state that in Muslim countries neither men nor women are properly educated to create a real family life, and woman has not the freedom or status necessary if she is to play her role. [39] Corruption came into Islam from outside, with the people who were converted and brought in their own 'customs and illusions.' They destroyed the original Islamic system of government, which defined the rights of rulers and ruled, and put in its place the rule of despotic force. All through society the strong learned to despise the weak, and men to despise women. [40]

Writing almost one hundred years later, Fanon discusses these outside forces in *Algeria Unveiled* in terms of colonialization.[d] "The method of presenting the Algerian as a prey fought over with equal ferocity by Islam and France with its Western culture reveals the whole approach of the occupier, his philosophy and his policy." [41] This fear is being reiterated in Egypt today as it tends to strain toward fundamentalism in response to the threat of invading Western culture.

Amin felt that the heart of the social problem was the position of women which could only be improved by education. [42] Education should not only be directed to the proper management of the household, it should also ensure that women could earn their own living. This was the only sure guarantee of women's rights; unless a women could support herself she would always be at the mercy of male tyranny, no matter what rights the laws gave her and would have to secure power for herself by devious means.[e] Education would end the

---

[c] Two of the most influential theoreticians of the contemporary women's movement, Shulaminth Firestone and Juliet Mitchell, have pointed out that the oppression of women neither began with modern capitalism, nor does it automatically disappear in socialist societies. Firestone argues that there is a universal sex class system inherent in the biological family, while Mitchell separates out the different structures of women's oppression (sexuality, reproduction, socialization of the young) located in the family. Mitchell argues that these structures differ historically but are everywhere oppressive in that they remove women from the field of production. Shulaminth Firestone, *The Dialectic of Sex, The Case of the Feminist Revolution*, (New York: Bantim Books, 1971). Juliet Mitchell, *Women's Estate*, (New York: Vintage, 1971).

[d] Another essay by Caulfield breaks down the assumption that women's experiences of male domination are "on a basic level everywhere the same". In pulling apart the customary views of male oppression she noted the critical point that westerners assume that colonialized peoples were, in her terms, "virtually unchanged representatives of the past". Mina Davis Caulfield, Universal Sex Oppression? A critique from Marxist Anthropology, *Catalyst*, Trent University, 1977, pp. 60-77.

[e] According to Nelson, in Egypt, and the Arab Middle East in general, where women are paramount in maintaining or possibly threatening the moral order, they have power. 'It is through

tyranny, and in doing so it would also end the veiling and seclusion of women. Amin, however, approached this subject with caution. His wish, he says, is not to abolish seclusion as such, for in a certain form it is necessary to safeguard virtue; it is rather to restore it to what the Shari'a lays down. [43]

Echoing Amin, on December 1944, Hoda Sharawi, Egypt's leading Feminist, at the 20th anniversary of the foundation of the Egyptian Women's Federation, suggests that the Federation's goal is the betterment of women through raised standards of education and preparation for marital life so that she may "make her share in the promotion of the well-being of the country in general." [44] These actions included the establishment of a health unit to treat sich women and children freely.

A Physician and Development Planner in the Ministry of Health, Dr. Wafik Hassouna has this to say about female education: [45]

> "I place the emphasis on educating women for responsible motherhood because I believe that only through the education of mothers and fathers can we expect the behavioural changes in the younger generation, who are, after all, the beneficiaries of the development plans on the drawing boards today. I would go so far as to suggest that because of the importance of this role that women who choose this option and participate fully in the education program would also be given remunerative compensation for their services as well as having social services channeled directly to them. I would also say that a whole system of continuing education and refresher education should be provided for women who wish to pursue a variety of career interests in their life. I strongly urge us to benefit from the experiences of other countries. Let us examine the statistics on the type of jobs women hold in countries in which they constitute a fairly large percentage of the labour force. If we do this we shall find that, all too often, the women have been assigned the menial, cryptoservant jobs and that, at the same time, their status has eroded because their contribution as responsible mother has not been accorded at least as equal a status as factory worker, in the sense that they have not received compensations—both in money and in kind—from society commensurate with the importance of their role. When we talk about education in Egypt, let us keep these points in mind. Let us seek together to identify what types of contributions we really need in Egypt to get ourselves moving in the right direction and then let us structure our system of rewards, status and sanctions so that those contributions which are most useful to the nation will also be those which are appropriately awarded."

The relationship of female education and levels of fertility has been established. [46] This relationship is recognized by the Population and Family Planning Board and the Government. Both have been making a considerable effort in organizing home handicrafts, purchasing the products from the

---

witchcraft, sorcery, divination, and curing that women are instrumental in influencing the lives of men.' Cynthia Nelson, "Public and Private Politics: Women in the Middle Eastern World" *American Ethnologist*, 1974, Volume 1, pp. 551-563.

women, and then marketing them. [47] This has had little impact on women as a whole, but has had some impact on physicians as they view themselves. A noted Egyptian Physician Feminist, Dr. Nuwwal Saadawi, in her book, *Women and Sex* states: [48]

> "Work is a human necessity whereas conception is nothing but a biological function in which all living things engage, from amoebae to apes ...

Unfortunately her views were met with reserve and resentment.

From the preceeding discussion, we can see two attitudes toward the education and emancipation of women in Egypt; education of women for labour and education of women for traditional roles. The interrelationship between Islamic ideals, education, feminism, and professionalism warrant further examination in order to understand the development of female emancipation in Egypt.

Historically, during the late 19th and early 20th century, education and social reform along western lines were viewed by the nationalists as prerequisites for independence. This meant reform in marriage and the family structure as well. On the other hand, another view desired a return toward traditional values arguing that female emancipation was in essence an imitation of western values which would only weaken the Islamic family unit.

The emancipationist view was usually associated with the thought of Mohammad ʾAbduh which represented the values of the upper classes. Whereas, the opposite view was associated with the petit bourgeoisie which represented the small-scale productive sector of poor peasants, small landowners and tenants, artesians and owners of small workshops, public service employees and military personnel.

The view of the petit bourgeoisie was represented in the Muslim Brotherhood and the Free Officer's movement of Nasser's time which demanded an end to foreign domination but continued to retain the traditional views toward women.

Therefore, it is the upper middle class in which intellectuals and those women in the profession of medicine, science and engineering have become professionally liberated, whereas the petit bourgeoisie tend to lag behind in this development.

In spite of the teachings of Islam, as in most of the world, women are often regarded as subordinate citizens and changes in status are occurring at a slow pace. Inheritance, property, and family laws explicitly regard two women as equal to one man.[f] Honour of the family resides in its female members, but is

---

[f] According to Hamamsy, although a girl inherits half as much as her brother, there is little demand for equality in inheritance rights by women. L. S. Hamamsy, "The Role of Women in the Development of Egypt", *Middle East Forum*, 1958, June, 1958.

an attribute possessed by and defended by men, usually her brothers.g Marriages are still customarily arranged by parents in the same social class, often tied by kinship, and children provide women with emotional satisfaction, power and prestige attributed to women with many sons by extended family networks.

Urban women with university education have traditionally entered the scientific and medical professions as well as social work and teaching. Secondary school training has allowed rural as well as urban women to become nurses and teachers.h

Here we have the dichotomy of Islam providing for female freedom and growth while culture dictates subordination. Under these conflicting theses, how does the Egyptian woman, as a healer and consumer of health services, deal with these issues.i

Women from the lower socio-economic groups resort to the Zar ceremonyj to relieve stress. [49] More research is indicated for women of Egypt from higher socio-economic groups so as to provide us with an understanding of how they themselves define and cope with stress. As Nelson and Olesen aptly state:

> "We must assume the standpoint of the participants, for to participate in the healing system is to participate in the moral order of the particular society or group: selves are defined in the exchange between healer and seeker; symbols are constructed which enter the lives of men and women and shape them as persons or link them to sacred orders. In short, seeking healing is not merely a medical matter, but is a moral issue in which constructions of self and illness shape and are shaped by definer and defined, healer and healed, persons and society. And it is to these issues that we should direct our research on women and their health. [50]

---

g 'In the Middle East where women are publicly acknowledged as having healing power, it is associated with supernatural and the fear that men have of women's sexuality or, better expressed, as the felt threat to male esteem of women's sexual misconduct.' Cynthia Nelson, "Public and Private Politics: Women in the Middle Eastern World", *American Ethnologist*, 1974, Volume 1, pp. 551-563.

h According to Navarro, within the labour force in the health sector of the United States, women constitute the majority of all producers a majority concentrated in the lower-middle class and working class echelons of the labour force. For this reason, sex and class are clearly interwined for most, though not all, women in the health sector. Vincente Navarro, Medicine Under Capitalism, Prodist, New York, 1976, p. 172.

i For a perspective of Western Women and Medicine see Joyce Leeson and Judith Gray, *Women and Medicine*, Travistock Publications, Great Britain, 1978.

j The Zar ceremony is a means of dealing with the demonic powers of evil who may cause illness and is usually used only when other methods, both traditional and allopathic have failed. Morsy, discussing Egyptian folk illnesses states that the ultimate cause of ʾ*uzr* may be traced to assymetrical power relations. The illness directs attention to personal grievances and distress and induces a temporary enhancement of social position among persons in subservient positions suffering from social stress and role conflict. Soheir Morsy, "Gender, Power, and Illness in an Egyptian Village", Ph.D. dissertation, Michigan State University, Department of Anthropology, cited by Barbara Pillsbury, "Traditional Health Care in the Near East" U.S. AID Report, Washington, D.C., Contract No. AID/NE-C-1395 (Mimiograph).

How are the healers in Middle Eastern society defined? For the Woman physician the concept of complementarity is valid here. According to Nelson [51] what is perhaps not appreciated by Western feminists is that what they view as oppression in the status of women in the Islamic Middle East is what has provided women with a traditional source of power as well as a legitimate authority within the large extended families. When women actually move into the productive work force they "generally find relatively little resistance with regard to employment from men. Instead of resistance and jealousy, women frequently meet encouragement from male colleagues." [52]

It is worth emphasizing in this respect that the pilot study leading to the present work [53] indicated that the woman physician did not view her role as any different from her male colleague; this is a clear implication that she views herself as an equal who is expected to perform her role in the same manner.

This may be so for the female physician in Egypt but one must question this assumption as it relates to other female healers, the *hakima* (diploma nurse), the *moamarida* (B.Sc. Nurse), and the *daya*, (traditional midwife). Lacking up to date Egyptian Research[k, l] one is tempted to agree with Navarro that in the system of Medicine women of this category are indeed in a subordinate position. [54]

However, the changing healing system will require more research not only into the receivers of the health system but also on the role of the *daya*, *hakima* and the High Institute of Nursing Graduates and the images of nurses in the Egyptian society and how these images influence the delivery of health services.

REFERENCES

[1] Parsons, T., *The Social System*, New York, The Free Press, 1951, pp. 428-473.
[2] Merton, R. K., *Social Theory and Social Structures*, New York, Free Press, 1968, pp. 86-91, 106-108.
[3] Linton, R., *The Study of Man*, New York, Appleton-Century, 1936, pp. 113-115, 126-128.
[4] Merton, *op. cit.* p. 423.
[5] Biddle, B. J. and Thomas, E. J., *Role Theory Concepts and Research*, New York, John Wiley and Sons, Inc., 1966, p. 35.

---

[k] See A. Fahmy, "The Hakima: Performance of a Professional Role," Unpublished Master's thesis, Dept. of Sociology and Anthropology and Psychology, American University in Cairo, 1969.

[l] For other analysis of nurses in Western medical systems, see Bonnie Bullough "Barriers to the Nurse Practitioner Movement: Problems of Women in a Women's Field", *International Journal of Health Services*, Vol. 15, no. 2, 1975, pp. 226; Virginia Cleland, "Sex Discrimination: Nursing's Most Pervasive Problem, *American Journal of Nursing*, Vol. 71, No. 8, August 1971, pp. 1542-7; Ellen Lewin, "Feminist Ideology and the Meaning of Work: The Case of Nursing", *Catalyst*, Trent University, 1977, pp. 78-103; and Virginia Olesen and Elvi Whittaker, *The Silent Dialogue*, San Francisco, Jessey-Bass, 1968.

[6] *Ibid.*, pp. 34-35.
[7] *Ibid.*, p. 34.
[8] Benne, K. D. and Sheats, P., 'Functional Roles of Group Members, *Journal of Social Issues*, 1948, Vol. 4, pp. 41-51.
[9] Sarbin, T. R., *Role Theory* in Lindzey, G. (ed.), *Handbook of Social Psychology*, Vol. 1, 1954, Cambridge, Mass., Addison-Wesley, p. 233.
[10] Goode, W. J., 'Community Within a Community: The Professions', *American Sociological Review*, Vol. 22, April 1977, pp. 194-200.
[11] Cole, D., *Nomad of the Nomads*, Chicago, Aldine Publishing Co., 1975.
[12] Evans-Pritchard, Sir E. E., *The Sanusi of Cyranaica*, Oxford University Press, 1949.
[13] Berger, M., *The Arab World Today*, New York, Doubleday & Co., 1964, pp. 42-71.
[14] Park, R. E., 'Human Migration and the Marginal Man', *American Journal of Sociology*, Vol. 33, May 1928, pp. 881-893.
[15] Stonequist, E. V., *The Marginal Man: A Study in Personality and Culture Conflict*, New York, Charles Scribner's Sons, 1937.
[16] Miller, D. C. and Form, W. M., *Industrial Sociology*, New York, Harper & Brothers, 1951, p. 631.
[17] Wardwell, W. I., 'A Marginal Professional Role: The Chiropracter', *Social Forces*, Vol. 30, March 1952, p. 340.
[18] Gamal Abdel Nasser, Proclamation of the National Charter, *President Nasser's Speeches and Interviews*, Cairo, Information Department, 1962, p. 335.
[19] *The Egyptian Gazette*, Thursday, April 19, 1979.
[20] *Ibid.*
[21] Kirk, D., 'Factors Affecting Moslem Natality', Paper Presented to International Conference on Family Planning Programs, Geneva, August 23-27, 1965, in *Muslim Attitudes Toward Family Planning*, New York, Population Council, 1967, p. 66.
[22] *Ibid.*, 72.
[23] Madkour, M. S., *Nazrat al-Islam ila Tanzim al-nasl*, Cairo, Dar al-Arabiya, 1965, p. 26.
[24] Ryder, N. B. and Westoff, C. F., *Reproduction in the United States*, Princeton University Press, Princeton, 1971.
[25] Mauldin, P., 'Fertility Studies: Knowledge, Attitude and Practice', *Studies in Family Planning*, No. 7, (June), pp. 1-10.
[26] Gadalla, S., *Is There Hope-Family and Fertility Planning in a Rural Egyptian Community*, The Social Research Center, The American University in Cairo Press and The Carolina Population Center, The University of North Carolina at Chapel Hill, 1978.
[27] *Ibid.*, pp. 38-39.
[28] Mauldin, P., 'Patterns of Fertility Decline in Developing Countries, 1950-1975', *Studies in Family Planning*, 9, No. 4, 1978, pp. 75-80.
[29] Chulalongkorn University Institute of Population Studies and National Statistical Office, Population Division, *The Survey of Fertility in Thailand: World Fertility Survey*, 1976, Report No. 1, p. 56.
[30] United Nations Population Division, 'New United Nations Projections: A Brief Summary of the Projections of Total Population as Assessed in 1973-74', *Population Bulletin of the United Nations*, no. 8, 1977.
[31] United Nations Population Division, 'Results of the Regional Consultations Subsequent to the World Population Conference', *Population Bulletin of the United Nations*, no. 8, 1977, cited by Nortman, D. L. and Hofstatter, E. in *Population and Family Planning Programs, A Population Council Fact Book*, The Population Council, New York, 1978, pp. 1-2.
[32] *Ibid.*
[33] Gadalla, *op. cit.* p. 239.
[34] International Labour Organization (ILO), *Rural Employment Problems in the United Arab Republic*, Geneva, 1969, p. 27.
[35] Al-Azhar University, Population Studies Research, Appendix A., Research Activities 1975-79, Mimiograph, p. 3-4.

[36] Saleh, S. A. W., 'Women in Islam: Their Status in Religious and Traditional Culture', *International Journal of the Sociology of the Family*, Volume 2, No. 1, 1972, pp. 1-8.
[37] Amin, Qasim, *Tahir al-Mar'a*, Cairo, 1899, p. 116, cited by Hourani, A., Arabic Thought in the Liberal Age 1798-1938, Oxford University Press, London, 1970, pp. 116-131.
[38] Amin, Qasim, *al-Mar'a al-jadida*, Cairo, 1901, p. 124, cited by Hourani, *ibid.*, pp. 116-131.
[39] Amin, Qasim, *Tahir al-Mar'a, op. cit.*
[40] *Ibid.*, pp. 12-14.
[41] Fanon, F., *A Dying Colonialism*, Monthly Review Press, 1965, pp. 35-67.
[42] Amin, Qasim, *al-Mar'a al-jadida, op. cit.* p. 20.
[43] Amin, Qasim, *Tahir al-Mar'a, op. cit.* pp. 27 and 83, cited by Hourani, pp. 116-131.
[44] Olesen, V., 'Styles and Sources of Social Change: Womens Movements as Critiques of Health Care Systems', *The Cairo Papers in Social Science, Womens Health and Development*, The American University in Cairo Press, Cairo, Volume one, Monograph one, December, 1977, pp. 21-34.
[45] Hassouna, W., 'Education of Women—For What?,' *The Cairo Papers in Social Science, Womens Health and Development*, The American University in Cairo Press, Cairo, Volume one, Monograph one, December, 1977, pp. 49-53.
[46] Schultz, P. T., *Fertility Patterns and Their Determinants in the Arab Middle East*, Rand Corp. RM-5978-FF, May 1970, p. 19.
[47] Waterbury, *op. cit*, p. 45.
[48] Saadawi, Dr. Nuwwal, Women and Sex, Dar ash-Shaab, Cairo, 1972.
[49] Kennedy, J. G., 'Nubian Zar Ceremonies as Psychotherapy', *Human Organization*, 4, 1967, pp. 185-194.
[50] Nelson, C. and Olesen, V., 'Preliminary Notes on Healing Systems, Social Control and Articulation of the Moral Order', *Cairo Papers in Social Science, Womens Health and Development*, The American University in Cairo Press, Cairo, Volume one, Monograph one, December, 1977, p. 20.
[51] *Ibid.*, p. 20.
[52] Mohsen, S., 'The Egyptian Woman: Between Modernity and Tradition', in Mathiasson, C. (ed.) *Many Sisters*, New York, Free Press, 1974, pp. 391-393.
[53] El-Mehairy, T. M. 'Medical Doctors: Managerial Abilities and Role Definitions', *Middle East Management Review*, Vol. II, No. 1. 1978, pp. 121-137.
[54] Navarro, V., *op. cit.*

CHAPTER SIX

RESEARCH METHODOLOGY AND FIELDWORK PROCEDURE

Pilot Questionnaire

Physician Questionnaire

The primary data was collected by means of a pretested questionnaire which was administered in an Arabic translation. The pilot study was originally done in the Governorate of Menoufia. Questions included responses to the physicians' felt need for additional education and training, their functions, an analysis of the level of competence of subordinate personnel, advantages and disadvantages in their present employment situation, and problems encountered in performing their jobs, as a female or a male, from the people in the community, from the staff in the clinic, from the supervisors in the Governorate and from the Administrators in the Ministry of Health.

Since bureaucracy was mentioned frequently in the pilot study, respondents were asked to state examples in answer to the above questions.

The frequent mention of bureaucracy is worth noting. A notable work by Morroe Berger attempts to apply the Weberian concepts of bureaucracy to a transitional society such as Egypt. [1] Although Berger attempted to discover how "bureaucratic" the Egyptian public service was, he concluded that the existing theory of bureaucracy was inadequate for analyzing the problems raised by the facts of the Egyptian society. More extensive research is needed into this area of study. Part of this study will attempt to analyze the physicians' examples of bureaucracy. These results might be highly instructive for practitioners of administration in transitional societies.

Respondents were asked to rate their administrative and supervisory skills on a scale of 1-5, the extent to which they are satisfied with their career, family relationships, social relationships, leisure time recreational activities and financial and social status.

Revised Version

As the study progressed, it was felt that feedback from the administrators was necessary to ascertain that the research was progressing in the right direction in terms of relevant issues and problems. It was also hoped that information elicited would provide insight as to role complementarity.

An interview was arranged with a Ministry of Health Administrator. The first interview proved to be disappointing even though the appointment was made in advance by a family member and colleague of the Administrator. Egyptian society places heavy emphasis on Gemeinschaft relationships and it is through these channels that a majority of my work was carried out.

Although eager to assist me, when asked direct questions his reply was that he would have to think about the answer. I returned the following week with a copy of my pilot study. An "appointment" in the context of Egyptian society does not necessarily mean exclusive right to the appointee. Riggs [2] aptly calls an administration model 'the sala model'. This model is predominantly present in a fused society. It is interesting to note that *sala* is an Arabic term used for a sitting room where guests are received.

This definition is not without applicability to the Egyptian environment. As I held the second interview, drinking coffee in a relaxed semi-informal atmosphere, I presented the administrator with my pilot study. I was quite astonished to find that he began reading the paper aloud to the other persons in the room, several of whom were in top administrative positions. During this narration, he continuously made comments, actually answering the questions which I had asked during the previous interview. This was complemented by the administrators present making additional comments as the reading of the paper progressed.

The following sums up some of their comments.

> "The Egyptian doctor is dissatisfied. He has been trained abroad in many cases, and has an idea of *how things should be*—then in Egypt he finds things to be different. This makes him frustrated. He is therefore functioning in a state of non-reality."

Bureaucracy was a frequent complaint of the Ministry of Health doctors. An administrator's response to comments cited in the paper was:

> "Bureaucracy—but what does the word mean to the doctors? There are many problems but the main one is career prospects. A doctor goes into the village and he is isolated. There is no one to talk to. No cinemas—nothing he is accustomed to. They (the village doctors) are usually young graduates who feel that they are being punished in the first place when they have vast responsibilities. They are neither trained nor have they had the chance to develop the administrative skills necessary. Previously, they had only their doctor supervisor (in the hospital training) to answer to—now they have lay village leaders and this can be problematic."
>
> "We have intensive training programmes, but they have much paper work which they resent. They also have problems because they cannot reprimand their subordinate staff since these people are from the village."
>
> "We now have instituted a rotation programme which permits the doctor to come to an urban area for one month every six months to keep him up to date and for psychological reasons. We also send much literature to the village to keep him up to date."

At this point I asked if Egypt was overproducing doctors as mentioned in a U.S. news article. [3]

> "We are not overproducing. We have enough rural units to absorb these doctors and health services are forever expanding."

In an attempt to guide me he concluded:

> "You must check to see how long a doctor is in a village. Compare those that have been in a village over 4 years with those who have been in a village less than 4 years."

Another administrator added,

> "You must concentrate only on the rural doctors. This is where many problems lie. Egypt is unique in that she has 5,000 of these units serving the people. We have the doctors to staff them. We can say to any doctor: "Go to the village," and he must go. The rural doctor faces problems with lack of supplies, isolation, fear for his career. He has many constraints. *No Egyptian doctor is satisfied.* One major constraint is salary. He makes 45 Egyptian pounds per month. This is not enough. So they either give up—they become absent—or they start charging for their visits, medicines, etc."

The foregoing comments reassured me of the relevance of the study in progress. It also presented dimensions of the role conflicts and complementarity. As a result, the final questionnaire was revised.

The revised questionnaire included value scales for Independence, Recognition, and Achievement. The scale was used for providing profiles for the different groups of physicians (Urban, Rural, Upper and Lower Egypt). The Hussein Value Scale [4] (Appendix 1) was developed for Egyptian culture in Arabic and has been used to test creativity. The values represented in the scale are similar to Herzberg's motivation factors, [5] and are the most consistant in producing job satisfaction, hence their inclusion in the study.

The combined value scales have a total of 66 items: 24 for achievement, 20 for independence and 22 for recognition. The respondent was instructed to select (i.e. check) the one item which best expressed his belief or opinion (Appendix 1). The items were randomized as is now customary to avoid psychological set.

Value Orientation

Here we will examine the physicians' value orientation to the three values of Achievement, Independence, and Recognition, viewed as motivating factors.

> "Value-orientation refers to those aspects of the actor's orientation which commit him to the observance of certain norms, standards, criteria of selection, whenever he is in a contingent situation which allows (and requires) him to make a choice. Whenever an actor is forced to choose among various means objects, whenever he is forced to choose among various goal objects, whenever he is forced to choose which need-disposition he will gratify, or how much he will gratify a need-disposition—whenever he is forced to make any choice whatever—his *value-orientations* may commit him to certain norms that guide him in his choices." [6]

Confusions arise in the discussion of values primarily because the speaker or researcher may have a general category in mind, another a particular limited type of value and perhaps yet another, a different specific type. The most widely known of the content groupings is Sprangers' (used in the Allport-Vernon test of values): theoretical, economic, aesthetic, social, political and religious. A major objection to these content classifications is that they are culture-bound.

The Value Scales

The value scales used in this study were constructed by an Egyptian specifically for the Egyptian culture. [7][a] Six scales were constructed by Hussein to tap the values of independence, truth, achievement, recognition and transcending the present (when the latter was viewed as rejection of the present and looking forward to the future), with 15 tests measuring five creative thinking abilities: ideational fluency, spontaneous flexibility, originality, sensitivity to problems, and maintenance of direction.

The objective of his study was to define the values of creative people as individuals with personalities dominated by individuality, distinction, and discrimination and was concerned with how far each of these is related to creative thinking.

He made two tests on his sample. The first was concerned with the value in question and the other concerned with creative thinking.

The final scale was administered to 100 subjects with a test-retest method and 15 days in between. [8] Reliability coefficients were determined for the value test and were found to be 0.88 for Achievement, 0.83 for Independence, and 0.78 for Recognition. Such reliability coefficients are rather high and indicate the possibility of using the value scales with a great degree of confidence as far as their alignment with the value desired for measurement.

These scales were then administered to 272 Egyptian students (Mean age 22.7 ± 2.83) from the faculties of arts and science. Data were analyzed using the methods of simple correlation, partial correlation, stepwise regression analysis, factorial analysis, and analysis of variance followed by t-test.

Since Hussein demonstrated that his scales represent an accurate measurement of certain values connected with creative thinking, it was felt that his scales would be the most appropriate for this study of Egyptian physicians.

The outcome of the analysis demonstrated the instrumentality of independence, truth, achievement, recognition, and transcending the present to the value of reform. According to Hussein, "Reform stands as an end-state value, whereas independence, truth, achievement, recognition, and transcending the present stand as instrumental to the former (reform)".

---

[a] See General Defence of Questionnaires in this chapter.

"Results also showed significant positive relationships between performance on tests of creativity and performance on the scales of values. It was found that, high, mild, and low performances on creativity tests were significantly different in their scores on any one of the value scales, more pronounced in the higher ones." [9]

The scales of Achievement, Independance, and Recognition were selected to develop a value profile of motivation for the Egyptian physician. The English translation appears in Appendix I. It was felt that the use of the Hussein scales would have more validity in the Egyptian case than culture-bound western scales.

If the physicians' value orientations differed from group to group, such differences might be due to variations in geographical regions of a culture, to life in the country versus life in the city, to class and economic status, to the location education was obtained or to some other variables. It was hoped that a value profile could be obtained for the three "motivating" values.

According to Parsons:

> "The most general term which can be applied to the phase of motivation is, perhaps, "satisfaction". There is an interest in things and modes of behaviour which yields satisfactions. One of the important components of this is undoubtedly "self-respect". So far, that is as moral norms are genuinely built into the structure of personality the individual's own state of satisfaction is dependent on the extent to which he lives up to them. This is above all true with respect to the standarts of his various roles, particularly in our context, the occupational role, and to the place he feels he "deserves" in the scale of stratification." [10]

Allowing for the limitations of group analysis, it is important to state here that this study is seeking to provide a broad picture of the Egyptian physicians' role. What follows here is an effort to explore plausible relations between variables.

Accepting Kluckhohns' warning that: "Indeed", the group value system, is an abstraction—a statement of central tendencies in a range of concrete variation. The abstraction is meaningful and useful, but we must never lose sight of the fact that it is an abstraction at a high level."]11] However, he goes on to say:

> "The convergence between personal values and *group* values will be found to vary; it will be greater on the part of representative or conforming individuals in relatively homogeneous cultures or subcultures. A value may be defined in psychological terms as that aspect of motivation which is determined by codes or standards as opposed to immediate situation. If the standards are those carefully abstracted to represent modalities more or less characteristic of some social unit, the value may be spoken of as a group value. If the reference is to the private form of a code that influences motivation in an individual, one speaks of a personal value. Gordon Allport has said that "shared value" constitutes a contradiction in

terms. This is doubtless true at the very concrete level. *But analytically, it is possible and useful to describe the central tendencies abstractly and to impute them to the group rather than to the individual.* [12]

MEDICAL STUDENT QUESTIONNAIRE

A questionnaire, translated into Arabic, was constructed to elicit information regarding medical student anticipatory socialization and role as a village doctor during their mandatory conscription. Open ended questions were asked, related to what he or she believed to be the needs of the villager, and the "world view" of the villager.

Other questions related to prior visits to rural health units, the importance of such visits, sociological knowledge gained in medical school, adequate preparation for village work from the educational system, and from his or her personal upbringing. They were asked why medical care in Urban Cairo is felt to be superior to rural areas if indeed it is and why medical care in urban Cairo is regarded or allegedly inferior to rural areas.

For a comparison with those physicians already in the rural units, an identical list of questions was included relating to the anticipatory disadvantages in the health services. They were also asked which items they anticipated to be advantageous in the rural health service and why they originally entered the faculty of medicine.

For the purpose of this study, Ain Shams University was selected. It is located in Cairo. One thousand students are graduated yearly from the faculty of medicine. This university was selected primarily because a) it is representative of the "Big 3" medical schools, the other two being Cairo University and Alexandria University, b) there were persons on the teaching faculty at the above university who could assist me in data collection.

The questionnaire was distributed to 105 fourth year and fifth (final) year medical students to obtain their projected views of village service in terms of anticipatory socialization and their clinical and psychological preparation for the village (Appendix II).

Students' age ranged between 22 and 27 years. The majority were 25 years of age. Only one student was married and one had attended a village elementary school.

INTERVIEWS

Interviews were conducted with three health administrators to ascertain if the research was proceeding in the proper direction. The results of the above were discussed at the beginning of this chapter. Opinions expressed at interviews by a physician who had just returned from the village will be offered as a relevant supplement to the questionnaire methodology.

CREDIBILITY OF THE DATA

Translation Linguistics

An old Arab proverb states: "With every language a (different) man", apt warning to the cross-lingual researcher in the Middle East whether he be an anthropologist, psychologist, or sociologist.

A native English speaker undertaking research in the Arab world must carefully consider problems of comparability in cross-lingual research.

There is a good reason to believe that apparent discrepancies (or correlations) between words and deeds are frequently a spurious artifact of the inadequate technology of social science—more apparent than real. Our techniques for tapping the phenomena interfere with and impinge upon those phenomena in ways that distort our findings—we create static with our instruments. [13]

Problems of comparability of meaning are introduced when questions are addressed to a society in which linguistic variations exist. A technique which is widely used to deal with this problem is called "back translation":

> There is general agreement on how the actual translation of the questions should be made. First, the original instrument is translated into the local language, and then another translator independently translates this translated version back into the original. The original and retranslated versions are compared and the discrepancies are clarified. [14]

However, Phillips in attempting to translate a simple survey instrument found back translation to be ineffective for use in Thailand. [15] The back translation procedure guarantees that the words translate accurately but it is necessary to know the extent to which those literally equivalent words and phrases convey the equivalent meanings in the two languages or cultures. In translating a string of words from one language into an equivalent string of words in another language, the cross-cultural researcher must fail in his efforts to achieve comparability when he fails to recognize that a vocabulary is not merely a string of words; within it are societal textures. [16]

It was therefore decided that care should be taken to translate accurately—not literally, not freely, but just accurately. In attempting the above, familiarity with the cultural context was a prerequisite since we cannot assume that valid correlations exist between two languages.

The technique used for the questionnaires was to have them translated conceptually by one person who was not a social scientist, then have a social scientist read the Arabic translation and original English version, make corrections, and return to the first person for review of the changes. In this way it was felt that bias might be eliminated. Retranslation of responses to the Arabic questionnaire were read aloud in English, the translator trying to keep within *the contextual meaning* of the phrases. These responses were recorded by the researcher onto precoded sheets.

In order to check the coding bias and translation error spot checks were made having a physician translate the questionnaire in the above manner.

The value scale was originally in Arabic and its validity established. [17] An English translation was made for my use only since the original Arabic was used in the questionnaire. The choice of this value scale was based on the assumption that "canned questionnaires from the west" are inapplicable for developing countries. The Hussein Value Scale [18] was designed for the Egyptian culture specifically.

Criterion Interview

Any act is an historical process, constructed by the actors as it unfolds. Its construction is influenced by alterations, and redefinitions of the immediate situation at which actors find themselves at various points in the flow of action. From this symbolic interactionist perspective we may expect that there is no theoretical basis for assuming that what people say correlates with whatever else they may do. [19]

What do people intend to convey when they answer our questions? Is the written word the same as the verbal explanation? [b]

My purpose in including interviews was to probe on randomly selected questions from the questionnaire to determine the validity of the data. This assisted me in verifying that the respondent's notion of what the questions means was the same as that intended by the investigator. Shuman describes a similar technique as a "random probe technique". [20]

Acknowledging the above problems, it was decided to include interviews with a physician who recently returned from the village service.

Social scientists seek to understand human behaviour by asking questions and observing action. As Mark Benney and Everett Hughes have stated "the interview, as itself a form of social rhetoric, is not merely a tool of sociology but a part of its very subject matter". [21]

Attempts in the interview were made to eliminate "courtesy" bias. The respondent in the Middle Eastern situation "tries to please". It is his cultural obligation to see to it that the interviewer is not distressed, disappointed, or offended. Mitchell suggests that a courtesy or hospitality bias is common in Asia everywhere from Japan to Turkey:

> The direction of the courtesy bias is different in different countries. For example, the humility of the Japanese is said to lead them to under-evaluate their own achievements, class positions, and the like. On the other hand, some researchers in the Middle East claim that respondents there tend to exaggerate their achievements, class position, knowledge of the world, and extent to which they

---

[b] An inrteresting discussion on this subject appears in 'The Open Souls Doctrine' in Harre', R. and Secord, P. F., *The Explanation of Social Behaviour*, London, Basil Blackwell and Mott Limited, 1976, pp. 105-123.

are modern rather than traditional. In practical terms, this means that the type of question-wording appropriate in Japan and the West would be inappropriate in Turkey and Iran. [22]

Interviews were carried out at the American University in Cairo campus. This location was convenient for both the respondent and the interviewer. A total of twelve interviews took place. Places of the interview were altered to relieve boredom but privacy was ensured. Interviews were terminated after one hour, since the respondent had some difficulty with speaking English. The interviews were conducted in the English language and it was felt that the slight difficulty with English would create some tension with consequent fatigue. Care was taken to make the respondent feel at ease and appreciated for his efforts.

A General Defence of Questionnaires

Ever since La Pierre's [23] well known demonstration of the inconsistency between expressed disposition and actual behaviour, there has been a tendency to look at attitude measurement with some scepticism. Certainly it is no longer possible to blandly assume a one to one correspondance between what a person states and what he does. The position take here however corresponds to the view of Cook and Selltiz (1964). [24] They argue than expressed attitude is a factor, along with other influences "into the determination of a variety of behaviours towards an object or class of objects including statements of feelings and beliefs about the object ..."

They assume two classes of variables in addition to an individual's expressed attitudinal disposition toward an object or class of objects:

(1) other characteristics of the individual
(2) other characteristics of the situation

Under (1) above occurs the variable "values he holds that are engaged in the situation." Enough has already been said about the Hussein Scale to claim a reasonable amount of confidence in the validity of the information yielded and its relevance to this subject matter.

As far as (2) is concerned, it is summarized as "prescriptions as to appropriate behaviour, the expectations of others in the situation with respect to the individual's behaviour, the possible and probable consequences of various acts on his part". It can fairly be held that prescriptive behaviour is considered in page 194 of the questionnaire and that "expectations of others in the situation" is reflexly implicit in subsections of the questionnaire itself i.e. interrelations with village leaders, the dayas and the endogenous healers. The writers name this approach—A Multiple Indicator Approach to Attitude Measurement. This synoptic approach goes far towards eliminating the numerous characteristics that make self report measures susceptible to distortions. Despite its critics the method has been the basis of major and prestigious work in the social sciences i.e. The Authoritarian Personality, The Kinsey Report and so on.

But can the "Social desirability" difficulty be acceptably eliminated by the multiple indicator approach? "Social desirability" is the term used to encapsulate such objections as: the purpose of the instrument is obvious to the respondent; the implications of his answers are obvious to him, and he can consciously monitor his responses. Thus a person who wishes to give a certain picture of himself whether in order to impress the tester favourably and to preserve his own self image—or for some other reason—can rather easily do so. This charge may be rebutted on two grounds: first of all the distortion noted has arisen largely from experience in research into political, class, and racial prejudice in North America, where respondents in academic settings feel themselves safer if they present themselves as "well adjusted, unprejudiced, rational, open minded and democratic", the values in fact of the white American middle class. The setting of the present investigation was quite different in that it examined a pragmatic rather than an idiological situation.

The charge of 'Social desirability' therefore is only very marginally applicable here. A final source of support for the validity of self report measures comes from Harre' and Secord (1976). [25] "Why not ask them?" is the basis of what they call the Open Souls Doctrine. What they ask is the basis, what is really at issue when the reliability of reports is questioned?

(1) The feeling, opinion, belief may not exist, or may not be reported. There exists no universal and independent check by which avowals and ascriptions can be decided as genuine reports distinguished from mistakes or lies.

(2) Retrospective commentary may in fact be retrospective falsification. Attributed feelings, beliefs, intentions were not attended to or did not exist in the course of an episode or series of episodes. Reports may be fictitious pseudomemories generated by the demand for commentary in a justificatory context.

Harre' and Secord's reply is along the following lines. "There are many cases in which a certain sort of remark is not ust a sign of, or a report of a state of mind but is a manifestation of that state of mind itself. For instance to complain verbally is a part of being discontented, because part of what is ascribed to a person who is described as 'discontented' is a tendency to complain. Indeed complaining may sometimes be the *whole* of discontent, though usually there may also be feelings of resentment, thoughts about better states of affairs, and so on. It is here that the philosophers' idea of logically adequate criteria will prove invaluable. This is the simple but pregnant idea that one cannot consistently deny that a person is discontented after accepting what they say as a genuine complaint. Similarly, under some circumstances, a report of a belief or of an intention may be exactly the manifestation of that belief or intention itself." [26]

This is precisely the basis upon which the whole of this inquiry rests.

Research Procedures

Method (Description of the study)

The subjects studied were a total of 136 physicians from Minia, Menoufia, and Cairo. Minia was selected as an indicator for rural Upper Egypt, N= 50. Menoufia was represented as an indicator for rural Lower Egypt, N= 50, and a Ministry of health Hospital was selected to represent urban Cairo, N= 36. A total of one hundred and eighty questionnaires were distributed 17% were women physicians. In addition, a sample of 105 (one hundred and twenty questionnaires were distributed) medical students was selected from the fourth and fifth year at the University of Ain Shams in order to obtain an understanding of the anticipatory socialization process.

Those physicians from Minia and Menoufia function as Rural Health Unit heads. The Cairo sample included resident and senior physicians, i.e. those having comparative administrative duties to the Rural Health Unit Heads.

Egypt, eager to reach the rural population has expanded her unique system of health delivery services to include over 5,000 units.[c] These units are primarily manned by newly graduated physicians.

All university graduates must serve at least one year mandatory service.

The Rural Health Unit

There are two types of health centres in Egypt: a combined health centre (magmuaa) and a health unit.

Most health units could be described as having three rooms for medical examination with an inner room (hall), a reception area (waiting room), a pharmacy room, a medical laboratory room, a doctors' office, a nurses' office and a room for storing records and registers. Often these units have an upper floor where the doctor stays. It is sparsely furnished but generally has a stove, refrigerator, electricity and running water.

The combined health centre has two storeys. The first floor usually has an emergency room, outpatient clinic room, and doctor and nurses' offices. The second floor consists of an operating room, utility rooms and generally three wards equipped with lavatories. Living accommodation for the doctors and nurses are on the second floor also. The centre sometimes has facilities for a library, a television room, washroom, garage and garden. Both types of units were included in the study.

---

[c] Conversation with a Director of Cairo University Hospitals.

Menoufia Governorate

Menoufia Governorate is located in the southern part of the Nile Delta between the two main branches of the Nile (Damietta and Rosetta). The Governorate is divided into eight counties which include eight urban towns and 302 rural villages. According to the 1976 preliminary census results, the population of Menoufia is 1.7 million people representing 4.7 percent of Egypt's total population. [27]

There are eight urban towns in Menoufia having a combined total population of approximately 300,000. This work is designed to study the rural areas since it is well known that, relative to the rural areas, the urban areas have superior and different services. The study of Cairo will compose the urban segment of the study.

The main features of the Governorate may be summarized as follows: [28]

1. Menoufia is the most rural, and the least urban governorate in Egypt. In 1976, the overwhelming majority of its population (80.3 percent) lived in rural villages; the proportion of its urban population (19.7 percent) was the lowest in the country.

2. Menoufia is one of the most densely populated rural governorates in Egypt. In 1976, its 1.7 million people were crowded into an area of 1,500 square kilometers; a population density of 1140 persons per square kilometer.

3. Menoufia is predominantly agricultural. In spite of highly productive and intensive farming, the overwhelming majority of the rural population suffers from low income. This is attributable to the very low land/man ratio and the very small fragmented landholdings which individual families cultivate. In 1976, the per capita share of agricultural land was less than 0.2 feddan.[d] Thus, each feddan or arable land supports 5.2 persons of the total population and provides means of livelihood for 4.2 persons of the rural population. Some 160,000 families cultivate 330,000 feddans (an average of two feddans per family) and the majority (60 percent) cultivate farms under two feddans.

4. Menoufia is characterized by a high emigration rate. Most of the migrants move from rural villages and settle in Cairo and other urban areas. The high emigration rate is one of the major consequences of the great population pressure on the small cultivated area and the lack of sufficient employment opportunities alternative to agriculture.

5. Menoufia, as throughout Egypt, has high birth rates and moderate death rates. Annual birth rates in the Governorate during the past forty years (1955-1975) have fluctuated between 48 and 38 per thousand population. Death rates, however, have shown a distinct decline from 30 to 15 per thousand population.

---

[d] One feddan equals 1.038 acres.

Based on preliminary results from the 1976 census, a demographic, economic and social profile on Menoufia is presented below. [29]

1. Demographic Indicators
   - Total population: 1.7 million
   - Menoufia's population as percent of Egypt's population: 4.7 percent
   - Rank of Menoufia with respect to population size in relation to other governorates: 10th out of 25 governorates
   - Population density in Menoufia: 1140 per km^2
   - Sex ratio: 104 males per 100 females
   - Urban population: 19.7 percent
   - Rural population: 80.3 percent
   - Average household size: 5.5 persons
   - Average No. of rooms per household: 3.2 rooms
   - Average No. of persons per room: 1.7 persons
   - Age composition of population: under 12 years old – 31.6 percent
     12-64 years old – 64.2 percent
     65 years old and over – 4.2 percent
   - Percent Christian: 1.98 percent
   - Population size in different census years:

Census Year	Population
1907	970,581
1917	1,072,616
1927	1,105,191
1937	1,159,701
1947	1,165,015
1960	1,347,953
1966	1,458,048
1976	1,710,892

2. Economic Indicators
   - Ratio of agricultural land to total population: 1 feddan per 5.2 persons
   - Ratio of agricultural land to rural population: 1 feddan per 4.2 persons
   - Percentage of economically active population (6 years old and over):
     Among males: 50.9 percent
     Among females: 9.7 percent
     Among total population: 30.7 percent
   - Percentage of homes with electricity:
     In rural areas: 34.4 percent

In urban areas:	64.5 percent
In governorate:	39.0 percent

- Percentage of homes with piped (running) water:

In rural areas:	2.4 percent
In urban areas:	38.6 percent
In governorate:	9.8 percent

3. Social Indicators
   - Educational Status (10 years old and over):

Illiterates:	57.0 percent
University educated:	1.3 percent

   - Marital Status of Males (18 years and over):

Single:	28.0 percent
Married:	68.3 percent
Divorced and widowers:	3.7 percent

   - Marital Status of Females (16 years old and over):

Single:	17.3 percent
Married:	65.3 percent
Divorced and widows:	17.4 percent

4. Service Delivery Systems

Number of Health Units:	134
Number of Social Units:	87
Number of Community Development Societies:	123
Number of Welfare Societies:	124
Number of Nurseries:	81

5. Administrative Units

Number of villages:	302
Number of towns:	8

Of the 134 Health Units in Menoufia, 50 were selected for the study from the three counties, Tala, Shebin El-Kom, and Shohada.

These counties were selected since they were part of an ongoing study by the Social Research Center at the American University in Cairo for household distribution of contraceptives, and serve as representative of Menoufia.

Minia Governorate

Minia Governorate is located between the Governorates of Beni-Suef to the north and Assuit to the south. Minia like all other provinces in southern Egypt, is extending in one direction only, following the valley of the Nile rendering communications and the exchange of ideas difficult. The Governorate is divided into nine counties. According to the 1976 preliminary census results, the population of Minia is 2.1 million people representing 5.5% of Egypt's total population. [30]

There are nine urban towns in Minia having a combined total population of approximately 400,000. This study included only the rural areas. Minia is characterized by having the majority of the population (79%) living in rural villages. Only 21% live in the urban area.

Based on preliminary results from the 1976 census, a demographic, economic, and social profile of Minia is presented below.

1. Demographic Indicators
    - Total population: 2.1 million
    - Minia's population as percent of Egypt's population: 5.5 percent
    - Rank of Minia with respect to population size in relation to other governorates: 8th out of 25 governorates
    - Sex ratio: 106 males per 100 females
    - Urban population: 21 percent
    - Rural population: 83.3 percent
    - Average household size: 3.0 rooms
    - Average No. of persons per room: 1.6 persons
    - Age composition of population:
      Percent under 12 years old 33.0 percent
      Percent 12-64 years old 63.5 percent
      Percent 65 years old and over: 3.5 percent
    - Percent Christian 19.8 percent
2. Economic Indicators
    - Percentage of economically active population (6 years old and over):
      Among males: 56.9 percent
      Among females: 5.8 percent
      Among total population: 32.2 percent
    - Percent of homes with electricity:
      In rural areas: 9.2 percent
      In urban areas: 60.0 percent
      In governorate: 9.0 percent
3. Social Indicators
    - Educational Status (10 years old and over):
      Illiterates: 52.0 percent
      University educated: 0.6 percent
    - Marital Status of Males (18 years old and over):

Single: 24.0 percent
Married: 73.0 percent
Divorced and widowers: 3.0 percent
— Marital Status of Females (16 years old and over):
Single: 11.7 percent
Married: 69.0 percent
Divorced and widows: 19.3 percent

The 50 units were selected as a representative sample of the province; accesibility via major automobile routes or train was also a major decisive factor.

A Minia unit usually serves a population of 5,000-10,000 persons.

The Urban Health System

Cairo population is 5.0 million people according to the 1976 census. [31]

A hospital was selected after consultations with an ex-Ministry of Health official as being a representative Cairo Ministry of Health hospital. Additional information regarding the Urban Health system was given in Chapter II.

Data Collection

Physicians' questionnaires in Menoufia were distributed and collected by research assistants of the Social Research Center of the American University in Cairo. Fifty questionnaires were distributed and collected.

The Minia questionnaires were distributed by Demonstrators and Lecture Assistants in the Faculty of Arts, Department of Social Studies, Minia University. This process was arranged through a University of Minia Professor. Fifty questionnaires were distributed and collected.

Eighty questionnaires were distributed for the Cairo sample through the assistance of the Hospital Director. Thirty six questionnaires were returned.

One hundred and twenty student questionnaires were distributed by two members of Ain Shams University Faculty in the School of Medicine. One hundred and five questionnaires were returned.

REFERENCES

[1] Berger, M., *Bureaucracy and Society in Modern Egypt: A Study of the Higher Civil Service*, Princeton, N.J., Princeton University Press, 1957.
[2] Riggs, F., *Administration in Developing Countries, The Theory of Prismatic Society*, Houghton Mifflin Company, Boston, 1964.
[3] 'Egypt's Doctor Woes', *San Francisco Cronicle*, Monday, October 17, 1977.
[4] Hussein, M. E. A., *The Specific Values of the Creative Person*, unpublished Ph.D. dissertation, Cairo University, Department of Phychology, 1978, (in Arabic).

[5] Herzberg, F., 'One More Time: How Do You Motivate Employees',' *Harvard Business Review*, January-February, 1968, pp. 52-62.
[6] Parsons, T., Shils, E. A., *Toward a General Theory of Action*, Harvard University Press, 1959, Cambridge Mass., pp. 59-60.
[7] Hussein, M. E., *The Specific Values of the Creative Person*, Cairo University, Department of Psychology, unpublished Ph.D. Dissertation, 1978, p. 194, (in Arabic).
[8] Hussein, M. E., *The Specific Values of the Creative Person*, Cairo University, Department of Psychology, unpublished Ph.D. Dissertation Abstract, 1978, Mimeograph (English).
[9] *Ibid*.
[10] Parsons, *op. cit.* p. 208
[11] Kluckhohn, C., *Values and Value Orientations* in Parsons, T. and Shils, E., *Toward a General Theory of Action*, Cambridge, Mass., Harvard University Press, pp. 388-433.
[12] *Ibid*, p. 416.
[13] Deutscher, Irwin, *Asking Questions Cross-Culturally: Some Problems of Linguistic Comparability* in Becker, H. (ed.) *Institutions and the Person*, Aldine Publishing Co., Chicago, 1968, pp. 319.
[14] Mitchell, R. E., 'Survey Materials Collected in Developing Countries: Sampling. Measurement and Interviewing Obstacles to Intra- and International Comparisons', *International Social Science Journal*, 1965, Vol. 17, No. 4. 1965, p. 681.
[15] Phillips, H. P., 'Problems of Translation and Meaning in Field Work', *Human Organization*, Winter, 1959-1960, Vol. 18, No. 4, p. 190.
[16] Mills, C. W., *Language, Logic and Culture*, in Horowitz, I. (ed.), *Power, Politics, and People*, New York, 1963, pp. 436-37.
[17] Hussein, *op. cit.*
[18] *Ibid*.
[19] Deutscher, I., 'Words and Deeds: Social Science and Social Policy', *Social Problems*, Winter 1966, Vol. 13, No. 3, pp. 325-54.
[20] Benney, M. and Hughes, E., 'Of Sociology and the Interview: Editorial Preface', *American Journal of Sociology*, Vol. 62, No. 2, Sept. 1956, pp. 138.
[21] Schuman, H., 'The Random Probe: A Technique for Evaluating the Validity of Closed Questions', *American Sociological Review*, Vol. 31, No. 2, April, 1966, p. 218.
[22] Mitchell, *op. cit.*
[23] LaPierre, R. T., 'Attitudes v. Actions', *Social Forces*, Vol. 13, pp. 230-237.
[24] Cook, S., and Selltiz, C., 'A Multiple-Indicator Approach to Attitude Measurement', *Psychological Bulletin*, Vol. 62, pp. 36-55.
[25] Harre', R. and Secord, P. F., *The Explanation of Social Behaviour*, London, Basil Blackwell and Mott Limited, 1976, pp. 105-123.
[26] *Ibid*.
[27] CAPMAS Report, Egyptian Population, 1976 census, mimiograph.
[28] Gadalla, S., *Proposed Action-Research Program for Promoting Family Planning, Health, and Social Welfare in Menoufia Governorate*, American University in Cairo, June, 1977, pp. 9-10.
[29] CAPMAS Report, *op. cit.*
[30] *Ibid*.
[31] *Ibid*.

CHAPTER SEVEN

SOME SPECULATIVE INTERPRETATIONS OF THE FINDINGS

Educational Evaluation

Table 7.1 gives the physicians' evaluation of their prior university education and their desire for additional education and/or training.

It is interesting to note that from the Cairo sample 67% aspired toward advanced education, and in the Menoufia sample 78% cited advanced education as their desire, whereas in the Minia sample only 26% aspired toward advanced education, the emphasis being placed upon training.

Menoufia is geographically closer to the urban centres of Cairo and Alexandria. The provincial capital of Shebin El-Kom is approximately 130 km. south of Alexandria and 65 km. north of Cairo. The province is extended in both directions facilitating access to the capital Cairo, whereas Minia, like all other provinces in southern Egypt, is extending in one direction only following the flow of the Nile rendering communications and the exchange of ideas more difficult.

A doctor from anywhere in Menoufia could be in Cairo within 1½ hours for a lecture, seminar or hospital training. The physician in Minia would require 4 hours to visit the capital. Menoufia is also characterized by more industrialization.

Table 7.1

Evaluation of University Education and Desire for Additional Education/Training

Sample	University Education		Additional Education for Improvement		Further Training Desired		
	Sufficient	Insufficient	Yes	No	Tr.*	Ed.*	None
Menoufia	62%	38%	86%	14%	70%	78%	6%
Minia	34%	66%	84%	16%	16%	26%	24%
Cairo	53%	47%	94%	6%	78%	67%	3%
Combined Sample Age over 40	85%	15%	95%	5%	65%	35%	25%

* Tr.-Training
  Ed.-Education

The establishment of universities increases the "urbanism" of a given province. Menoufia has a longer history in this respect. For example, the nucleus of the University of Menoufia started back as far as 1943. Minia University nucleus started only within the last ten years.

The marked differences between the Menoufia and Minia sample may be explained by the geographically determined value system of the culture.

Another explanation may be that the difference is correlated to the academic abilities of the respondents. Graduating students possessing higher grades are distributed geographically closer to Cairo.

The quality of institutional roles and individual personalities in the health delivery system, as in all other systems, is related to the ethos of the particular culture, and the specific role expectations and personal dispositions to its values. On the one hand, the expectations the physician derives, at least in part, from the values of the culture in which the health unit is situated. On the other, the dispositions of the physicians are internalizations of the values (or sub-values) of the culture (or sub-culture) in which the physician was socialized.

In answer to the question: "Do you feel that your university education adequately prepared you for your profession?", 62% of the Menoufia sample felt that they had been adequately prepared. In the Minia sample, 34% felt that they had been adequately prepared and 53% in the Cairo sample felt that they had adequate preparation. See Table 7.1.

Respondents were asked "Would you like to receive additional education or training to carry out your work more effectively?" In Menoufia 86% indicated a desire for additional education and/or training. The Cairo sample showed that 94% of the respondents desired additional education and/or training. In Minia 84% indicated this desire.

But how do the medical students view their preparation for future practice? The following section seeks to answer this question.

Altruism Submerged

The students were asked if they viewed the mandatory village service as a form of punishment, moral obligation, a means of serving others, a means of repaying society for their education, a means of preventing them from pursuing their career academically, a part of their educational process, or a valuable experience. Table 7.2 summarizes their replies and illustrates that only 56% of the students viewed it as a means of serving others while 50% saw it as a valuable experience. Apparently there is an eagerness to make their medical knowledge pay off, which points up to the reality that the developing physicians are entrepreneurs with a profit motive. Thirty-three percent (33%) felt it was part of the educational process, emphasizing their desire for more clinical practice. Fifty percent (50%) of the respondents stated they were looking forward to this service whereas thirty-nine percent (39%) stated they were not. Eleven percent (11%) did not reply.

Table 7.2

Medical Students' View of Mandatory Village Service

Mandatory Village Service Viewed As:	% Replying Yes
Punishment	5
Moral obligation	26
A means of serving others	56
A means of repaying society for your education	20
A means of preventing you from pursuing your career academically	10
A part of your educational process	33
A valuable experience	50
Other	6

Although looking forward to the service and wanting to serve, students expressed some fear of the unknown and an element of unpreparedness for their role as "village doctor".

Statements expressing insecurity were "Those who go to the village should be more experienced" (5th year student), "How could you throw a new graduate into such an environment without adequate orientation and with poor facilities?" (5th year student), "The system is all wrong, the doctor should be under guidance" (4th year student), "No contact between most of the students and the villagers makes us apprehensive because of their ignorance and poverty" (4th year student).

Only thirty percent (30%) of the respondents had been to a rural health unit, and of those only 16% (5 students) visited the unit as part of their formal education. An overwhelming seventy-eight percent (78%) felt that such visits would prepare them for their mandatory village service.

Seventy-five percent (75%) stated that they did not believe their education was adequately preparing them to work in rural areas. Why do these students feel apprehensive and inadequate for fulfilling their role expectation? The most frequent explanation, almost a plea for more information, was the lack of knowledge about the socio-psychological factors of the villagers. As one student stated, "They should have a course called 'Medicine for the Egyptian Countryside'." "We do not concentrate on the endemic diseases in Egypt and education (perhaps the student)[a] is *lost* within the international picture." "I have never been accustomed—I would feel I am in the jungle." These and similar answers demonstrate how fear, isolation, and a feeling of inadequacy threaten the role fulfilment of the future village doctor. This was once again reiterated in their response to the question "Do you believe the villagers share the same cultural background as you?" Seventy-seven percent (77%) replied no, and 16% replied yes.

---

[a] The statement appearing in brackets is my addition.

Asked if they believe an understanding of the villagers' "world view" was essential for providing adequate care for the village population, eighty-three percent (83%) felt this knowledge was essential. Seventy-four percent (74%) indicated that it was not included within their medical education, and sixty-seven (67%) stated that they would like to see it included.

The students were asked to describe the "world-view" of the villagers. In general, negative traits were mentioned. These included witchcraft, limited health awareness, high fertility rate, misunderstanding of religion, poverty, illiteracy, etc.

Hence we find the dimension of altruism submerged by fear, inadequacy and lack of understanding. The unselfish concern for others, the idealism of the student is buried by the educational system's constraints and the profit motive.

Urban Care Superiority

Table 7.3 summarizes the responses to selected questions about urban medical care by the 105 medical students. They rated it either superior or inferior to rural medical care.

Asked if they planned to stay in the rural area after their mandatory service, seventy-eight percent (78%) replied no, ten percent (10%) replied yes and twelve percent (12%) did not reply.

In general, the literature rarely mentions the positive aspects of rural health service. The non-rural physicians and medical students, who are the majority

Table 7.3

Students's Views About Urban/Rural Medical Care

Questions and Responses	Percent
Why is medical care in urban Cairo superior to rural areas?	
More physicians	52%
More continuing education and professional stimulus for urban physicians	50%
Less problems of time and distance	25%
Superior facilities	88%
Other reasons	21%
Why is medical care in urban Cairo inferior to rural areas?	
Less personalized care	45%
Physicians and facilities are less responsive to patients' needs	25%
Less cooperative and coordinated medical community	26%
Other reasons	6%
No response*	32%

* The no response answers could represent the feeling that they did not believe urban Cairo care inferior in all categories.

in Egypt, may have an unrealistically negative view of village practice. Such negativity increases the problems of recruiting physicians for rural communities. However, with Egypt's unique and comprehensive scheme of mandatory service, recruitment is not a problem. The problem lies in the existing negativity toward rural practice which may have been reinforced in medical schools as prior research had indicated. [1, 2, 3]

Field visits to rural areas may be a positive approach toward overcoming prejudices and fears. Steinwald and Steinwald have stated:

> ... a primary value of preceptorships and similar rural programs may lie in their role as sources of information about unfamiliar life and medical practice styles, and that an increased orientation of rural programs toward urban-reared students may prove fruitful. [4]

Theoretical Implications

Sarbin [5] refers to position of a person in a social structure as a set of expectations or acquired anticipatory reactions i.e. he learns to expect or anticipate actions from other persons and others have expectations of him.

In this instance the respondent or actor is carving out a pattern of social behaviour, i.e. role, which would seem to be situationally appropriate to the expectations of his group, in this instance the university (see Figure 7.1). Sargent, for example, says, "A person's role is a pattern or type of social behaviour which seems situationally appropriate to him in terms of the demands and expectations of those in his group." [6] He concludes that in this sense, roles "have ingredients of cultural, of personal, and of situational determination. But never is a role wholly cultural, wholly personal, or wholly situational." [7]

If the doctor performs his "role" to the satisfaction of the three other incumbents (Figure 7.1) and they likewise fulfill his expectations, it could hence be inferred that the doctor feels the university education prepared him for his profession, as was the case in Menoufia (+62%) and Cairo (+53%). These professionals rank higher in scholastic achievement.

Minia physicians on the other hand, with a negative score (-66%), indicate that a set of expectations are not fulfilled, i.e. they rank lower in scholastic achievement. The usual determining factor for placing physicians distant from the periphery of Cairo is based upon this determination. This demonstrates a positive relationship between scholastic achievement and fulfilment of expectation.

Figure 7.1 illustrates what is termed a position-centric model. The focal position, i.e. doctor, is specified by its relationships to three counter positions. In this case, the practical supervisory staff, classroom professor, and student body.

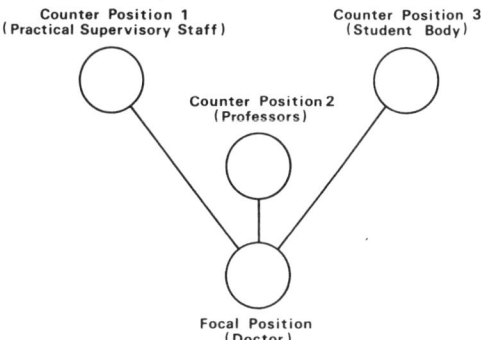

Figure 7.1. A Position-centric Model

By responding to the question "Do you feel you need additional education or training to carry out your present work more effectively, Minia (+ 84%) correlates with the negative (-66%) response of the question: "Do you feel that your university education adequately prepared you for your profession?". However, by Menoufia and Cairo answering positively, a discrepancy results which may indicate that although the actor may have considered his education adequate for preparing him for his profession, he nevertheless feels the need for further education or training. This may in turn mean that he "does not feel" that he is performing effectively, i.e. he doubts his fulfillment of role expectations.

We have just reviewed the physicians' education as he sees it in the circumstance of practice and in anticipation of that practice. In Chapter V a brief review of the descriptive sub sets of roles was given. In the following pages, we examine the roles of therapist, manager, educator and mediator in the practice of medicine as well as the physicians' self-evaluation of his own role performance. Table 7.4 illustrates the self assessed role definitions by two groups of rural physicians and one group of urban physicians.

Sub Sets of Roles and Praxis as Therapist

Here the term number-of-roles is used to mean the "roles" of administrator, supervisor, teacher, healer, etc. As might be expected, there was a consensus among the physicians viewing their role as primarily "healer". Eighty-six percent (86%) from the Minia sample, eighty-four percent (84%) from the Menoufia sample, and ninety-two percent (92%) from the Cairo sample indicated Medical Care as their major function.

As Manager

Fifty-six percent (56%) of the Menoufia sample viewed themselves as "Administrator", whereas, thirty-two percent (32%) of the Minia sample and

Table 7.4

Self Assessed Role Definitions by Two Groups of Rural Physicians and One Group of Urban Physicians

Sample	Administration	Supervision	Combined Administration & Supervision	Teaching	Medical Care	Other Items**
Minia n=50	32%	42%	74%	42%	86%	61
Menoufia n=50	56%	34%	90%	36%	84%	47
Cairo n=36	28%	17%	45%	28%	92%	14

* More than one option was permitted
** Family Planning was included in this category

twenty-eight percent (28%) of the Cairo sample viewed this role as a major function. The role of "Supervisor" was stated by fourty-two percent (42%) of the Minia sample, thirty-four percent (34%) of the Menoufia sample and only seventeen percent (17%) of the Cairo sample. It is interesting to note here that a major complaint of the Menoufia physicians was "over-employment", sometimes called masked unemployment, that is, employing more than one person to do a job which can be performed by a single individual. Veterans who fought in the two previous Egyptian/Israeli wars are hired by the Government in the rural health units and serve as orderlies.

Egypt, following the Socialist tradition, attempts to spread the meagre wealth of the country. This humanitarian gesture, however, sometimes has negative aspects in that "many employees must have two jobs to survive—they work in the rural health unit and farm their lands rendering supervision difficult."[b]

By combining the percentages for "Administrator" and "Supervisor" we have the following results: Menoufia 90%, Minia 74%, and Cairo 45%; this clearly indicates that the rural samples viewed this aspect of role, (i.e. the managerial aspect) as significant. Problems of red tape, especially paperwork, were a frequent complaint in the rural samples.

In the geographically distant areas, the role of "teacher" was cited more frequently. Forty-two percent (42%) of the Minia sample found this to be of major importance, whereas, only twenty-eight percent (28%) of the Cairo sample mentioned this role.

---

[b] This statement was made during a conversation with an informant, a young physician with experience in a rural health unit.

As Educator

Given the option to state "other" roles, the Minia sample indicated 61 items, the Menoufia sample stated 47 items and the Cairo sample mentioned only 14 items.

The role of "teacher" was exemplified by defining other roles as "giving health guidance", "giving health seminars", "showing films", "creating health awareness", "instructing and lecturing on general health". The rural physicians of Minia and Menoufia frequently mentioned the above, whereas, the Cairo physicians only mentioned "social help". However, the role of "teacher" was the function most often stated by the Minia sample which is located geographically most distant and isolated from Cairo.

As Mediator

The Physician immersed in the milieu of southern Egyptian society, accepts the role of mediator. Acting as "mediator among the villagers", "attending peoples' meetings", "attending meetings of the village council", and "attending meetings of the board of social development", were all mentioned by the Minia sample.

The Menoufia physician tends to find himself more in a mediator-leader role with "solving conflicts", "leading role in the community", and "leader".

The urban physician of Cairo, on the other hand, indicated his role in this manner only as, "solving the social problems of the nursing staff". They primarily viewed their role within the narrow strata of administrator, supervisor and teacher with little diversification in "other role definitions".

However, this was not the case with the Menoufia sample and especially the Minia sample who viewed their roles as Mediator and Village Leader. Here we find the sample to be functionally differentiated.

Hence we have within a culture (the medical profession), a division of subcultures, illustrated by the upper Egypt, lower Egypt, and urban (Cairo) sectors, possessing divergent values and perceiving their roles in different ways. A possible explanation for these varying subjective judgements lies in the concept of marginality which will be discussed later in this chapter.

Role Performance

Terms commonly used to describe behaviour, that is overt behaviour, include words such as "performance" and "role performance". However, behaviour viewed as action may be covertly represented as well, as a tendency to behave, a desire, an intention. [8] We shall use the term performance for overt behaviour, self defined, classified as action, and the term attitude for covert tendencies to engage in behaviour that, if made overt, would be designated as action. (Parsons, [9] and Parsons and Shils [10] have classified behaviour by the criterion of action.)

"Work performance", "school performance", and "sex-role behaviour" are examples of designations of performance repertoires. The term "role performance" usually refers to the performances of a particular category of persons, where the common features of the performances are left undesignated. Various criteria are found for determining the basis upon which performances are classified. References to "work performance" and "school performance" derive from a classification in terms of institutional context. Classifications of performances by designations of "leader" versus "follower" or "task performance" versus "socioemotional performance" illustrate the operation of functional criteria. All of these are arbitrary designations of the content of performance. [11] Our interest here is in the perceptions of actors, rather than the perceptions of the observer.

Respondents were asked: "The Ministry of Health specifies the functions for each physician's job description; on a scale of 1-5, rate how well you are fulfilling the functions given for your position".[c]

Table 7.5 summarizes the results of such self-evaluation, and the mean scores of each group of physicians. There was a significant difference in the mean scores, as tested by the variance analysis shown in Table 7.6, which might be attributed at least partially to geographical location.

Table 7.5

Fulfilling Position According to Ministry of Health Specifications

Rank	5	4	3	2	1	No answer*	Mean Score*
Minia n=50	4%	22%	52%	18%	2%	2%	3.1 ± 0.7
Menoufia n=50	36%	32%	16%	2%	14%	14%	4.2 ± 0.7
Cairo n=36	28%	19%	17%	8%	0	28%	3.0 ± 1.1

Figure 7.2 is a graphical representation of the contents of Table 7.5 and shows clearly a normal distribution around the middle of the scale of "fulfillment of position according to the Ministry of Health specifications" for Minia (isolated). On the other hand, the Cairo (urban) and Menoufia (less isolated) show a shift of distribution towards the higher range of the scale.

Only four percent (4%) of the Minia sample rated their job performance at the maximum level of 5. The majority, fifty-two percent (52%), however, rated themselves with a score of 3.

---

[c] Appendix I.

SOME SPECULATIVE INTERPRETATIONS OF THE FINDINGS

Table 7.6

Analysis of Variance for Mean Scores in Table 7.5

Source	d.f.	Sum of Squares	Mean Squares
Among	2	29	14.5
Within	115	89	0.77
Total	117	118	—

$F = 18.83 > F_{0.05}(2,115) = 3.07$

* Mean scores and analysis of variance excluded the no-answers.

This contrasts significantly with the self-rating of the Menoufia physicians of whom thirty-six percent (36%) rated their performance on the scale at 5 and thirty-two percent (32%) on the scale at 4. This Menoufia group viewed their major role as "administrator-supervisor". Twenty-eight percent (28%) of the Cairo sample rated their level of performance on the scale at 5. It is interesting to note that from this sample twenty-eight percent (28%) did not reply. However, a diversity of other roles usually does not contribute to the development of a coherent occupational identity:

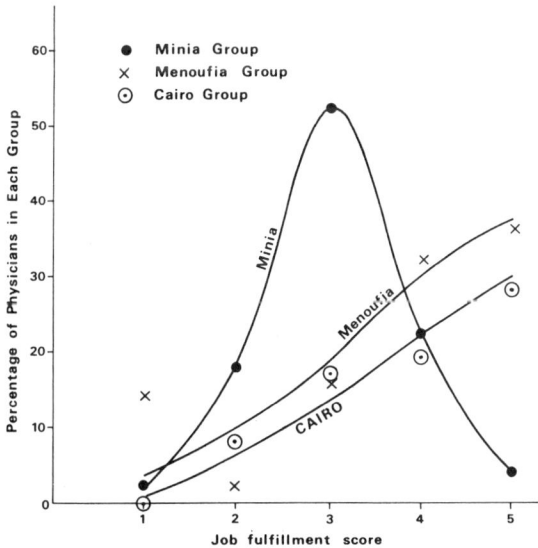

Figure 7.2. Distribution of Job Fulfillment Scores

Kinds of work tend to be named, to become well-defined occupations, and an important part of a person's work-based identity grows out of his relationship to his occupational title. These names carry a great deal of symbolic meaning, which tends to be incorporated into the identity. In the first place, they specify an area of endeavor belonging to those bearing the name and locate this area in relation to similar kinds of activity in a broader field. Secondly, they imply a great deal about the characteristics of their bearers, and these meanings are often systematized into elaborate ideologies which itemize the qualities, interests, and capabilities of those so identified. [12]

The process of identification and the nature and functioning of identity in conduct is a problem which warrants discussion. Foote [13] has illustrated that individuals identify themselves in terms of the names and categories current in the groups in which they are participating. They apply labels to themselves and learn how they ought to behave, thus acquiring a set of perspectives in terms of which their conduct is shaped.

The Minia group, by virtue of isolation from other interacting groups such as family, colleagues, or urban relationships, identify as part of the group (community), assuming the symbolic role of mediator. The attachment to his occupational title of Doctor as he acquires a self in harmony with his present environment gives him a sense of belonging but a less coherent occupational identity.

Minia Role Performance

As previously indicated, only four percent (4%) of the Minia sample rated their performance on the scale at 5.

It is relevant here to review the reasons why the Minia physician viewed his expectations in relation to the Ministry of Health definitions for his position in this manner. Those physicians who categorized their role on the scale of 4 or 5 gave some of the following reasons:

"I fear God in my work."

"I try to satisfy my conscience by helping all the patients at any time and sometimes give them my personal medications."

Several felt they were fulfilling their job properly "within the limits of the society and facilities" or "because the facilities were adequate." However, relations with the village council chief and "his ability to get the services and medications necessary for the unit" and "the village leaders are cooperative with me in the health projects" emphasizing the Gemeinshaft rural relationship in Minia is worth noting.

Those respondents who rated their performance on the scale at 3 frequently stated their inability to perform up to the Ministry of Health standards "because the work centres around administration which takes most of the time" or "because I am not well versed with the administrative side."

Other reasons frequently mentioned were: "lack of facilities", "workers inefficient".

Minia respondents who rated themselves lower than 3 gave reasons such as "inadequate facilities", "working conditions uncomfortable".

MENOUFIA ROLE PERFORMANCE

Thirty-six percent (36%) of the Menoufia sample rated their performance at 5. Let us consider some of the reasons. Frequently stated was "I am doing all my duties." and "I do everything I am asked to do". Also stated was "I love my work, so I commit myself to my duties—I'm there all the time". Those who felt their work fulfillment was not up to standard stated: "Administrative work takes all the time", "Lack of personal experience—inability to digest all new things", and "Lack of equipment".

CAIRO ROLE PERFORMANCE

Some of the statements of the Cairo physicians (28%) who ranked their performance at 5 were: "Because of devotion and honesty in work and taking care of the patient without looking at financial or social gains", "I do my work at its best taking into consideration pleasing God in doing my humanitarian work", "Because I am a resident and must do my job properly", and "I am committed to what the Ministry requires in attendance and work and additionally by participating in any work within my capabilities".

Reasons for rating their performance at 3 included: "Low salary, low quality of lodging", "Lack of facilities", and "Not enough experience". Other reasons stated for poor performance included: "Because of the bad conditions of work and crowding every week with on-call and lack of financial and moral incentives", and "Day to day pressures".

However, the Minia group tended to "identify" more strongly with the village population, assuming the role of mediator and generally participating in village functions. On the other hand, the feeling of alienation is expressed in the statement: "I'm from Cairo and not prepared mentally to work in a village."

Merton observes that a marginal man is one who aspires to membership in a group that denies him admission. [14] More isolated from family, friends and colleagues, the physician may aspire to identify more closely to the village patient/populace more than his Menoufia or Cairo colleagues. This is further elaborated by the fact that the Minia physician has ranked lower on the general exams, making him/her an "intellectual inferior". These doctors are, therefore, labelled as poor achievers and carry with them the stigma of being somewhat lower in abilities since the placement system is clearly understood by the community he serves.

A significant number of the Minia physicians were also educated in southern (less prestigious) universities. Admittance to these universities is usually based upon a lower Thanawia Amma grade. This would, in effect, within the profession, prevent them from belonging to the elite group of Cairo and Menoufia.

Another factor to consider is that a number of Minia's physicians were born in village areas. This would once again tend to reinforce alienation and hence marginality.

Finally, the visibility of the role performance has a distorting effect on the recognition he or she receives as has been implicit in Blau [15] and Merton's [16] work. This visibility can be reinforcing. Also, isolation of the Minia physician restricts the number of professional partners in what Whyte [17] has called "long narrow hierarchies ... are relatively low in economic efficiency and in employees' morale". In such organizations people are prevented from "discovering what their strengths and weaknesses are" and from "feeling that they themselves have really mastered their jobs." [18]

But when we come to "adjustment", i.e. more satisfaction with work, the marginal man appears more satisfied in his surroundings—more adaptive as will be illustrated in the following discussion.

Satisfaction as Exchange Theory

Interdependences between and among indivuals may be illustrated by the physician and the sick person and the well community. The existence of employment of the physician depends upon the illness of the patient, just as the existence of crime and criminals provides gainful employment for the police.

If these phenomena are examined closely, there appear to be two different determining relationships. The first involves behavioural facilitation or hindrance, whereas the second entails rewards and costs accruing to the person. [19] This conceptualization is generally viewed in the context of a two-person relationship. However, here we are considering the hindrances, facilitations, rewards and costs in terms of individual or group behaviour; groups being delineated into role boundaries such as: the community boundary, the professional boundary, the familial boundary, and the occupational boundary. These boundaries are viewed conceptually as linkages of facilitation and hindrance. The units of behaviour or "acts" are defined more exactly by the following examples.

There may be "mutual facilitation" in which group members facilitate the performance of one another, such as effective subordinate personnel facilitating the performance of medical procedures, for example, proper maintenance of the office, surgical supplies, etc.

"Mutual facilitation" is illustrated in Allport's study of "co-acting" groups in which a task was performed alone and with a control group performing a task in the company of others. Results indicated that "social facilitation" was presumed to occur partly because of the awareness of the sight of others doing the same thing. [20]

"Mutual hindrance" occurs when either hinder the performance of the other, for example, relatives and excessive number of visitors which impede the work of the physician. In this study hindrances may include other aspects, such as the result of over-employment (in the occupational boundary) in which three or four persons are employed to do the job of one person, which results in overcrowding the clinic and inefficiency.[d]

Therefore, we see the behaviour of others acting alone or in a group which creates a situation in which they function as facilitator or hinderer. As a result of this interaction, the consequences could be measured as rewards (positive aspects) or costs (negative aspects). Costs may be any factors which inhibit the performance of behaviour, which may be considered a material or psychological loss or an aversive condition. The greater the inhibitor of performance, the greater the cost. Therefore, costs may be high if insecurity is present, when great mental effort is required, or if conflicts are present. Costs, derived thus, are cumulative in their effect.

Homans discusses the values of activity and its costs (which at the same time are the lost values of alternative activities), psychological profit and investment. According to Homans, the secret of human exchange is the possibility that an actor can offer the other person behaviour which is more valuable to him than costly to the actor, and obtain from him behaviour which is more valuable to the actor than costly to the other person. This exchange does not concern commodities but activities, the value of these activities varying with regard to quality and quantity. [21]

Rewards are gratifications or satisfactions a person enjoys. A reward is constituted by providing the means whereby a drive is reduced or a need fulfilled. The amount of reward as a result of such an experience is measurable here in this study in terms of "satisfactions" and the cost measurable in terms of "dissatisfactions".

In this context a preliminary hypothesis would be: If the costs are high for an incumbent of a position as a result of conflicts, anxieties, etc., he will attempt to increase his rewards so that his goals can be satisfied. The foregoing is achieved by the reduction of the levels of aspiration.

Levels of aspiration refer to goal striving and is a fundamental concept in the analysis of achievement-related behaviours. Occupational goals and personal standards concerning how well one should perform in a given situation can be considered under the rubric of level of aspiration. Since many goals are possible, one's level of aspiration involves a decision or choice among various alternatives. Levels of aspiration have been shown to be influenced by in-

---

[d] *Op. cit.* Conversation with informant.

dividual differences, group standards, cultural factors, failure, and conflict. [22, 23]

The degree of variability in the measure of job satisfaction of incumbents of the same position in different geographical locations is a phenomen which will be explored in this chapter.

JOB SATISFACTION OVERALL

Dissatisfactions

The explanations of frustration among general practitioners give more or less emphasis to such factors as the structural conditions under which doctors practice, their attitudes, the nature of their medical education, and the character of demands made upon them. [24]

In a study of physicians, it is important to report the negative aspects of practice, so that they may be reduced or limited. This is especially relevant from the standpoint of policymaking. It is often misconceptually believed that rural practice has little to offer the physician and that he suffers from major dissatisfaction. This aspect has been documented by a number of authors. [25, 26, 27, 28, 29, 30]

Table 7.7 illustrates the responses to "disadvantages in the present employment situation" of the Cairo, Menoufia, and Minia samples.

The response to "conditions of work, isolation, hours, etc." followed an expected sequence.
In Minia, the most isolated, sixty percent (60%) mentioned this aspect, and forty-two percent (42%) of the Menoufia sample felt this was a problem. In Cairo, only twenty-five percent (25%) felt this was a disadvantage.

"Managerial responsibilities, bookkeeping" appear to be the major dissatisfaction in the rural areas of Minia (80%) and Menoufia (90%). I discussed this aspect of "paperwork" with my informant. Each unit has a "Kateb" (clerk) to help with the paperwork. This person's usual education is two years above secondary school studies. His duties include recording all the certificates. He is also held responsible for the furniture. However, he is not required to record drugs. "If he takes the medicine it would given him power and he might lock the cupboard—it would be good for him to take only the paperwork, but I must *trust* him," stated the informant. Other problems given were, "They (the 'Katebs') think they know better than the doctor since he is new and they have been there a long time". In response to the question if the nurse could record the medicines, he said, "She may make errors". He later stated, "I chose one farmer to help me separate the medications—he could read".

Obviously, trust and the desire for accuracy was an important aspect in the physician opting to do much of the paperwork himself. However, recording

Table 7.7

Physicians' Dissatisfactions

Item of Dissatisfaction	Percentage of Sample Citing Item		
	Cairo n=36	Menoufia n=50	Minia n=50
In Present Employment Situation:			
Conditions of work, isolation, hours, etc.	25	42	60
Managerial responsibilities, bookkeeping	22	90	80
Prejudice against women in medicine	0	4	14
Problems of family versus career	18	20	34
Lack of prestige of the profession	17	18	4
Mechanical aspects of medical work, repetition tediousness	31	26	32
Salary	72	58	44
Community problems surrounding your work	33	28	52
Relations with supervisors	18	10	12
Lack of equipment and supplies	61	68	80
Inadequate staff	22	12	64
Other	3	24	22
In General Environment Affecting Private Life:			
Housing	53	44	66
Transportation	67	44	66
Children's education	11	16	26
Cost of living	72	72	46
Other	11	14	4

medications, etc. is a cumbersome task which requires several entries and many physicians felt that such duplication was unneccessary.

It is interesting to note that in the more conservative and traditional area of Minia "prejudice against women in medicine" was more marked (14%) although only four percent (4%) of the Menoufia sample stated this as a disadvantage. This was not mentioned at all by the Cairo sample. Therefore, a total of only 9 physicians out of 136 felt this was a problem. The major reason cited for this problem was that it is "difficult for a woman to go out at night—especially without proper transportation".

For "Problems of family versus career", thirty-four percent (34%) of the Minia sample found this problematic, whereas, twenty percent (20%) from Menoufia and eighteen percent (18%) from Cairo stated this problem. A plausible explanation for this is that the Minia physician may leave his family behind in Cairo for better educational opportunities. Twenty-six percent (26%) of the Minia sample cited "children's education" as a problem, whereas, sixteen percent (16%) of the Menoufia sample and only eleven percent (11%) of the Cairo sample mentioned his aspect.

As an indication that the communities in the Minia governorate confer more prestige on the physician, only four percent (4%) of the Minia sample complained of lack of prestige of their profession as opposed to seventeen percent (17%) and eighteen percent (18%) for Cairo and Menoufia respectively.

"The mechanical aspects of medical work, repitition, and tediousness" were found to be almost equally disadvantageous with thirty-one percent (31%) for Cairo, twenty-six percent (26%) for Menoufia, and thirty-two percent (32%) for Minia.

Dissatisfaction with salary was correlated to a problem in the general environment affecting private life, cost of living, as illustrated in Table 7.7. The Minia group showed the least dissatisfaction with salary and cost of living. It should be mentioned here that the Minia sample included the highest percentage of physicians who had been more than one year on the job (84% compared to 76% for Menoufia and 50% for Cairo). This may afford them greater opportunity for 'private' consultations. Also, the fact that the more central areas of Menoufia and Cairo would naturally have a higher cost of living index.

The Minia physician, acting the role of mediator and leader cited more dissatisfactions with "community problems surrounding his/her work" (fifty-two percent, 52%). Only twenty-eight percent (28%) of the Menoufia sample mentioned this problem, whereas, thirty-three percent (33%) of the Cairo sample found this to be problematic. It should be noted here that the Cairo hospital is located in one of the native areas. Some of the statements cited by these physicians, reinforcing this theme, were "problems with visitors" and "problems from relatives", "fear of some patients", and "to be a male physician is an advantage, because it takes a *strong man* to deal with these people".

The Cairo respondents found "relations with supervisors" more problematic (eighteen percent, 18%) than did the rural physicians (Minia twelve percent, 12%, and Menoufia ten percent, 10%). The rural physician is more often alone, without a supervisor, unlike the urban hospital where the physician often interacts with his chief daily.

"Lack of equipment and supplies" was a major complaint from the Minia sample (eighty percent, 80%). However, it is interesting to note that although Cairo is the urban centre, sixty-one percent (61%) of the sample as compared with sixty-eight percent (68%) of the Menoufia sample stated this dissatisfaction.

In the category of "other disadvantages" only three items were specified by the Cairo sample as opposed to twenty-four items for Menoufia and twenty-two items for Minia. Some of the "other dissatisfactions in the present employment situation" were:

Menoufia

"If they desire us to maintain a scientific level, why don't they allow us to study from our positions?"
"Lack of seriousness of subordinates—inefficiency"
"Media campaigns against doctors"

Cairo

"Not allowed to practice outside"

Minia

"Bribery and favouritism"
"Lack of efficiency (professional and supporting staff)"

Because it was felt that problems in the general environment affect one's private life which in turn is relevant to dissatisfaction in the employment situation, respondents were asked to consider their problems with housing, transportation, children's education, and cost of living.

Problems in housing were specified by all three groups: Minia sixty-six percent (66%), Cairo fifty-three percent (53%), and Menoufia forty-four percent (44%). This is to be expected due to the acute housing shortage; a tenant may have to pay the landlord up to 5,000 Egyptian pounds[b] key money. This is considered illegal by the government; however, it may be the only way for a newly married physician to obtain a *flat to rent*. This amount is not applied toward the rent nor returned and in effect is a "lost investment".

Village transportation is problematic. A doctor may travel to a patient by motorcycle, taxi, foot, donkey, or "feluca" (sail boat), as indicated by sixty-six percent (66%) of the Minia sample and forty-four percent (44%) of the Menoufia sample. However, a young doctor may opt for an apartment for his new bride and have to use public transportation, which is not an easy task in Cairo with the "population explosion". It may take one hour to find a taxi "going your way". Even the physician with his own automobile today in Cairo finds the traffic problem an impossible situation. The Cairo sample indicated this dissatisfaction with sixty-seven percent (67%).

Satisfactions

It is equally important to document satisfactions of practice not only from the attitudinal point of view, but to present an accurate picture for statistical analysis. Reporting the dissatisfactions for the three samples would give an inaccurate analysis if given alone. The satisfactions of Egyptian physicians are presented for comparative analysis. Table 7.8 illustrates the job satisfactions for all three samples.

"Job fulfillment" was accorded high percentages by Minia and Cairo, ninety percent (90%) and ninety-two percent (92%) respectively. Menoufia rated this aspect with seventy-eight percent (78%).

Table 7.8

Physicians' Satisfactions

Item of Satisfaction	Percentage of Sample Citing Item		
	Cairo n=36	Menoufia n=50	Minia n=50
In Present Employment Situation:			
Job fulfillment	92	78	90
Professional development	31	28	56
Promotional opportunities	6	4	16
Prestige	8	10	28
Financial rewards	6	4	22
Social relations	11	28	50
Contribution to the health and welfare of the people	61	70	86
Other	3	10	2
General:			
Your career or occupation	61	54	72
Your future job prospects	44	46	80
Family relationships	89	80	90
Leisure time recreational activities	31	16	64
Financial status	47	36	80
Social relationships	83	88	74
Social status	78	86	84
Relationships with colleagues	94	82	92
Effectiveness of the medical syndicate	14	24	32

"Relationships with colleagues" was also rated high: Cairo ninety-four percent (94%), Minia ninety-two percent (92%), and Menoufia eighty-two percent (82%). Other professional items were rated significantly lower, such as "professional development": Minia fifty-six percent (56%), Cairo thirty-one percent (31%), and Menoufia twenty-eight percent (28%). In general, "career satisfaction" was rated: Minia seventy-two percent (72%), Cairo sixty-one percent (61%), and Menoufia fifty-four percent (54%).

It is interesting to note that eighty percent (80%) of the Minia sample rated "future job prospects" as satisfactory, whereas, Menoufia with forty-six percent (46%) and Cairo with forty-four percent (44%) were less optimistic.

"Promotional opportunities" were also rated more optimistically by Minia, sixteen percent (16%), as opposed to Menoufia, four percent (4%), and Cairo, six percent (6%).

Minia, most distant from the medical syndicate rated their satisfaction with its effectiveness at thirty-two percent (32%). Menoufia rated their satisfaction with twenty-four percent (24%) and Cairo, perhaps more likely to have higher expectations, rated their satisfaction at fourteen percent (14%).

An article in the Egyptian Gazette editorial asks why one never hears of any startling contributions by the Medical Association or individual grouping of doctors in the matter of public health. A reason may be difficulties of co-ordination or publicity—"If there was a prevalent attitude that prevention is better than cure one feels a lot more would have been done." [31]

The rural-southern physician derived, as would be expected, more prestige satisfaction (twenty-eight percent) compared with his colleagues: Menoufia (ten percent) and Cairo (eight percent). Likewise, the Mediator-Leader "Marginal Man" obtained more satisfaction from the "Contribution to the health and welfare of the people", being cited by eighty-six percent of the sample. Significantly, the Menoufia physician also expressed more satisfaction than their Cairo colleagues with this item (70% versus 61%).

The "Marginal Man" also found more satisfaction in his personal life as shown in Table 7.8. It is significant that Egypt, although striving for rapid industrialization, still maintains extended family ties. The third most satisfactory aspect in his/her life was "family relationships" exemplifying the important role family plays in all aspects of Egyptian life. Minia cited it with ninety percent (90%), Cairo eighty-nine percent (89%), and Menoufia eighty percent (80%).

Some samples of the "other reasons for satisfaction" given were:

Menoufia

"Gaining an understanding of rural people"
"Treating people and loving them"
"Doing an important human job"
"God's satisfaction"

Minia

"The profession itself is an advantage"

Medical Student Expectations of Rural Job Satisfactions and Dissatisfactions

The literature rarely mentions the positive aspects of rural practice. Press releases, feedback from other colleagues and senior professionals emphasize the negative aspects (for example, isolation, problems from the community, inadequate professional support, and the disadvantages of rural living). As a result, medical students may have a view of rural practice that is unrealistically negative. Unfortunately, the existing negativity toward rural practice may be reinforced in medical schools. [32, 33]

It was, therefore, felt that the student's views of his/her anticipated service in terms of satisfaction and dissatisfaction would provide insight for anticipatory socialization. Table 7.9 gives the results as compared with the combined Minia/Menoufia physicians sample. Cairo was eliminated from this comparison since the statement asked the respondents for their anticipatory views about the *rural* areas. As was previously mentioned, fourth and fifth year students were combined since no significant difference existed. Not all items were included in the student questionnaire; only those items rated by the students are being presented for comparison of perceptions versus realities.

Table 7.9

Medical Students' Anticipated Disadvantages in Rural Areas Compared with Rural Physicians

Disadvantages (Dissatisfactions)	Combined Minia/Menoufia Rural Sample %	Combined 4th/5th yr. Students %
Conditions of work, Isolation, hours, etc.	51	55
Managerial responsibilities, bookkeeping	85	22
Prejudice against women in medicine	9	6
Problems of family versus career	27	31
Lack of prestige of the profession	11	12
Mechanical aspects of medical work, repetition, tediousness	29	24
Salary	51	50
Community problems surrounding your work	40	23
Relations with supervisors	11	8
Lack of equipment and supplies	74	78
Inadequate staff	38	26
Other	23	19

As can be observed from Table 7.9, the students' perceptions were generally "accurate"; however, the realities of practice present more managerial responsibilities, more community problems, and less adequately trained staff than anticipated. Some of the other medical students' anticipated disadvantages included:

"Lack of psychological preparedness"
"Poor communication between units and hospitals"
"Lack of cleanliness"
"Lack of contacts with research and new techniques"
"Less opportunities for contacts with specialists and higher education"
"The feeling that one is exiled in the villages"
"Ganging among the workers against the doctor"
"Lack of financial or social advantages"
"Lack of civilized life i.e. electricity and entertainment"

A major concern and item most often mentioned was the lack of continuing education. The students in this sample were from one of the prestigeous universities, hence, more academically inclined.

Table 7.10 indicates the perceived advantages of the medical students as compared with the "realities" of the physicians from Minia and Menoufia. As can be observed, the medical students viewed their anticipated satisfactions to a lesser degree than their colleagues already in the field. This was especially demonstrated by a lower rating for social relations, contribution to the health and welfare of the people, prestige, and job fulfillment. However, some of the other reasons cited for job fulfillment were insightful:

"The specialists are in the city so it is hard for a beginner to start practice."
"Difficulties involved in the crowded big cities"
"Quiet away from the pollution and everyday problems e.g. transport"
"Financial benefits"
"An opportunity to get away from the mad nervous cities"

On the other hand, the statement "No advantages ... the new doctor is not qualified to be responsible for 5,000 people", expresses self-doubts.

Table 7.10
Medical Students' Anticipated Advantages in Rural Areas Compared with Rural Physicians

Advantages (Satisfactions)	Combined Minia/Menoufia Rural Sample	Combined 4th/5th yr. Students
	%	%
Job fulfillment	84	70
Professional development	42	40
Promotional opportunities	10	6
Prestige	19	5
Financial rewards	13	14
Social relations	39	21
Contribution to the health and welfare of the people	78	59
Other	6	3

Satisfaction and Dissatisfaction Indices

To express the satisfactions and dissatisfactions of each sample as a whole, the scores of each individual within were cumulated and an arithmetic mean obtained, i.e. a mean score. The mean scores might be arbitrarily referred to henceforth, as a satisfaction index; dissatisfaction index in the case of dissatisfactions.

Table 7.11 gives the mean scores for satisfactions and dissatisfactions of the three samples together with the standard deviations.

By statistically (t-distribution) comparing the mean scores (at $\alpha = 0.10$, justifiable for the standard deviations obtained and given in Table 7.11), the results confirmed that the mean scores for satisfactions and dissatisfactions were higher in Minia than in Menoufia than in Cairo. The accepted statistical differences are shown in Table 7.12 as percentages of the total possible mean score of 17.

In certain cases the difference appears to be rather small. However, analysis of variance for the 3 differently located groups indicated a significant difference at $\alpha = 0.05$ (Tables 7.13 and 7.14), the significance being more pronounced for the satisfactions mean scores.

Table 7.11

Mean Scores for Satisfactions and Dissatisfactions

Sample	Satisfactions	Dissatisfactions
Minia n = 49	10.1 ± 2.5	7.0 ± 2.0
Menoufia n = 49	7.6 ± 2.0	5.9 ± 3.1
Cairo n = 35	7.5 ± 2.3	3.3 ± 2.4

Table 7.12

Statistical Differences Between Mean Scores for Satisfactions and Dissatisfactions

| Samples Compared | Differences in % of Total Possible Mean Score (17) | | |
	Minia > Menoufia	Minia > Cairo	Menoufia > Cairo
Satisfactions	11.0	12.8	1.8
Dissatisfactions	2.4	8.2	5.9

Table 7.13

Variance Analysis of Satisfaction Mean Scores

Source	d.f.	Sum of Squares	Mean Squares
Among	2	207	103.50
Within	130	680	5.23
Total	132	887	

$F = 19.78 > F_{0.05}$ (2, 130) = 3.07

Table 7.14

Variance Analysis of Dissatisfaction Mean Scores

Source	d.f.	Sum of Squares	Mean Squares
Among	2	57	28.50
Within	130	857	6.59
Total	132	914	

$F = 4.32 > F_{0.05}$ (2, 130) = 3.07

Attempts at Role Integration

The mean scores for the three groups in Table 7.11 indicate that the degree of satisfaction was most pronounced in Minia. The following explains this phenomenon theoretically.

Initially we find the Minia Sample with a high degree of dissatisfaction in conditions of work, isolation, problems of family versus career, community problems, inadequate staff and lack of equipment and supplies. Then we are presented with the high level of Minia's satisfactions with social rewards, job fulfillment, future job prospects, financial status, leisure time recreational activities.

On the assumption that human beings seeks to reduce tensions—a postulate of several social science theories, [34] for example, cognitive dissonance, we will consider how the Minia physician adapts himself to the built-in strains of his profession.

Here a ritualistic type of adaptation can be identified. According to Merton [35] it involves the abandoning or scaling down of the costly cultural goals of great pecuniary success and rapid social mobility to the point where one's aspirations can be satisfied.

One device for allaying anxieties is to lower one's level of aspiration—permanently. High aspirations invite frustration and danger whereas lower aspirations produce satisfaction and security. It is, in short, the mode of adaptation of individuals seeking a private escape from the dangers and frustrations which seem to them inherent in the competition for major cultural goals by abandoning these goals and clinging all the more closely to the safe routines and the institutional norms. [36]

Supporting this argument, the voiced desire for advanced education and training was considerably lower in the Minia sample, sixteen percent (16%) aspiring for additional training and only twenty-six percent 26%) aspiring for further education. This was considerably lower than their colleagues in Menoufia of whom seventy percent (70%) desired additional education. The Cairo sample, likewise, demonstrated the same pattern with seventy-eight percent (78%) desiring further training and sixty-seven percent (67%) desiring additional education to improve their position in the medical profession.

This argument will be further supported in the analysis of the value scales for achievement, independance, and recognition.

Work load, i.e. number of patients seen daily, was not correlated with the job satisfaction index in this analysis. It was felt that this would not be an accurate indicator since it is difficult to ascertain the circumstances involved. During participant observation, it was noted that the physician spent approximately two minutes with each patient because of the great numbers. The patient cited his/her complaint and the physician wrote out the prescription. A patient requiring more time was given it, in spite of the heavy demand on time. Naturally it would be impossible to compare this physician's work load with a surgeon in the Cairo hospital who had spent the entire morning in the operating theatre for three cases.

In addition, since it is not permitted for those physicians doing their mandatory practice to have private patients, these figures would not be reported on the questionnaire. However, my informant stated that "In the rural areas the average doctor sees thirty to fifty patients daily. If he gave them all the medications they desired, they would not come for private consultation. The doctor "saves" some of the good vitamins, etc. for his "private" patients who are charged L.E. 0.50 or 1.00 per visit. The patient is not charged for the medication. The small units generally have 5-10 private patients per evening."

Asked what the difference in care of a private versus public patient is, he replied, "Follow-up for the private patient is better; he gets more care; a *social relationship* is developed; he does not come alone but comes with the whole family." [e]

It may be noted that according to Freidson, "job satisfaction is inevitably a function of the alternative careers which exist at any particular time and of the symbolic and material rewards of these alternatives." [37]

In order to develop the preceding analysis, a more in-depth study of the hindrance and facilator aspects of role is considered in the following section.

Marginality Versus Complementarity

Struggle and conflicts between patient and physician have been documented almost 2500 years ago in the Hippocratic corpus which presented the doctors' complaints about the non-professional criteria that people use to select their physicians, [38] criticism of patients, insisting on doubtful remedies [39] or more conventional remedies such as "barley water, wine, and hydromel" and not following the doctor's orders. [40] The problems presented in these historical documents are applicable today especially in more traditional societies where the physician comes from a different sub-culture. The physicians often find the patients very troublesome as a result of different social-class origins. Sigerist's assumption that health care is primarily a social relationship is worth consideration. [41]

> In every medical action there are always two parties involved, the physician and the patient or, in a broader sense, the medical corps and society. Medicine is nothing else than the manifold relations between these two groups. The history of medicine, therefore, cannot limit itself to the history of the science, institutions and characters of medicine, but must include the history of the patient in society, that of the physician, and the history of the relations between physician and patient.

---

[e] *Ibid.*

Sigerist's assertion deserves special consideration in a transitional society [42] where physicians who are trained in major cities to learn Western expertise and methodology go to the rural areas or serve the urban poor populace, usually migrants from rural areas. Conflicts may be endemic in the role relationship between physician and patient due to the differences in perspectives.

The scope of this chapter is to examine the frictions experienced with subordinate staff, the community, the supervisors, and the Ministry of Health. As was mentioned in the previous chapter, we are considering interaction here as either group or individual phenomena, delineated into boundaries of occupation, community and profession. The concepts are based on Freidson's analysis that some relationships have inherent conflict. These conflicts are partially due to the "cultural differences", but others are due to the power structure. [43] However, Parsons states that Weber's monocratic model of rational-legal bureaucracy is an inappropriate work setting for the professional, and that an organization resembling a "company of equals" with only minimal hierarchical differentiation and supervision is instead the appropriate model. [44] His argument is inapplicable to the Egyptian case where hierarchical structure prevails both within the professional boundary and between the professional and subordinate staff.

Scaling of Data

Data for the forthcoming analysis was assimilated from open-ended questions which provided more detailed descriptions of the conflicts present. Categories were constructed from the problems stated and statements were then placed within the specified categories by the researcher. In an attempt to prevent bias, the statements were again read by a native Egyptian who once again re-categorized them. Any discrepancies were discussed and the items were re-categorized if necessary. Percentages are given for the frequencies statements were made within the following categories:

1. Problems from the community
2. Cultural traditions facilitating your work
3. Cultural traditions impeding your work
4. Problems from subordinate staff
5. Problems with supervisors
6. Problems with the Ministry of Health

Problems from the Community

Referring to Figure 7.3, the "Community Boundary" includes the traditional healer, the village leader or religious leader (sheikh), and the consumer (village or city patient). It is within this boundary that the following problems, as defined by the physician, will be discussed.

Respondents were asked the question "As a male or female physician, what are the problems you are encountering in performing your job from the people in the community?" Classifications for this question included:

1. Inconsiderateness of the doctor (unappreciative of doctor)
2. Lack of discipline (excessive visitors, poor manners)
3. Poverty/Lack of education (poor health habits, poor personal hygiene, poor nutrition)
4. "Primitive"/traditional belief system (complications from traditional healers, village medical students, village council leaders)
5. Lack of confidence (doctor, medicine, free treatment)
6. Status of women
7. Demanding (more services, over-ulitization of existing services)
8. No reply

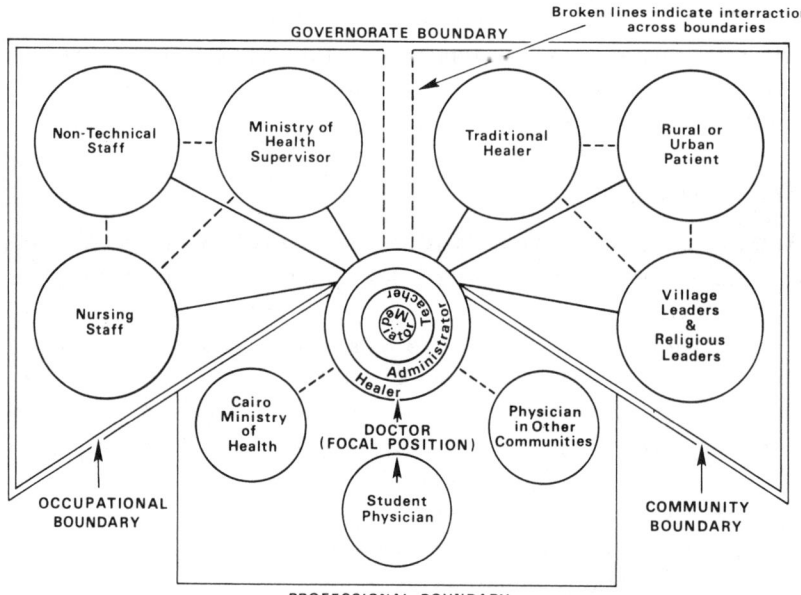

Figure 7.3. Role Structure of the Egyptian Health Delivery System

Table 7.15 gives the results for this category. In the first item (Inconsiderateness of the doctor) fifteen percent (15%) of the Cairo sample stated this problem, whereas only seven percent (7%) of the Menoufia sample and three percent (3%) of the Minia sample cited it.

Some examples stated were "Lack of estimation of the doctor" (Cairo), "Lack of appreciation of the doctor as a human being who needs rest and should not be disturbed with trivial questions outside office hours, especially

Table 7.15

Problems From the Community as Stated by Physicians

Items	Percentage of sample citing item		
	Cairo	Menoufia	Minia
1. Inconsiderateness of doctor	15	7	3
2. Lack of discipline	24	5	0
3. Poverty/Lack of education	16	35	49
4. "Primitive"/Traditional belief system	8	18	21
5. Lack of confidence	22	18	19
6. Status of women	0	2	0
7. Demanding	5	9	5
8. No reply	10	6	3
	100	100	100

between one a.m. and six a.m." (Cairo), and "Lack of gratitude" (Menoufia).

Item number 2 (Lack of discipline) which included "excessive visitors" (i.e. not observing visiting hours, wanting to live-in with the patient) and "poor manners" (including argumentative behaviour) accounted for twenty-four percent (24%) of the problems listed in this category for Cairo, only five percent (5%) for the Menoufia sample, and no one (0%) from the Minia sample mentioned this problem. It is important to understand why the patients behave this way. The practice of medicine is permeated with objective uncertainty and the less educated patient may not "cooperate" with the physician.

The more educated patient will have a higher expectation of the physician and possess more knowledge; therefore, the patient tries to control in some way what the physician does to him or his loved ones. Also, this behaviour is more likely to occur when the patient defines his illness as potentially more critical than when he views his illness as minor. This would be applicable to the Cairo sample also as more critically ill patients are often sent to the city physician.

Item number 3 (Poverty/lack of education) was seen as a major problem in Minia, forty nine percent (49%), and Menoufia, thirty-five percent (35%), whereas only sixteen percent (16%) of the Cairo sample specified this problem. As can be seen in the demographic data cited on pages 98-102, the illiteracy rate is high in Minia and Menoufia. The more rural and southern areas have marked illiteracy, and the villager is generally poorer than his city cousin. As can be observed from Table 7.15, "Primitive"/traditional belief system quantitatively increases in that direction: Cairo eight percent (8%), Menoufia eighteen percent (18%), and Minia twenty-one percent (21%). It is not surprising that traditional healers play a role in Egyptian society;

however, considering the amount of concern often voiced about traditional healers, it is surprising that the degree of dissatisfaction voiced is quantitatively low compared with "Poverty/lack of education", and as a group significantly lower than item 5, Lack of confidence. Perhaps this indicates that the over-emphasis of culture in modern medical programmes *in terms of obstacles to change* may need rethinking. It is this overemphasis that carries the elitist implication that it is specifically the culture of the masses that constitutes the more crucial obstacles to the improvement of public health. However, it may be a serious limitation to continue to focus *only* on culture, which places the blame on the developing people as has been done the past.

The serious lack of confidence demonstrates that the ideology and organization of "Western Medicine" and agents of change may need challenging. Twenty-two percent (22%) of the Cairo sample indicated lack of confidence from the community, eighteen percent (18%) of the Menoufia sample and nineteen percent (19%) of the Minia sample indicated this problem.

Simmel has stated that "our modern life is based to a much larger extent than is usually realized upon the faith in the honesty of the other ... We base our gravest decisions on a complex system of conceptions, most of which presuppose the confidence that we will not be betrayed." [45] Simmel evidently was writing about Western Societies where one has confidence in the mechanic's ability to repair a car as well as the physician's ability to prescribe the proper medication and treatment. To the Middle Easterner, this confidence is nonexistent. Berger has discussed this in length in his Arab World Today. [46] One logically assumes in Egypt that the mechanic will not do the job properly and therefore, it follows, that the physician may not do *his* job properly. This lack of confidence and trust permeates the society by virtue of the client's expectations having been repeatedly unfulfilled, reinforcing this attitude.

In spite of the low percentage, i.e. Menoufia's two percent (2%) and no response in Minia or Cairo, for the item of "Status of women", it deserves consideration. The examples stated were, "Women come in advanced stages of diseases due to the negligence of husband and father", and "The weak position of women". It is interesting that no male physician cited this problem. A hierarchy appears to exist within the family which determines who will go to the doctor and seek expensive treatment. Although the treatment in the rural health unit is free, the cost of a day's wages, medications which must be purchased if unavailable at the clinic, and the reluctance of Middle Eastern village women to be seen by a male doctor all contribute to this factor.

Scarce resources are more frequently allocated to men, especially male household heads, than to women. It is explained that a man's illness is more detrimental to household welfare since resources may have to be diverted to hire wage hands to work in the family land in his place. One survey of village family expenditures for illness during a four-month period revealed an average of L.E. 2.20 for men versus 1.50 for women. [47]

Age is also a major factor in evaluating the severity of an illness and may intervene with the factor of gender. A woman who has gained the high status of mother of an adult son receive prompt and more costly treatment than a young childless daughter-in-law or a male infant in the same household or maybe even than the adult son's wife. [48, 49]

Item number 7, (Demanding ... more services or over-utilizing existing services) was cited by Cairo five percent (5%), Menoufia nine percent (9%), and Minia five percent (5%).

The patterns of utilization in well-defined situations needs further study. Why are hospitals and physicians' services used at different rates in various regions and cities? Are those persons "over-utilizing the services" residing within the proximity of the clinic or hospital, thereby creating a picture of masked utilization, or do they come from distant places which could render the "cost" in terms of a lost work day, etc. greater? Utilization is dependent on such factors as illness levels, age and sex composition of the population, presence or absence of health facilities, family income, residence, and the perceptions of providers and recipients of health services. As Anderson aptly states:

> "Finally, it is hoped that sociologists can contribute to more sophisticated, i.e. realistic thinking in the medical care field. There is a tendency among many in the medical care field to assume that there is no limit to the amount of hospital or physicians' services people would use if facilities were available and services were free and there were no diliberate controls of any kind. There seems to be no concept of an equilibrium of use—and it is this concept which can usefully be explored by sociologists to serve both sociology and medical care." [50]

Cultural differences between physician and patient have received considerable attention. [51] It has been suggested that the physician should try to reduce conflict by adjusting himself to the patient's expectations, for example, behaving in a more relaxed informal way rather than assuming a 'professional' attitude. [52] It should be added here, however, that the professional facade of the new graduate serves to aid him during this period of uncertainty. Perhaps what is most needed is to bring social sciences into the Egyptian Medical Schools so that he/she may learn more about the village and indigent patient *as a person*. Only then can they be equipped to be understanding and tolerant, thereby, adjusting themselves to the expectations of the patient that may contradict their own.

What are these cultural traditions that hinder or facilitate their practice? More published information exists on local health practices in Egypt than in any other country of the Middle East. A cursory review of the literature is provided in chapter two to assist the reader in understanding the health related cultural traditions of the "traditional" Egyptian.

Hindering Traditions

Table 7.16 presents the cultural traditions impeding one's work, as seen by the physician. It should be noted here that the traditions listed encompass the occupational and professional as well as the community boundaries. It should also be mentioned here that the term "traditions" was conceptually viewed by the physicians in very broad terms to include items such as poverty, lack of confidence, as well as traditional beliefs. This is the physicians' perceptions of the "Egyptian cultural traditions". The physician's reality is therefore being presented. [53]

Table 7.16

Cultural Traditions Stated by Physicians as Impeding Their Work

Cultural Tradition	Percentage of sample citing "tradition"		
	Cairo	Menoufia	Minia
1. Negative social traits	40	9	8
2. Traditional healers	0	9	1
3. Poverty/Lack of education	24	30	38
4. Traditional beliefs/Fatalism	2	14	21
5. Native treatment	2	4	4
6. Unco-operative	4	8	14
7. Lack of confidence (in doctor, medicine, free treatment)	4	1	0
8. No reply			

The most significant finding was that "Negative social traits" was the major complaint from the Cairo sample. This item included: bribery, favouritism, gossiping, procrastination, lack of discipline, and lack of respect. Only nine percent (9%) of the Menoufia sample and eight percent (8%) of the Minia sample cited these complaints. The urban physician, more dissatisfied with his role, found the patient "lacking in character", "violent", having a "loss of traditions". He complained of "frequent visits to the patient by relatives", and "insisting to accompany him to the hospital". As was mentioned previously, the hospital studied was in one of the more native crowded quarters of Cairo. It would be interesting to know if physicians working in less densely populated areas and/or in private hospitals share these views. Clearly the expectations of both patient and practitioner are not being met.

In May, 1977, The World Health Assembly of WHO passed a resolution to promote traditional medicine. [54] This was an effort to encourage all member nations to conduct research on and seek ways of utilizing their indigenous practitioners. The resolution was proposed by certain member nations and has subsequently stimulated others, such as Egypt, to consider (or reconsider) the training and upgrading of their traditional practitioners. [55]

Is this a genuine problem today, or are the traditional healers becoming obsolete? Current research indicates that the village barber is becoming less involved with community medicine since the influx of more rural health units. [56]

Only nine percent (9%) of the Menoufia sample and one percent (1%) of the Minia sample cited this problem. No physician from Cairo made this complaint.

Just why the physicians have reported so few complaints about the traditional healer needs more examination. Is it because a symbiotic relationship prevails, or do they in their status-bound ivory tower deny their existence?

The role of traditional medicine in health care is receiving increasingly more attention. The WHO meeting convened by the WHO Regional office for Africa on the promotion and development of traditional medicine defined traditional medicine as follows:

> "... The sum total of all the knowledge and practices, whether explicable or not, used in diagnosis, prevention and elimination of physical, mental or social imbalance and relying exclusively on practical experience and observation handed down from generation to generation, whether verbally or in writing.
>
> Traditional medicine might also be considered as a solid amalgamation of dynamic medical know-how and ancestral experience.
>
> Traditional African medicine might also be considered to be the sum total of practices, measures, ingredients and procedures of all kinds, whether material or not, which from time immemorial had enabled the African to guard against disease, to alleviate his sufferings and to cure himself." [57]

The traditional healer was defined by the regional office expert group as:[f]

> "... a person who is recognized by the community in which he lives as competent to provide health care by using vegetable, animal and mineral substances and certain other methods based on the social, cultural and religious background as well as on the knowledge, attitudes and beliefs that are prevalent in the community regarding physical, mental and social well-being and the causation of disease and disability." [58]

---

[f] The traditional healer is not to be confused with the auxiliary defined by Basch as "any of a wide range of trained medical workers who have vocational and practical qualifications, with or without diploma, beyond regular schooling and who work normally under the direct or remote supervision of a professional. Both professional and auxiliary personnel are usually *credentialed* as opposed to the traditional healers who often work in the same communities". Basch, P. F., International Health, Oxford University Press, Inc., N.Y., 1978, p. 308.

For a discussion on the auxiliary, see Frankenberg, R. and Leeson, J., 'The Sociology of Health Dilemmas in the Post-Colonial World: Intermediate Technology and Medical Care in Zambia, Zaire, and China', in DeKadt, E., and William, G. (ed.), *Sociology and Development*, Tavistock Publications, London, 1974, pp. 255-278.

The People's Republic of China's medical system has received considerable attention in recent years; they have had for centuries a tradition of healers who used traditional methods because of the inaccessibility of Western medicines and treatment. These flourished into the 1930s and 1940s. [59] The Government's success in introducing nearly one million barefoot doctors and eliminating various forms of traditional healers within one generation without creating insurmountable conflicts between these healers and the barefoot doctors raises the question of how this was accomplished. It is speculated upon in the light of Landy's concept of role adaptation as it applied to healers and barefoot doctors. In discussing the role adaptation, he posits that "the curer's status does not become attenuated ... when the expectations of his community are such that the technology if not the values, of scientific medicine is perceived by them so clearly superior that they distinctly prefer it to their own." [60] Thus the barefoot doctor represents one form of role adaptation whereby he becomes the "healer for all seasons." [61] Although it is impossible to explain this phenomenon fully, the combining of Chinese medicine with that of Western medicine may have facilitated this trend. The traditional curers may have been drawn into the orbit of "scientific medicine", and in order to remain as a curer, the Government has assigned him with a role within the health scheme subject to his undergoing more health training and ideological realignment. [62]

Answers to these questions are found only by in-depth analysis of historical and social contexts. Some countries suffering from the vestiges of colonial administration still rely heavily on "imported" health care systems. A world wide struggle continues to exist in the medical division of labour. According to Leslie, advocates of cosmopolitan medicine attempt to: [63]

1. Standardize the curricula for training health specialists.
2. Reserve the legal practice of medicine to individuals with requisite training.
3. Enforce a hierarchy of medical authority dominated by doctors who form a self-governing profession with the right to define and to supervise the work of paramedical specialists.
4. Limit access of lay men or of other kinds of curers to the technology of cosmopolitan medicine.
5. To eliminate or narrowly restrict all other forms of medical practice.

Seen in this context, the actual systems of different countries are compromise structures of cosmopolitan medical workers and of other kinds of health specialists; their models projected by their critics or admirers are ideological tools in the struggle to gain or keep power, and to control their course of development. [64] g For example, in India, in spite of an existing

---

g These indigenous systems include: Ayurveda, which is based upon Sanskrit texts, Yunani, Greek medicine and Siddha which is a tradition of humoral medicine in India.

dual system of professionalized indigenous[h] and cosmopolitan medicine, it is not without conflicts, especially between practitioners of those systems who compete for positions and legitimacy within the state sanctioned medical bureaucracies. Newman, [65] found that the practitioners of indigenous medicine in the rural areas of two states in India outnumbered the modern allopathic physicians. In another study by Chuttani and others [66] it was reported that nearly 63% of a group of such practitioners had no qualifications at all; however, more than 2/3 of those studied practised the modern allopathic system and used modern medicines. In yet another study, Alexander and Shivaswamy [67] have reported that the traditional healers treated about eight times the number of patients treated by the state health care. It also indicated a positive attitude toward participation in family planning and immunization programmes. Leeson and Frankenberg, [68] in their study of the patients of traditional doctors in Lusaka, have found that other considerations enter into the decision-making process as to whom the patients seek for cure, such as convenience, and the desire for an explanation, particularly if a cure is delayed. These illustrations indicate that the indigenous medical system is acceptable to the masses. Djukanovic and Mach [69] have recommended the training of indigenous healers and integrating them into the general health system as an alternative approach to meeting the basic needs of peoples in developing countries.

In Egypt, the *Daya* (midwife) has survived the modernizing influences in society. [70] Other indigenous practitioners such as floor cleaners in hospitals have been found to be effective in treating their neighbours after hours.

A recent study of formal and informal healing systems in four villages in Egypt indicated that professionals suffer from a status-bound aloofness, while informal healers have closer ties with their patients and the local community, are attentive to non-somatic aspects of illness and respond to the patient's doubts and fears more sympathetically than the doctor, thus humanizing the health process. [71]

However, the interplay and trust among villagers, traditional healers, and medical doctors can be aptly illustrated by the following account:

> "... My boy fell while playing in school with his friends. When he came home he complained of pain in his arm. I sent for the bone-settler.[i] While massaging the arm the boy pointed out to me a spot under his arm where pain was localized. I looked at it and found that it was swollen. The bone settler said that it was due to the fall, but I instructed him to stop massaging and let the child alone. I immediately took the boy to the health unit to see the doctor. I found out that he was

---

[h] See Frankenberg, R., 'Allopathic Medicine, Profession and Capitalistic Ideology in India', Paper Prepared for the Ninth World Congress of Sociology at Uppsala, August 14-19, 1978, Ronald Frankenberg, Dept. of Sociology, University of Keele, Staffordshire, 1978.

[i] Written here as in the original, "bone-settler" is most probably intended to be bone-setter.

on holiday, so I went to the health barber. He said that the boy had an internal abscess and he could operate on it. I told him don't do that, but just give him something to relieve the pain. He gave him some pills and an injection, and we waited until the next day when the doctor came and operated. Afterwards we went several times to another health barber who also works in the health unit's clinic to dress the wound and give the boy some penicillin injections." [72]

Thus we find that whereas the physician lacks an understanding of the needs of the patient, a symbiotic relationship with the traditional healer persists.

"Incha Allah", "Rabena ous keda", and "Rabena Mawgood", (If God wills, God wishes it, and God is present) are often heard spoken in Egypt. This fatalistic "Trust in Allah" often presents problems to the practitioner of modern medicine. Item number 4, in Table 7.16 "Traditional beliefs/fatalism" (including religious beliefs) was viewed as problematic by only two percent (2%) of the urban sample; however, the rural areas, which are more traditional, cited difficulty with these traditions: fourteen percent (14%) and twenty-one percent (21%) for Menoufia and Minia respectively.

It is interesting to note that twenty-four percent (24%) of the Cairo sample, twenty-five percent (25%) of the Menoufia sample and four percent (4%) of the Minia sample did not answer this question. Does this indicate lack of knowledge as to what "cultural traditons" include or is it a total lack of understanding of the cultural milieu?

Supporting the argument previously mentioned, both rural and urban patients apparently are not utilizing native healers as previously had been the case and are more often resorting to modern medicine as indicated in the responses from Cairo (two percent), Menoufia (four percent), and Minia (four percent), which mention "native treatment" as impeding work.

Lack of co-operation and not following instructions, were mentioned in this category by four percent (4%) from Cairo, eight percent from Menoufia and fourteen percent (14%) from Minia.

Lack of confidence in the doctor, medicine and free treatment was mentioned by only four percent (4%) of the Cairo sample, one percent (1%) of the Menoufia sample and none from the Minia sample.

Facilitating Traditions

It is important to know the traditions facilitating the physician's work so that they may be used as building blocks upon which to develop and maintain change. Change here would include the reduction of conflict inherent in the physician-patient relationships. Table 7.17 illustrates the items for the category of Cultural Traditions Facilitating Work. It is interesting to note that "Morals/Religion" accounted for three percent (3%) in the Cairo sample, fifteen percent (15%) in the Menoufia sample, and only one percent (1%) of the

Minia sample. It would not be unusual to expect a difference between the rural and urban sample; however, the discrepancy with the Minia sample warrants consideration. Minia has a higher percentage of Christians [73] as compared with other governorates. It may be that the Moslem physicians are not as attuned to the religious beliefs of the Christian patient as he would be to those of the same religion as himself.

Table 7.17

Cultural Traditions Stated by Physicians as Facilitating Their Work

Cultural Tradition	Percentage of sample citing "tradition"		
	Cairo	Menoufia	Minia
1. Morals/Religion	3	15	1
2. Respect/Obedience	25	25	26
3. Kind/Naive/Hospitable	22	20	37
4. Appreciative	3	4	0
5. Health Awareness	6	7	1
6. No reply	41	29	34

Research indicates that on important occasions patients do not readily do what they are told by their physicians. [74, 75, 76, 77, 78] They insist upon following lay advice and self-medication. This makes the professional task difficult when the patient refuses to co-operate for his own good. Therefore, when the patient is "respectful, obedient, kind, naive, or hospitable", conflict is reduced. Item 2, "Respect/Obedience", was mentioned by twenty-five percent (25%) of the Menoufia sample and twenty-six percent (26%) of the Minia sample, whereas, Item 3, "Kind/Naive/Hospitable", was cited by twenty-two percent (22%) of the Cairo sample, twenty percent (20%) of the Menoufia sample, and thirty-seven percent (37%) of the Minia sample.

A small percentage i.e. Cairo three percent (3%), Menoufia four percent (4%) and Minia, none, found their patients "appreciative". Likewise, only six percent (6%) of the Cairo sample, seven percent (7%) of the Menoufia sample and one percent (1%) of the Minia sample cited "Health Awareness".

Student Comments on Cultural Traditions

What do the medical students believe to be the "world view" of the villager? Students in the fourth and fifth year of their medical education were asked: "What do you understand the villagers 'world view' to be? (World view includes: beliefs, traditions, values, and attitudes)."

Some of their comments were:

> "They still hold to values and inherited principles, but their medical and health awareness is very limited; for example, they believe in witchcraft and visit sheikhs

because of their high illiteracy. Most of them do not put enough effort to combat diseases and restrict reproduction."

(Male, fourth year medical student)

"Lack of enough entertainment and methods of entertainment, little socialization, different traditions for women and their lack of freedom, backward view of the woman and her work."

(Female, fifth year medical student)

"The great desire for a large family, no motivation for birth control, a great desire from the woman to reproduce in order to attach her husband to her, preference of males over females makes a woman prove herself by reproduction, misunderstanding of religion concerning birth control, illiteracy especially among women, lack of responsibility to children or country because of privileges gained from the state for the children."

(Female, fifth year medical student)

"Old outlook and outdated beliefs, witchcraft."

(Male, fifth year medical student)

"Bad health habits, like cleanliness, he may do the abolution (for prayers) in the canal and get Bilharziosis in order to conform to certain traditions, they dislike educated people".

(Male, fifth year medical student)

"They lack ambition and driving force to effect changes, but some of them reach the highest ranks. Most stick to religious beliefs; they care about inherited traditions and habits."

(Male, fifth year medical student)

"They leave everything "up to God", especially in diseases, so preventive medicine is lost; there are the traditions and bad customs for treatment which are usually harmful to the patient; also bad beliefs like the numbers in the man's family are connected with his virility and are subject to boasting; wrong understanding of religious beliefs."

(Male, fifth year medical student)

"There are many wrong beliefs like fatalism and many traditions which must be changed, because it does not go with our life now, like polygamy and the man being the unchallenged boss of the family."

(Female, fifth year medical student)

Conflict Across Classes and Sub-cultures

What is illustrated by the students' views is their conceptual framework through which illness is viewed as reflected in the teaching orthodoxy of medical schools. Many of the conceptions of the sick role reflect a middle class orientation of values upon which the physician and patient agree. This pattern emphasizes individual responsibility and the mastery of the individual in the occupational sphere and time. The rural patient as well as the indigent urban client may not share these values. Individual responsibility may be nonexistent by virtue of the ethos of predestination and responsibility to kin, in Egypt the extended family.

The many family members who accompany the patient to the clinic, the numerous visitors to the hospital are supplementing this "individual responsibility", therefore, the relationship between patient and physician must encompass these significant others. This relationship is seldom a dyadic model. It is generally a role of multiple relationships in which the clinic staff serve as intermediaries.

Linton in *The Study of Man* says that statuses are the "polar positions" in reciprocal behaviour patterns. [79] He further states in the "Cultural Background of Personality": "The place in a particular system which a certain individual occupies at a particular time will be referred to as his status with respect to that system." [80] Parsons defines status as a "... place in the relationship system considered as a structure, that is a patterned system of parts." [81] Newcomb gives this point especial emphasis:

> Thus the positions, which are the smallest element—the construction blocks—of societies and organized groups, are interrelated and consistent because they are organized to common ends. From one point of view, then, societies and organized groups are structures of positions which are organized to reach certain goals. Since every position is a part of an inclusive system of positions, no one position has any meaning apart from the other positions to which it is related. [82]

The nature of the present problem is outlined in the last sentence of Newcomb's statement.

This concept, as it applies to the rural health system, is illustrated in Figure 7.4.

Mastery of one's self is a difficult task when mastery of the environment becomes impossible. Poverty and illness are then explained in supernatural terms of the "evil eye" or "God's will". The encroaching dry desert, the daily toil under Egypt's sun, and the poverty, with the knowledge that others have more, contribute to the futility of individual responsibility.

Other concepts, such as time, deserve consideration. The peasant puts the seed into the ground and leaves it up to Allah. He rises at dawn with the call of the *muezzin* to prayers and the rising sun. His months are divided according to the times of prayer. Therefore, the physician's concept of time for taking medications and treatments is uncomprehensible to the peasant. He may wear a watch, but his inner timing is at one with nature.

Let us examine the possibility of removing the blinders of "civilization" that obscure the sight of the physician. Research has indicated that the physician should try to arrange his patient relationships to fulfil the client's expectations. Saunders' statement describes the cultural differences between patient and practitioner:

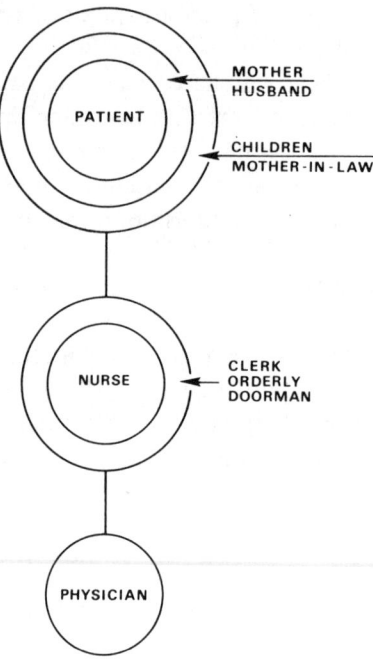

Figure 7.4. Structure of the Rural Health Unit

When the practice of medicine involves the application of elements of the institution of medicine in one culture to the people of another, or from one subculture to members of another subculture within the same cultural group, what is done or attempted by those in the healing roles may not be fully understood or correctly evaluated by those in the patient roles. Conversely, the responses of those on the patient side of the interaction may not conform to the expectations of those on the healing side. To the extent that this occurs, the relationship may be unsatisfactory to everyone concerned.

When persons of widely dissimilar cultural or subcultural orientations are brought together in a therapeutic relationship, the probability of a mutually satisfactory outcome may be increased if those in the healing roles know something of their own culture and that of the patient and are aware of the extent to which behavior on both sides of the relationship is influenced by cultural factors. An even higher probability of satisfaction may result if the professional people are willing and able to modify elements from their medicine so as to make them fit the expectations of the laymen with whom they are working. [83]

The medical delivery system, like any formal organization, must adapt itself to its external environment. Homans would term its adaptation to the environment its "external system". [84] In Parson's formulation an organization must come to terms with systems in its external situation since its "output" normally is a function of the "input" from the external system. [85]

Is the cultural gap too great to facilitate understanding? Is the time period spent by most rural physicians too short to "acculturate" them to the rural sub-culture? What can bridge this gap? As was mentioned by one doctor, "What we need is a course in special studies which would teach us about the life of the farmer, the nature of their work, their way of thinking, how to treat him and how to advise him"[j], in short, a course in rural sociology. Emphasis must be placed upon the sociological aspects of patient care. However, the assistance of intermediaries in the delivery of health care should not be overlooked. These assistants come from the village, are semi-trained in the "language of medicine" and can stand between the indigenous population and Western trained medical professionals. Research is needed in understanding the abilities, skills, and problems of those personnel who function within the occupational boundary and whose position flows into the village boundary.[k] This was illustrated in the statement, "I must often repeat the instructions to the patient ... they need repetition. The nurse also can explain, but she usually sends them to me ... It all depends upon my relations with the staff; they can discourage the patients from coming in, since most of them are from the village. ... Because of this it is very important to change the doctor's place if he has difficulty with the personnel."[l]

The problems encountered with subordinate staff are reviewed to understand the conflicts inherent in this relationship.

Problems With Subordinate Staff

We shall argue that in formal organizations like the Health System, there are inherent forces which tend to create disagreements between administrators and subordinates.

The Cairo physicians rated their subordinate personnel with sixty-one percent (61%) in the category of Lack of Discipline. This was in response to the question "What problems are you incurring with your subordiante staff?" Some Cairo examples include:

> "Nurses speak to the doctor in an unacceptable manner. The nurse will not bring things immediately; if questioned, she answers back."
>
> "Technicians in the laboratories and radiography do not co-operate, ... they act as though they own the place. During shifts, if you ask for certain analysis or X-ray, they always reply that they do not have the facilities."
>
> "Noncommittment to execute instructions in the absence of a supervisor."
>
> "Lack of co-operation in work; ... if a doctor asks an orderly for a sphygmomanometer, he would not get it."

---

[j] *Op. cit.* Conversation with informant.
[k] See Figure 7.3.
[l] *Op. cit.* Conversation with informant.

The above complaints, as given in Table 7.18 were also mentioned by thirty-three percent (33%) of the Menoufia sample and twelve percent (12%) of the Minia sample. Freidson points out:

> ... "it seems to be assumed that technical expertise, unlike "arbitrary" administrative authority, is in someway neutrally functional and therefore so self-evidently true as to automatically produce co-operation or obedience in others as well as the efficient attainment of ends. In Goludner's analysis, for example, we are told that as long as the *end* of technical expertise is accepted by workers, the expert's recommendation of means to that end will also be accepted automatically, or at least without serious question in a "representative" or "expert" bureaucracy. [86] The implication is that when all workers can participate in setting ends in a complex organization, technical expertise can guide the way production is carried out without the necessitiy of exercising "punishment-centered" authority. Similarly, the implication in Parsons' comparison [87] of the authority of office with the authority of expertise is that while the former arbitrarily compels obedience, the latter is in someway naturally compelling by virtue of the fact that expertise and not office gives "orders." [88]

Table 7.18

Problems with Subordinate Staff as Cited by Physicians

Item	Cairo	Menoufia	Minia
	(percent)		
Lack of discipline	61	33	12
Lack of responsibility	9	26	52
Inconsiderate of doctor	4	5	1
Nepotism, bribery	0	4	3
Insufficient numbers	0	2	13
Overemployment	0	8	0
Lack of incentives	0	2	0
No reply	26	20	9

The authority of expertise is problematic, requiring in its pure functional form the not always successful effort of persuading others that its "orders" are appropriate. [89] Rather than concentrate exclusively on the reasons why the physicians are dissatisfied with their subordinate personnel, let us consider plausible explanations for the behaviour of the subordinate. According to Gouldner's and Parsons' analysis one would expect subordinate personnel in the health system to obey the authority of expertise. This is not the case within the Egyptian Health System as the Cairo sample indicated. What is the reason for such discrepancy? What factors contribute to the difference between the Cairo sample (61%) and the Minia sample (12%) (Table 7.18)? Considering the item "Lack of discipline" an answer may be partially found in the theory of relative deprivation.

Relative Deprivation

In the Egyptian case, the subordinate personnel lack identification with the prime goals of the organization and lack an important voice in setting the formal level and direction of work. As a result, their work has become mechanical and meaningless, a minute segment of an intricate mosaic of specialized activities that they are in no position to perceive or understand, and so the worker becomes alienated. The para-professional worker is, like the industrial worker, subordinated to the authority of others. [90] This lack of goals and subordination contribute to the lack of co-operation, absenteeism, and the lack of assuming responsibility. The concept of relative deprivation appears applicable here. This concept assumes that persons may feel that they are deprived of some desired state or thing, in comparison with some standard, or with the real or imagined condition of other people. [91]

"When inequalities are stable, pervasive, ritualized, and strongly defended and enforced, the accompanying ideologies typically emphasize great social, cultural or biological differences between the superordinate and the subordinate." [92] But there is today a "... general worldwide revolt against the 'premise of inequality'." [93] In addition, urbanization and mobility juxtapose sharp and obvious inequalities that formerly were more nearly insulated by geographical and social barriers. [94]

Williams defines a set of conditions favouring the development of "class" or other massive collective awareness of inequalities and relative deprivation to include:

1. Massing; concentration of population: functional proximity of similarly situated persons
2. Differential interaction within-category and across-category (class, ethnic, racial, and so on)
3. Number of collectivities, categories, or strata: few
4. Continuous or discontinuous character of the categories, collectivities, or strata: clear boundaries, with little overlap of category memberships and referents
5. Social instability: a large amount of "uprooting" (rapid shifts in interaction patterns, referents, norms, and so on)
6. Degree of social mobility:
   a. intergenerational: high
   b. career: moderate
   c. short-term: low
7. Degree of "objective" inequalities: high
8. Variables in which inequalities exist (income, wealth, education, occupational prestige, authority, power, safety, life-style): differentials in power and income seem of primary importance but any of the main aspects may become crucial under some conditions. It is a safe generalization that conspicuous coincidence of several types of inequalities sharpens boundaries and tends to enhance collective awareness. [95]

These conditions personify the Egyptian situation. Cairo is characterized by massive immigration from the countryside. Crowding and concentrations of population are the result in more popular quarters where often subordinate medical personnel live.

Reponses of relative deprivation are maximized by: rapid social change, high geographical mobility, high education, more exposure to mass media and high rates of upward and downward social mobility. Egypt is characterized by the foregoing, although the rate of upward mobility in terms of status is still minimal; however, technicians and labourers are experiencing more financial stability and as a consequence are slightly more upwardly mobile in Cairo.

Hirschman suggests that poor people in developing countries initially accept vast inequalities in the belief that eventually they themselves also will benefit from economic development. He calls this case the "tunnel effect". [96] He cites an example to explain this effect. If two lines of automobiles are stopped in a tunnel and one finally begins to move, the initial reaction of drivers in the lane still stalled is not relative deprivation and resentment but relief and hope ("my turn will come soon"). Only if one's own movement is then inordinately delayed does the positive mood give way to frustration. However, the "tunnel effect" is temporary if hope is repeatedly deferred and others move ahead, disillusionment is likely to be marked and the sense of relative deprivation is strong. [97] Therefore, relative deprivation is one among many components affecting social behaviour within the medical delivery system.

Inefficiency and low technical standards was the major problem stated by fifty-two percent (52%) of the Minia sample. This complaint was voiced by twenty-six percent (26%) of the Menoufia sample and only nine percent (9%) of the Cairo sample. Cairo, the nation's capital, would naturally have more better trained individuals. This factor apparently decreases in the southern direction.

In a conversation, the necessity of training the "Daya" (midwife) in a "large hospital for better experience" was stressed.[m]

Other items included in the Problems with Subordinate Staff were:

Inconsiderateness of doctor: Cairo four percent, Menoufia five percent and Minia, the most rural only one percent.

Bribery and Nepotism: not mentioned in the Cairo sample, was mentioned by four percent and three percent of the Menoufia and Minia samples respectively. Nepotism would be expected in rural areas where Gemeinshaft relationships prevail.

It was felt that insufficient numbers of subordinate personnel was a problem in Minia (thirteen percent); however, only two percent (2%) of the Menoufia sample considered this a problem. In fact, the Menoufia sample

---

[m] *Ibid.*

complained of overemployment (eight percent), illustrated by the following examples:

... "Overemployment ... the hiring of veterans after the 1973 war ... they just play sports, drink tea or smoke the goza (water pipe)."

"I had thirty people working at my health unit ... I needed only six or eight." [n]

It was also felt that the doctor should be "trained how to train nurses." [o]

Part of the inefficiency in the rural areas may be attributed to workers having more than one job. As was stated: "All the workers had more than one job except the nurse and me." [p]

Some of the Minia examples include:

"They give out medications incorrectly, because of their lack of knowledge."

"Low standard in preparing the workers, so that they can guide and care for patients."

"... accustomed to a certain system of work, since they have been there for 20 years."

"... giving wrong and unscientific instructions to the people ... behaving like a doctor."

As the above examples indicate, more effort should be put forth in training subordinate staff. But, is the Egyptian doctor ready to relinquish some of his "power"? The aspect of professional dominance has often been a subject of analysis. [98] It was stated in a conversation that "Nurses could not learn to take blood pressures." [q] These data indicate the need to train doctors how to train others. This may be an answer to the health delivery system dilemma.

The lack of available incentives was mentioned by only two percent of the Menoufia sample; however, it was stated that "adequate overtime payment will *encourage* the technical staff." [r]

It is interesting to note that in spite of the Cairo sample being most dissatisfied with their personnel in terms of lack of discipline, absenteeism, etc., (61%), twenty-six percent of the Cairo sample did not complete this question, twenty percent of the Menoufia sample, and only nine percent of the Minia sample did not reply.

Problems With Supervisors

As in the physician-subordinate relationship, there are inherent forces within the health system which tend to create conflicts between the physician

---

[n] *Ibid.*
[o] *Ibid.*
[p] *Ibid.*
[q] *Ibid.*
[r] *Ibid.*

and his supervisor from the Ministry of Health. Analysis will be based on certain definitions and assumptions defined by Gross et al. These assumptions are:

1. A formal organization is defined as a social system with "a primacy of orientation to the attainment of a specific goal." [99]

2. To achieve this goal, formal provisions must be made to break it down into specific tasks whose achievement is delegated to incumbents of formally established positions.

3. The achievement of the goal of the organization is contingent on the achievement of tasks by position incumbents.

4. The general function of a position incumbent who has authority over incumbents of other positions is to see that the particular set of tasks for which his subordinates are responsible is accomplished and that they contribute to the achievement of the "higher" order task(s) for which he is himself responsible.

5. In order to achieve the task(s) for which his position has been formally created, the incumbent of any position must make decisions or choices among possible alterntive courses of action.

6. Any decision of an incumbent of a position in a formal organization will have an effect not only on the achievement of the task(s) of that position, but also on the achievement of "higher" and "lower" order tasks for which incumbents of other positions are held accountable, and ultimately on the achievement of the goal of the organization.

7. From the viewpoint of the incumbent of a particular position, his primacy of orientation is not to the organizational goal but to achievement of the task(s) for which his position has been created and for which he is held accountable.

8. In order to carry out the task(s) of a position, an incumbent will feel that it is necessary to have as complete control as possible over the factors and conditions impinging on decisions for which he will be held accountable.

9. An overriding assumption which it is necessary to make in order to deduce hypotheses from these eight propositions is that incumbents of positions in formal organizations are motivated to achieve the tasks for which they are held accountable. [100]

These assumptions used by Gross for analyzing the school system [101] will serve here in the analysis of the health system.

If decisions of an incumbent of a position in a formal organization will have an effect not only on the achievement of the task(s) of that position, but also on the achievement of "higher" and "lower" order tasks for which incumbents of other positions are held accountable, and ultimately, on the achievement of the goal of the organization (Proposition 6) and if both the superordinate (Ministry of Health Supervisors and Ministry of Health Administrators) and subordinate (physician) desire to have complete control over the factors affecting their respective tasks (Proposition 8), and if both are motivated to achieve their formal tasks (Proposition 9), then the following hypothesis may be used to illustrate the influence of proximity in role relationships between incumbents in counter positions.

Incumbents in a subordinate position (physicians) geographically and physically closer to the incumbents of a superordinate position (Ministry of Health Administrators and Ministry Supervisors) will define more conflicts attributed to bureaucracy in their work.

Let us consider the data concerning "problems with supervisors". Respondents were asked to answer the question, "As a male or female physician, what are the problems you are encountering, in performing your job, from the supervisors in the governorate and from the administrators in the Ministry of Health." Data was scaled using the same procedure discussed previously. Tables 7.19 and 7.20 illustrate the responses given.

Using the item of red tape (bureaucracy) in citing the problems with supervisors, twenty-two percent (22%) of the Cairo sample, seventeen percent (17%) of the Menoufia sample and only eight percent (8%) of the Minia sample indicated these conflicts.

Table 7.19

Problems Encountered by the Physicians With the Governorate Supervisors

Problem	Cairo	Menoufia	Minia
	(Percentage of sample citing problem)		
Favouritism	2	0	0
Inability to communicate	0	4	0
Interference from non-medical administrators	2	4	2
Red Tape (Bureaucracy)	22	17	8
Lack of Understanding/Lack of Confidence	20	13	13
Not Responsible/No follow-up	5	4	9
Inadequate Supplies	3	0	2
No reply	46	58	66

Table 7.20

Problems Encountered by the Physicians With the Ministry of Health Administrators

Problem	Cairo	Menoufia	Minia
	(Percentage of sample citing problem)		
Farouritism	8	0	0
Inability to communicate	0	8	2
Interference from non-medical administrators	0	0	0
Red Tape (Bureaucracy)	37	12	14
Lack of Understanding/Lack of Confidence	14	21	23
Not Responsible/No follow-up	8	3	7
Inadequate Supplies	0	2	12
No reply	33	54	42

Referring to problems with the Ministry of Health, thirty-seven percent (37%) of the Cairo sample, twelve percent (12%) of the Menoufia sample and fourteen percent (14%) of the Minia sample defined this problem.

The above implies that subordinates in day-to-day contact with their superordinates feel the strain of conflict more than those physicians in health units more distant from Cairo who have autonomy in executing their work. Autonomy is "the quality or state of being independent, free, and self-directing." [102] In the case of professions, autonomy apparently refers primarily to control over the content and the terms of work. That is to say, the professional is self-directing in his work. [103]

Complaints about supervisors from the Cairo respondents were:

"... Routine ... They complicate the papers required for files of work, vacations, raises and promotions, in addition to administrative complications"

"... Utilizing their positions to install their authority and gain more rights than they are entitled to or having more facilities"

"... The authorities from the local government impose their authority on the health units and this creates animosity between them and the doctor"

"... my personal conviction that it is impossible to grant any personal request for any doctor without a complaint to higher supervisors"

The Minia and Menoufia sample viewed their problems with the Ministry of Health supervisors as:

"... appearances, during inspections they are concerned about trivialities"
"... away from the situation ... see them occasionally."

The physician's dissatisfactions with his supervisors appear to correlate with his dissatisfaction with his subordinates in terms of how he views their discipline and co-operation. Therefore, it appears that incumbents in a subordinate position (physicians) geographically and physically closer to their superordinates (Ministry of Health Supervisors and Administrators) will define more conflicts with their subordinates (technical staff, nurses, etc.).

In examining this relationship, it is relevant to discuss a conclusion Riecken and Homans reached in their review of small group research:

In examining research on the research sentiment, activity, and norms, we have generalized the findings to one basic hypothesis, which may be stated as follows: a member O of a group chooses or likes a member P to the degree that P's activities realize O's norms and values. [104]

Therefore, we could add that not only will member O "choose or like" P, but he will also evaluate P's performance of his job highly to the degree that P's activities realize O's expectations for him, as Gross and his associates found. With their data, this additional proposition lead to the prediction that the more the school board conforms to professional standards, the more highly the superintendent will evaluate the performance of the board. [105]

Lack of understanding and concern of the doctors' problems by the Ministry of Health Administrators was felt more by the Minia sample (23%) and the Menoufia sample (21%); less so by the Cairo sample (14%). These administrators are located in Cairo and the rural physician feels a genuine "Lack of concern from these officials."

> "... People of the Ministry cannot evaluate the heavy work of the rural physician among people who are different in thinking, and interests in family planning ... a doctor's efficiency is measured by the number of people who visit the clinic, and they consider him responsible for the success of the programme in spite of his achievements in other fields"
>
> "... Lack of attention to people who visit the Ministry ... they say 'come tomorrow'"
>
> "... Lack of appreciation of the responsibility of the field doctor ... shifting from one place to another ... they do not take into consideration if a doctor is established."
>
> "... Not sending medical bulletins ... not preparing adequate accommodation"
>
> "... Delay in answering enquiries"

Problems with the Ministry of Health (Governorate) supervisors were greater in Cairo, the group more closely supervised, where 20% of the sample cited "Lack of understanding/Lack of confidence", whereas, in the Minia and Menoufia samples only thirteen percent from each mentioned this problem.

Some of the Cairo physicians' comments are presented:

> "... Not taking a young doctor seriously ... his opinions and ideas"
>
> "... Lack of appreciation of the working conditions"
>
> "... Lack of concern about new doctors ... if you want a transfer, they refuse"

Indicating an element of mistrust, the question referring to problems with supervisors in the Ministry of Health was not answered by forty-six percent (46%) of the Cairo sample, fifty-eight percent (58%) of the Menoufia sample, and sixty-six percent (66%) of the most rural southern sample, Minia.

These figures were also high for replies to problems with the Ministry of Health Administrators. Fifty-four percent (54%) of the Menoufia sample, forty-two percent (42%) of the Minia sample and thirty-three percent (33%) of the Cairo sample refused to answer this question.

It is interesting to note that in spite of some complaints about inadequate supplies, only three percent of the Cairo sample, two percent of the Minia sample and none from the Menoufia sample mentioned this complaint in relation to their supervisors from the Governorate (Ministry of Health). However, 12% of the most distant Minia sample felt the Ministry of Health Administrators were slow in delivering supplies. Only two percent of the Menoufia sample mentioned this problem and none of the Cairo physicians mentioned this complaint. This demonstrates two things: First, the subordinate (physician) views this aspect (lack of supplies) as negligible in terms of conflict with superordinates. As a major dissatisfaction, given in Table 7.7, "Lack of Supplies" was considered a major problem. However, when this researcher visited the health units, an adequate supply of medications (including many of foreign manufacture) was available. Second, most of the physicians' problems with the Ministry of Health Administrators and their Supervisors are of a socio-psychological nature, primarily red tape (bureaucracy) and a felt lack of understanding of the physicians' problems and needs.

The foregoing has considered the doctors' analysis of problems with superiors and subordinates. In the following section we will review how the physicians rate their own administrative and supervisory skills.

The Illustrating Case of Managerial Experience

There is a growing belief that better management of health services is essential if higher standards of health and of health care are to be achieved. Without effective management, attempts to improve the organization, structure, and functioning of services will be unsuccessful. [106]

There is already a widening gap between what is known and what is being practised in the field; in addition, the results of management research in the health field are not readily available and not necessarily transferable from one country to another. Problems frequently appear in terms of shortages of manpower of various kinds and the lack of staff with managerial capabilities is regarded as especially serious. [107]

To gain insight into the managerial problems of the health delivery system, respondents were asked to rate themselves on a scale of 1-5 for the following administrative and supervisory skills:

a. ability to plan, organize, manage, and evaluate services of the unit or clinic
b. ability to plan, implement and evaluate the nursing and midwifery staff (services, resources, in-service training, etc.) of the unit or clinic
c. ability to co-ordinate the medical component with services
d. ability to supervise, counsel, guide, and support staff and to interpret their needs.
e. ability to promote the leadership skills of staff undergoing practical training
f. ability to help staff to develop and advance professionally
g. ability to record information, use data, and make comprehensive and comprehensible reports
h. ability to recognize problems, arrive at decisions based on a critical

assessment of the situation, initiate a course of action (with or without the aid of others), and evaluate own performance

i. ability to exchange views and co-operate with colleagues and superiors
j. ability to exchange views and co-operate with local leaders in your community

The purpose here is not skill measurement, but to gain an understanding of the perceptions of abilities as the physician fulfills his role. The scores are recorded in Table 7.21. Results fail to demonstrate significant differences

Table 7.21

Physicians Self Rated Administrative and Supervisory Skills

Question	Mean Scores (out of 5) ± Standard Deviation		
	Minia (n=49)	Menoufia (n=48)	Cairo (n=35)
39. Ability to plan, organize, manage, and evaluate services of the unit or clinic	3.8 ± 0.7	3.8 ± 1.0	3.2 ± 1.2
40. Ability to plan, implement and evaluate the nursing and mid-wifery staff (services, resources, in-service training, etc.) of the unit or clinic	3.2 ± 0.9	3.6 ± 1.0	3.9 ± 1.3
41. Ability to coordinate the medical component with services	3.7 ± 0.7	3.8 ± 1.0	3.3 ± 1.0
42. Ability to supervise, counsel, guide, and support staff and to interpret their needs	3.7 ± 0.7	4.4 ± 0.7	3.7 ± 1.0
43. Ability to promote the leadership skills of staff undergoing practical training	3.5 ± 0.9	3.8 ± 1.0	3.2 ± 1.2
44. Ability to help staff to develop and advance professionally	3.4 ± 1.1	3.8 ± 1.0	3.7 ± 1.1
45. Ability to record information, use data, and make comprehensive and comprehensible reports	3.6 ± 1.0	3.7 ± 1.1	3.3 ± 1.1
46. Ability to recognize problems, arrive at decisions based on a critical assessment of the situation, initiate a course of action (with or without the aid of others), and evaluate own performance	3.5 ± 0.9	4.0 ± 1.2	3.6 ± 1.0
47. Ability to exchange views and cooperate with colleagues and superiors	3.8 ± 0.9	4.2 ± 1.0	4.3 ± 0.9
48. Ability to exchange views and cooperate with local leaders in your community	3.4 ± 1.1	3.8 ± 1.2	3.2 ± 1.3

Note: The fluctuating scores do not exceed 5 as an upper limit.

between the different groups. This obvious observation was substantiated by variance analysis at α = 0.05. This is also clearly illustrated by Figures 7.5-7.14. The mean scores ranged between 3.20 and 4.40, indicating a relatively high self-rating of managerial skills, which require consideration:

1) Why did the incumbents perceive (rate) their skills relatively high on the scale?

2) Why did the incumbents as a group in all three geographical locations fall within the median range of 3.20 to 4.40?

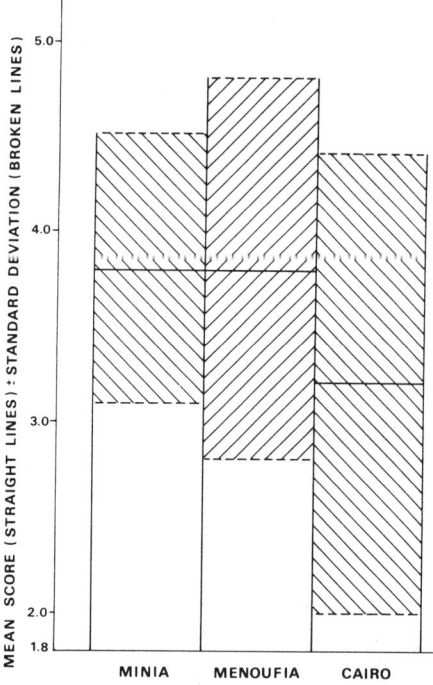

Firgure 7.5. Physicians' Self Rated Administrative and Supervisory Skills: Group Scores to Question 39: Ability to Plan, Organize, Manage, and Evaluate Services of the Unit or Clinic.

Homogeneity Principle

People with similar backgrounds will have been exposed to similar influences and, therefore, will develop similar role definitions. That is, people with similar background characteristics develop similar constellations of expectations, and when encountering new situations, the similarity in background will tend to result in similar definitions of the new situations. [108]

The group studied could be defined as homogeneous by virtue of their professional training, social status, sex, and age. It is assumed that socialization

SOME SPECULATIVE INTERPRETATIONS OF THE FINDINGS 155

of a physician is relatively uniform in Egypt irrespective of the school attended since the university curriculum is uniform. A higher council of Universities co-ordinates the academic activities of all universities, and all physicians are trained in university hospitals. These hospitals are budgeted from the Ministry of Higher Education.

The professionalization of a doctor stresses autonomy and self assuredness. Autonomy means "the quality or state of being independent, free, and self-directing." [109]

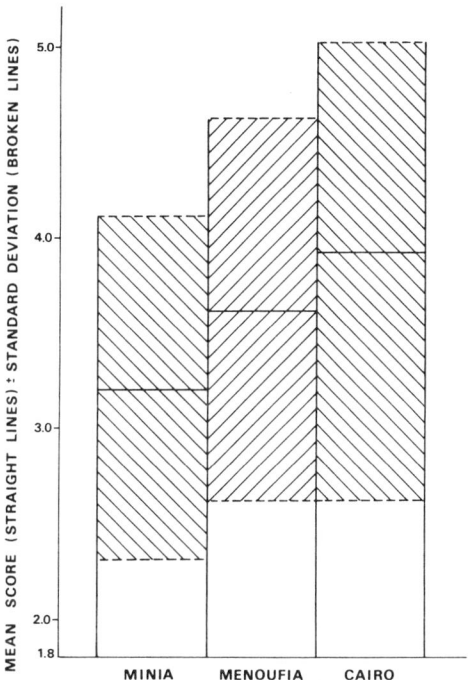

Figure 7.6. Physicians' Self Rated Administrative and Supervisory Skills: Group Scores to Question 40: Ability to Plan, Implement and Evaluate the Nursing and Midwifery Staff (Services, Resources, Inservice Training, etc.) of the Unit or Clinic.

In the case of professions, autonomy refers primarily to control over the content and the terms of work. That is, the professional is self-directing in his work. [110]

All were admitted to the faculty of medicine by virtue of superior grades. In addition, the majority are from the same social status. Of the total number of respondents who answered these questions (n = 132), only twenty-three were female (17%). This figure fits into the national average as reported by Merriam: [111]

156 SOME SPECULATIVE INTERPRETATIONS OF THE FINDINGS

The number of women graduates from the scientific faculties has grown rapidly in the last fifteen years. Of the total number of women graduates in different scientific fields, 32 percent of the medical science graduates as of 1966 came from the 1963 and 1965 classes, and 95 percent of the 1966 pool of university graduates were already employed in 1967. The other sciences—agriculture, science, and engineering also showed a progressively greater increase in the share of young graduates employed as of 1967, and their shares rise even faster between 1967 and 1977. [112]

The pool of scientists with post-graduate degrees has also increased its contribution from women in the past fifteen years. The greatest female share of those with an M.S. degree or higher is in the medical sciences with a 23 percent share of the 4,221 professionals, followed closely by the physical scientists, of whom women constitute 22 percent. Women represent only seven percent of the total number of engineers and technicians with post-graduate degrees, although they have a slightly better share of women graduates of 1973 and 1976. [113]

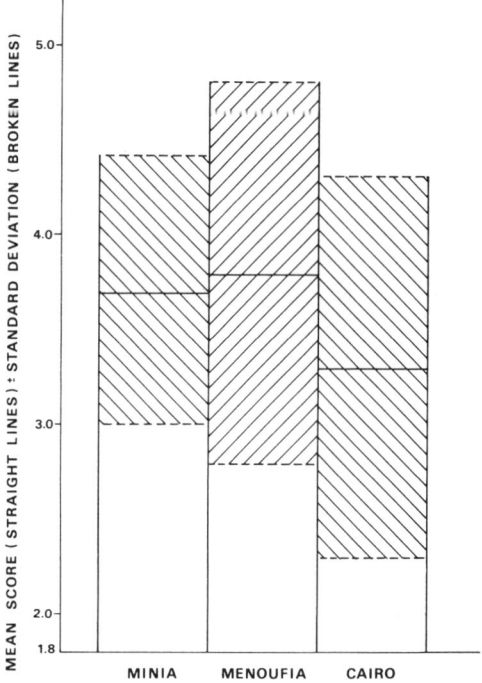

Figure 7.7. Physicians' Self Rated Administrative and Supervisory Skills: Group Scores to Question 41: Ability to Coordinate the Medical Component with Services.

Another aspect of homogeneity is age. The majority, i.e. (90%), 123 subjects are under forty years of age.

Sub Group Analysis

Because the range of dispersion in the individual scores was relatively high as indicated by the standard deviations, an analysis of sub groups was attempted.

Often, comparisons of job performance by males and females are based on sweeping generalizations about culturally determined or biological differences. However, there is nothing to suggest that either nature or nurture produces males in the Egyptian society who are inherently superior to females as far as administration is concerned. [114]

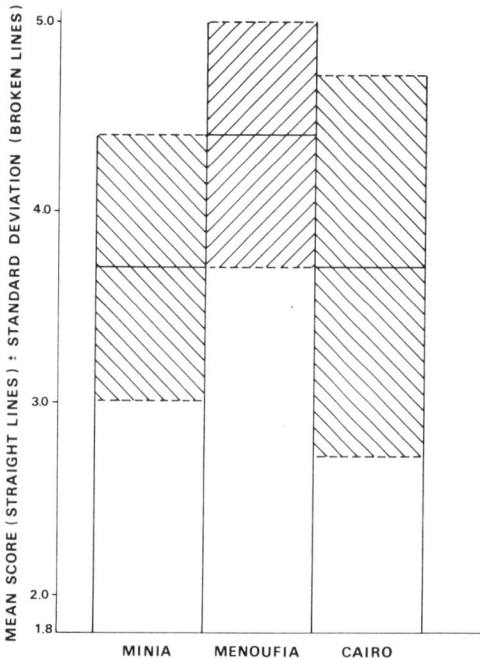

Figure 7.8. Physicians' Self Rated Administrative and Supervisory Skills: Group Scores to Question 42: Ability to Supervise, Counsel, Guide, and Support Staff and to Interpret their Needs.

Female doctors do not overtly aspire to administrative positions. Part of this reluctance is culturally derived. Freudian theory may have also inhibited female doctors from openly aspiring to adminstrative positions, with its emphasis on the particularity of sexual roles. [115]

Actual job performance differences have not been explored in Egypt's medical profession. However, Scotch's study of manpower in a community centre field social agency, which included evaluation of worker performance by sex, indicated higher scores in administrative skills by females than males. [116]

Only the Menoufia and Minia samples are being considered here, since the Cairo sample included only two women. In spite of the small samples (Minia n = 9, and Menoufia n = 12) the discrepancies of their self rating is worth mentioning. Their scores are presented in Table 7.22.

158   SOME SPECULATIVE INTERPRETATIONS OF THE FINDINGS

The marked differences between the Menoufia and Minia samples may be explained by the geographically determined value system of the culture.

The quality of institutional roles and individual personalities in the health delivery system, as in all other systems, is related to the ethos of the particular culture, and the specific role expectations and personal dispositions to its values. On the one hand, the expectations the physician derives, at least in part, from the values of the culture in which the health unit is situated, and on the other, the dispositions of the physicians, are internalizations of the values (or sub-values) of the culture (or sub-culture) in which the physician was socialized. [117]

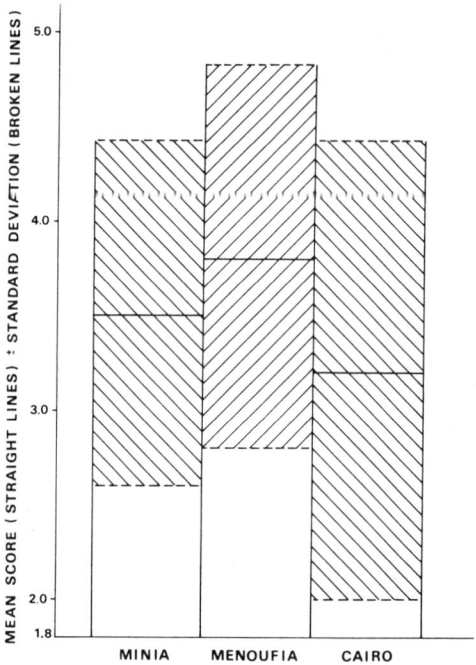

Figure 7.9. Physicians' Self Rated Administrative and Supervisory Skills: Group Scores to Question 43: Ability to Promote the Leadership Skills of Staff Undergoing Practical Training.

The mean scores for the female Minia sample ranged from a low 2.60 to 3.9, whereas the more central to cosmopolitan Cairo, Menoufia, had a mean range from 3.4 to a high 4.4.

Since the over 40 years of age sample size from Minia and Menoufia were small (n = 4 and n = 6 respectively), only the Cairo sample is being considered here. For the nine subjects who were forty, six of the ten questions were rated 4.0 and above, clearly demonstrating self confidence in the over 40 years age group. Their scores are presented in Table 7.22.

Table 7.22

Physicians Self Rated Administrative and Supervisory Skills

(Sub Group Analysis)
Mean Scores

Question	Female n=9 Minia	Female n=12 Menoufia	Over 40 Years n=9 Cairo
39. Ability to plan, organize, manage, and evaluate services of the unit or clinic	3.9	3.9	4.1
40. Ability to plan, implement and evaluate the nursing and midwifery staff (services, resources, in-service training, etc.) of the unit or clinic	3.2	3.3	3.4
41. Ability to coordinate the medical component with services	3.2	4.0	3.7
42. Ability to supervise, counsel, guide, and support staff and to interpret their needs	3.4	4.4	4.3
43. Ability to promote the leadership skills of staff undergoing practical training	2.9	4.1	4.1
44. Ability to help staff to develop and advance professionally	2.9	3.8	4.3
45. Ability to record information, use data, and make comprehensive and comprehensible reports	3.0	3.4	3.7
46. Ability to recognize problems, arrive at decisions based on a criticial assessment of the situation, initiate a course of action (with or without the aid of others), and evaluate own performance	3.2	3.7	3.8
47. Ability to exchange views and cooperate with colleagues and superiors	3.6	4.1	4.1
48. Ability to exchange views and cooperate with local leaders in your community	2.6	4.0	4.0

As can be noted in Table 7.21, the standard deviation increases in Cairo with Minia having the lowest dispersion. This trend corresponds with the length of time subjects within each group have been on the job, the criterion being more than one year. Minia, with the lowest dispersion figures, had only eight respondents (16%) who had been in their position one year or less. In Menoufia, twelve respondents (24%) had been at their positions one year, or less and eighteen respondents from the Cairo sample (50%) had been there one year or less.

Although the sample sizes in the sub groups were to small to make statistical correlations, the general trends indicated may be worth further research.

It should be again emphasized here that this section does not attempt to measure the physicians' managerial skills, but the self perceptions of their abilities. These findings may serve in the development of managerial training programmes, an essential for improving the health delivery system in Egypt. The management consultant, if aware of the physicians' "mind set" as to his perceived abilities will be better prepared to understand the reasons for his suggestions being negatively received.

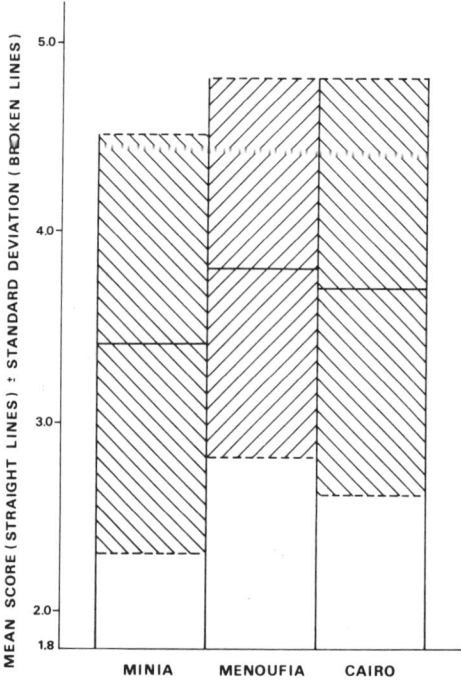

Figure 7.10. Physicians' Self Rated Administrative and Supervisory Skills: Group Scores to Question 44: Ability to Help Staff to Develop and Advance Professionally.

People often think of themselves or define their jobs in terms of stereotypes or of past education or experience, rather than with their job requirements in mind. For instance, physicians who accept positions as heads of programmes very often have a difficult time seeing themselves as "administrators". The basic training of a physician prepares that person to make medical decisions for individual patients, to take a strong and knowledgeable position and to give direct orders to medical staff with the complete expectation of full compliance. Such an approach in an administrative setting may result in excellent services for a few but no services for many others. [118]

The autonomous physician, over one year in his position, perceives his managerial skills positively. How one makes decisions, establishes their validity, reacts to other persons' ideas, and examines attitudes, values, and assumptions is all part of what is referred to as "mind-set". If mind-set remains fixed and rigid, other changes will probably not take place. Countries can easily

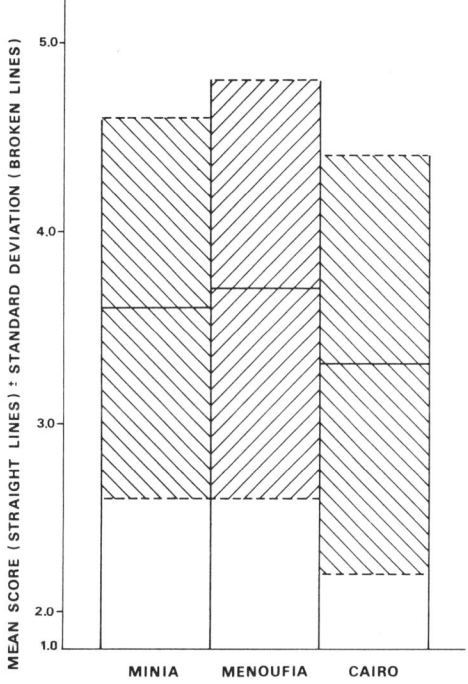

Figure 7.11. Physicians' Self Rated Administrative and Supervisory Skills: Group Scores to Question 45: Ability to Record Information, Use Data, and Make Comprehensive and Comprehensible Reports.

adapt new management techniques, purchase modern computers with printout arrangements, fill-out enormous quantities of forms, and collect great quantities of data; yet in spite of these new techniques, the decisions may continue to be made in an authoritarian manner, with little or no use made of the information collected and organized. [119]

If a change takes place in the way people think of their jobs and responsibilities, then other, programmatic changes can take place. The tendency to make decisions exclusively on an intuitive basis rather than with the use of available data can be overcome; therefore, training programmes having an impact on mind-set should be considered.

Subordinate Professional Competence

A study of the physician's evaluation of his subordinate staffs' technical and professional competence is considered here. The technical and professional abilities are being viewed as distinct from the section which examined the "problems with subordinate staff" in terms of behavioural problems such as lack of discipline and responsibility.

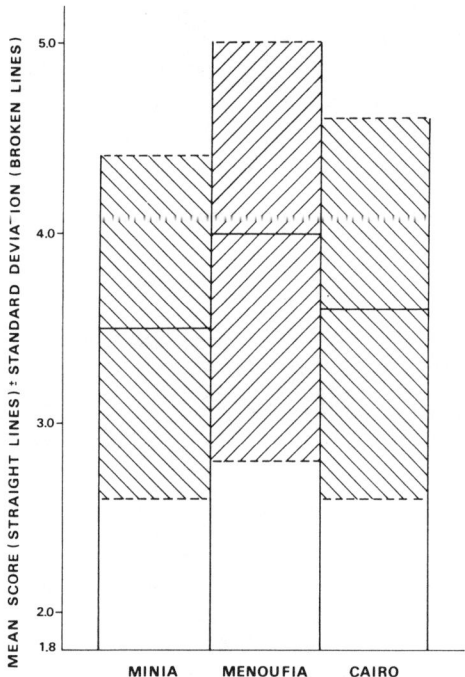

Figure 7.12. Physicians' Self Rated Administrative and Supervisory Skills: Group Scores to Question 46: Ability to Recognize Problems, Arrive at Decisions based on a Critical Assessment of the Situation, and Evaluate own Performance.

Physicians were asked to state the general level of competence of other subordinate personnel at their unit in the following skills: history taking, counselling, clinical procedures, and follow-up care. These results are represented in Table 7.23 and Figures 7.15-7.18.

Health administration in most developing countries takes place under conditions of inadequate communication in widely scattered locations. This creates very special managerial needs for dealing with the problems of training, supervision, and programme feedback. These problems call for:

SOME SPECULATIVE INTERPRETATIONS OF THE FINDINGS 163

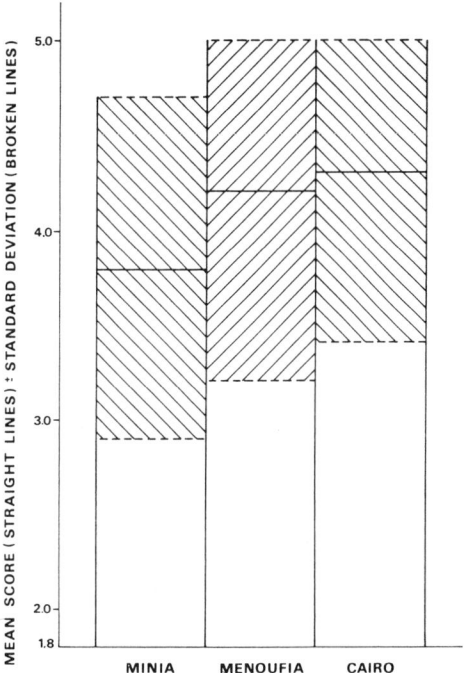

Figure 7.13. Physicians' Self Rated Administrative and Supervisory Skills: Group Scores to Question 47: Ability to Exchange Views and Cooperate with Colleagues and Superiors.

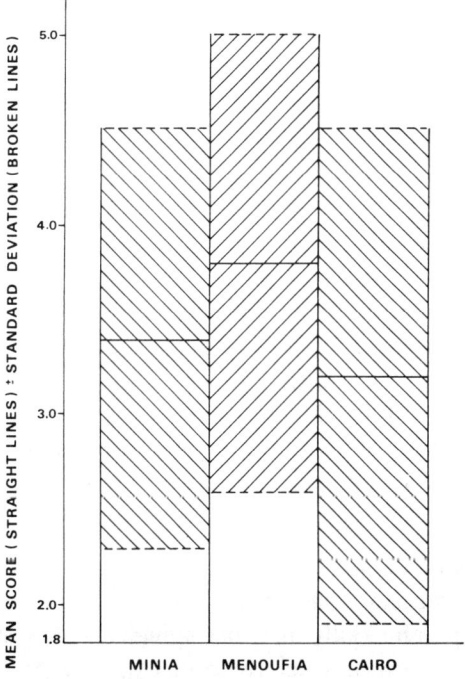

Figure 7.14. Physicians' Self Rated Administrative and Supervisory Skills: Group Scores to Question 48: Ability to Exchange Views and Cooperate with Local Leaders in your Community.

(1) Knowledge on the part of management of what individuals working in remote areas can do,
(2) What they are doing
(3) What they should be doing given local problems and needs.

Table 7.23

Professional Competence of Subordinate Staff as Evaluated by Physicians

	Minia n = 50 %	Menoufia n = 50 %	Cairo n = 36 %
History Taking			
Good	2	20	31
Fair	68	42	53
Poor	20	24	8
No Answer	10	14	8
Counseling			
Good	12	30	36
Fair	52	42	42
Poor	26	16	14
No Answer	10	12	8
Clinical Procedures			
Good	4	16	44
Fair	16	28	42
Poor	70	28	8
No Answer	10	28	6
Follow Up			
Good	6	34	22
Fair	34	28	47
Poor	50	20	19
No Answer	10	18	12

The Cairo sample rated their subordinates significantly higher than did their colleagues in Menoufia and Minia. This would appear logical since more educational opportunities exist in the urban city.

With a larger group of respondents, in the Cairo sample, above 40 years of age, we could attribute this difference to power. A basic premise, borrowed from Golembiewsky, [120] Likert [121] and Gross, [122] is that effective supervision is directly related to the amount of power with which the supervisor has to work. The power variable, here defined as control of the job-site, is a function of:

    a. the design of the job
    b. the organizational structure
    c. the training and skills that the individual, his subordinates, and his superiors have with which to do their jobs. [123]

SOME SPECULATIVE INTERPRETATIONS OF THE FINDINGS

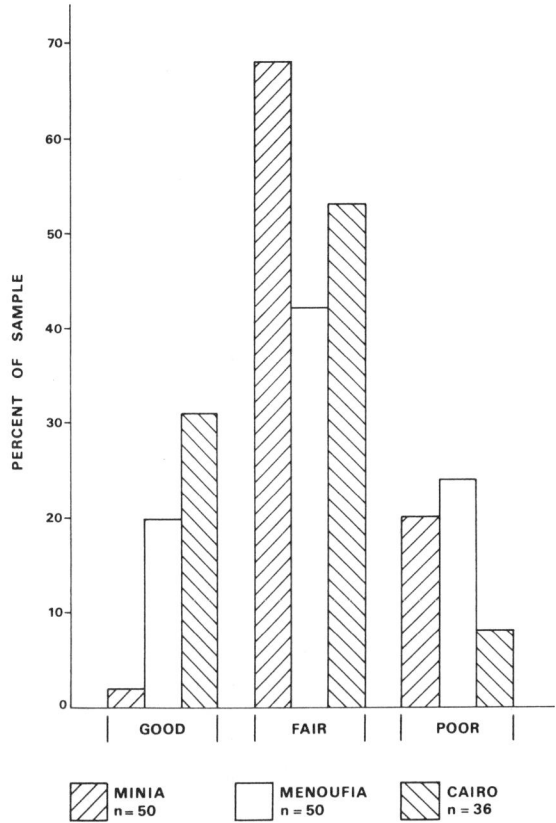

Figure 7.15. History Taking Competence of Subordinate Staff as Evaluated by Physicians.

It is assumed that although the Minia and Menoufia samples have greater autonomy by virtue of their isolation, the Cairo physicians would have more power by virtue of the organizational structure.

Power is frequently limited by poorly designed jobs, unclear lines of authority, inadequate training, lack of authority to hire and fire subordinates, the use of seniority in promotions, and weak criteria for rating of employees' performance. [124]

Because of the isolation factor, the rural areas are troubled with the above problems more than the urban areas; however, because supervisory power is significantly affected by the methods of supervision and activation used with employees, this factor is most amenable to modification by training which provides us with a point of intervention to improve management processes and performance in the medical services.

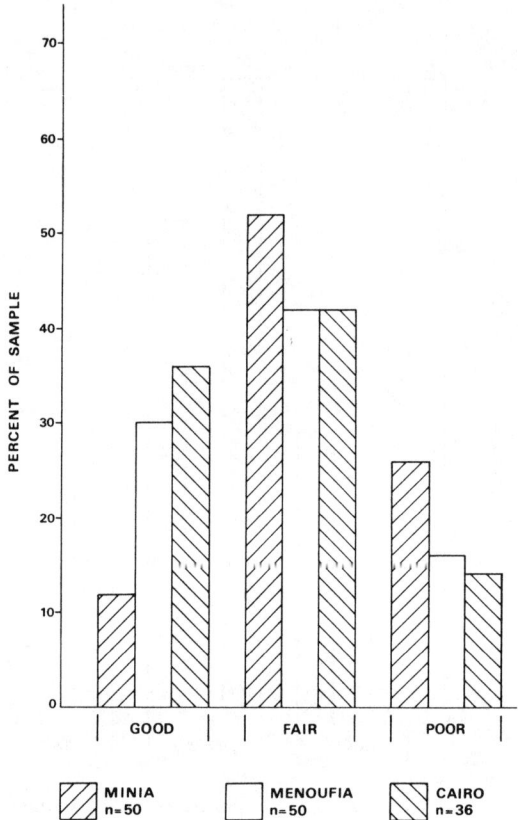

Figure 7.16. Counselling Competence of Subordinate Staff as Evaluated by Physicians.

REFERENCES

[1] Bynum, G., Sanches, R., and Odegard, B., 'Medical Education: A Causal Agent in Physicians' Maldistribution. *Journal Medical Education*, 471 922, November 1972.
[2] Loveland, G. C., 'Rural Practice: What Health Professionals Look For', *Journal Kansas Medical Society*, 1973, Vol. 74, pp. 234-235.
[3] Lane, J. R., Lane, L. B. and Leinhardt, S., 'Medical Manpower Models: Need, Demand and Supply', *Inquiry*, Vol. 12, 1975, pp. 97-125.
[4] Steinwald, B. and Steinwald, C., 'The Effect Preceptorship and Rural Training Programs on Physicians' Practice Location Decisions', *Medical Care*, Vol. 136, 1975, pp. 219-228.
[5] Sarbin, T. R., *Role Theory* in Lindzey, G. (ed.) *Handbook of Social Psychology*, Cambridge, Addison-Wesley Publishing Company, Vol. 1, 1954, p. 225.
[6] Sargent, S., *Concepts of Role and Ego in Contemporary Psychology*, in Roher, J. H. and Muzafer, S. (ed.), *Social Psychology of the Crossroads*, New York, Harper and Brothers, 1951, p. 360.
[7] *Ibid.*, p. 359.
[8] Biddle and Thomas, *op. cit.* p. 26.
[8] Parsons, T., *The Social System*, Glencoe, Illinois, The Free Press, 1951.
[10] Parsons, T. and Shills, E. A., *Toward a General Theory of Action*, Cambridge, Mass., Harvard University press, 1951.

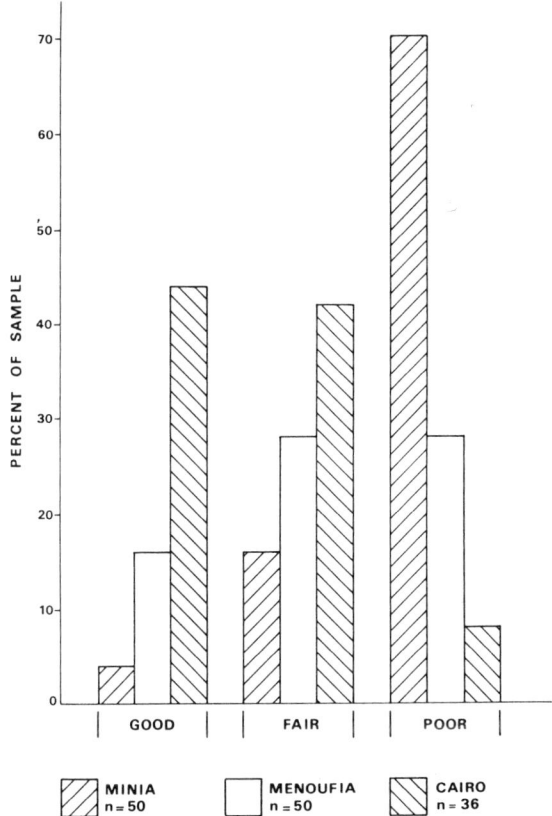

Figure 7.17. Clinical Procedures Competence of Subordinate Staff as Evaluated by Physicians.

[11] Biddle and Thomas, *op. cit.* pp. 26-28.
[12] Becker, H. S. and Carper, J., 'Elements of Identification with an Occupation', *American Sociological Review*, Vol. 21, June 1956, pp. 341-348.
[13] Foote, N. N., 'Identification as the Basis for a Theory of Motivation', *American Sociological Review*, February 1951, pp. 14-21.
[14] Merton, *op. cit.* pp. 290-291.
[15] Blau, P. M., *The Organization of Academic Work*, New York, Wiley, 1973, pp. 123-128.
[16] Merton, *op. cit.* pp. 373-376.
[17] Whyte, W. F., *Small Groups and Large Organizations*, in Rohrer, J. and Sherif, M. (ed.), *Social Psychology at the Crossroads*, New York, Harper and Bros., 1951, pp. 297-312.
[18] *Ibid.*
[19] Biddle, B. J. and Thomas E. J., *Role Theory Concepts and Research*, New York, John Wiley and Sons, Inc., 1966, p. 36-39.
[20] Allport, F. H., *Social Psychology*, Boston, Houghton Mifflin, 1924.
[21] Homans, C. C., *Social Behaviour: Its Elementary Forms*, New York, Harcourt, Brace and World, 1961.
[22] Easton, E., *A System Analysis of Political Life*, New York, John Wiley, 1965, p. 17.
[23] Lewin, K., Dembo, T., Festinger, L. and Sears, P. S., *Level of Aspiration*, in Hunt, J. M. V. (ed.), *Personality and the Behavioral Disorders*, Vol. 1, New York, Ronald Press, 1944, pp. 333-378.

168   SOME SPECULATIVE INTERPRETATIONS OF THE FINDINGS

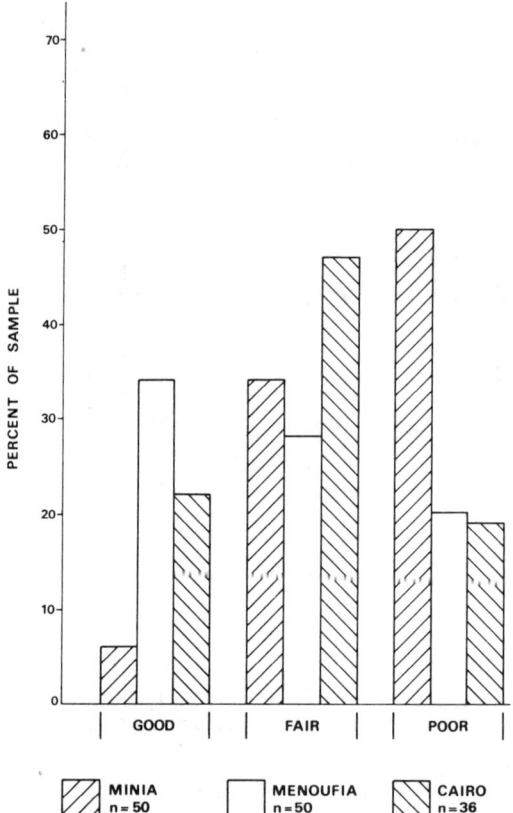

Figure 7.18. Follow-up Competence of Subordinate Staff as Evaluated by Physicians.

[24] Atkinson, J. W., *An Introduction to Motivation*, Princeton, N.J., Van Nostrand, 1964, p. 99.
[25] Mechanic, D., *Medical Sociology: A Selected View*, New York, Free Press, 1968.
Stewart, C. I., Jr. and Corazon, M. S., *Increasing The Supply of Medical Personnel*, American Enterprise Institute for Public Policy Research, Washington, D.C., 1973, pp. 31-33.
[26] Fuchs, V. R., *Who Shall Live? Health, Economics and Social Choice*, Basic Books, Inc., New York, 1974, pp. 13-15, 69-70.
[27] Roemer, M. L. and Anzel, D. M., 'Health Needs and Services of the Rural Poor', part 2, *Medical Care Review*, 1968, pp. 461-491.
[28] McCormack, R. C. and Miller, C. W., 'The Economic Feasibility of Rural Group Practice: Influence of Non-Physician Practitioners in Primary Care', *Medical Care*, Vol. 10, 1973, pp. 73-80.
[29] Hughes, E. E., 'Rural Medical Service', *New York State Journal of Medicine*, Vol. 65, 1965, pp. 345-347.
[30] Mechanic, D., *Public Expectations and Health Care*, New York, Wiley-Interscience, 1972, p. 287.
[31] *The Egyptian Gazette*, August 26, 1978.
[32] Bynum, G., Sanchez, R. and Odegard, B., 'Medical Education: A Causal Agent in Physicians' Maldistribution', *Journal of Medical Education*, Vol. 47, No. 922, November 1972.

[33] Loveland, G. C., 'Rural Practice: What Health Professionals Look For', *Journal Kansas Medical Society*, Vol. 74, 1973, pp. 234-235.
[34] Brown, R., *Models of Attitude Change* in Brown, R., Galanter, E., Edkhard, H. and Mandler, G. (ed.), *New Directions in Psychology*, New York, Holt, Rinehart and Winston, 1962, pp. 3-85.
[35] Merton, R. K., *Social Theory and Social Structures*, New York, Free Press, 1968, pp. 140-141.
[36] *Ibid.*
[37] Freidson, E., *Professional Dominance: The Social Structure of Medical Care*, Aldine-Atherton Press, New York, 1970, pp. 152-153.
[38] Jones, W. H. S., *Hippocrates* (Trans.), London, 1943, Vol. II, pp. 67, 281, 311.
[39] *Ibid.*, Vol. 1, p. 317.
[40] *Ibid.*, Vol. 11, p. 67.
[41] Marti-Ibanez, F., *Henry Sigerist on the History of Medicine*, New York, M.D. Publications, Inc., 1960, p. 26.
[42] Riggs, F., *Administration in Developing Countries the Theory of Prismatic Society*, Boston, Houghton Mifflin Co., 1964.
[43] Freidson, E., *Professional Dominance: The Social Structure of Medical Care*, Aldine Publishing Co., Chicago, 1970, p. 24.
[44] Parsons, T., *The Social System*, New York, The Free Press, 1951, Chapter 10.
[45] Wolff, K. H. (ed. and trans.), *The Sociology of Georg Simmel*, Glencoe, Illinois, The Free Press, 1950, p. 313.
[46] Berger, M., *The Arab World Today*, Doubleday and Co., Inc., New York, 1964.
[47] Pillsbury, B., *Traditional Health Care in the Near East*, A Report Prepared for the U.S. Agency for the U.S. Agency for International Development, Washington, D.C., March 1978, Contract No. AID/NE-C-1395.
[48] Morsey, S., *Illness Concepts and Structural Constraints: Health Care in an Egyptian Village*, Paper read at the Middle East Studies Association Annual Meeting, New York City, November 9-12, 1977.
[49] Blackmann, W. S., *The Fellahin of Upper Egypt Their Religious, Social and Industrial Life Today with Special Reference to Survivals from Ancient Times*, Reprint, New York, Barnes and Noble, 1968.
[50] Anderson, O. W., *The Utilization of Health Services*, in Freeman, H., Levine, S., Reeder, L. (ed.), *Handbook of Medical Sociology*, Englewood Cliffs, New Jersey, 1963, pp. 349-365.
[51] Mead, M., *Cultural Patterns and Technical Change*, International Documents Service (UNESCO), Columbia University Press, New York, 1955.
[52] Clark, M., *Health in the Mexican-American Community*, University of California Press, Berkeley, Calif., 1959, p. 215.
[53] Berger, P., *The Social Construction of Reality*, Doubleday & Co., New York, 1967.
[54] Resolution of the World Health Assembly, 30.49.
[55] Pillsbury, *op. cit.* p. 7.
[56] Nada, A., *The Village Barber*, unpublished paper, 1978.
[57] AFRO Technical Report Series, No. 1, 1976 (African Traditional Medicine Report of the Regional Expert Committee), Technical Report Series 622, WHO Geneva, 1978, pp. 3-4.
[58] *Ibid.*
[59] Crozier, R., *Traditional Medicine in Modern China*, Cambridge, Mass., Harvard University Press, 1968.
[60] Landy, D., 'Role Adaptation: Traditional Curers Under the Impact of Western Medicine. *American Ethnologist* Volume 1, pp. 103-107, cited by New, P. K. and New, M. L. in 'The Links Between Health and the Political Structure in New China', Human Organization, Volume 34, pp. 237-251, 1975.
[61] New, P. K. and New, M. L., 'The Links Between Health and the Political Structure in New China', *Human Organization*, Volume 34, pp. 237-251, 1975.
[62] *Ibid.*
[63] Leslie, C. M., 'Pluralism and Integration, the Indian and Chineese Medical System', in

Alexander, E. R., Kleinman, A. M. and Kunstadter, P. (ed.), *Medicine in Chinese Cultures*, The John E. Fogarty International Center, National Institute of Health, Washington, D.C., 1974.
[64] *Ibid.*
[65] Neumann, A. K., Bhatia, J. S., Andrew, S. and Murphy, A. K., 'Role of the Indigenous Medicine Practitioner in Two areas of India: Report of a Study', *Social Science and Medicine*, Volume 5, 1973, p. 137.
[66] Chuttani, C. S., Bhatia, J. C., Bhatia, A. K., Bhandari, A. C., Vir Dharam and Timmappaya, A., 'Study of Private Medical Practitioners in Rural Areas of a Few States in India', *Indian Journal of Medical Education*, Volume 12, p. 248, 1973.
[67] Alexander, C. A. and Shivaswamy, M. K., 'Traditional Healers in a Region of Mysore', *Social Science and Medicine*, Volume 5, p. 595.
[68] Leeson, J. and Frankenberg, R., 'The Patients of Traditional Doctors in Lusaka', *African Social Research*, Volume 23, June 1977, pp. 217-234.
[69] Djukanovic, V. and Mach, E.P. (ed.), *Alternative Approaches to Meeting Basic Health Needs in Developing Countries*, A joint UNICEF/WHO Study, World Health Organization, Geneva, 1975.
[70] Hamamsy, L., 'The Daya of Egypt, Survival in a Modernizing Society', *Caltech Population Program Occasional Papers*, Series 1, No. 8. The California Institute of Technology, Pasadena, California, 1973, Reprint Series No. 22, The American University in Cairo, Social Research Center, Cairo.
[71] Nadim, Nawal El-Messiri, *Rural Health Care in Egypt*, Ottawa, Ontario, IDRC-TS15e, 1980.
[72] *Ibid.*, p. 37.
[73] CAPMAS Report, Egyptian Population, 1976 census, mimiograph.
[74] Paul, B. D. and Miller, B., *Health, Culture and Community*, Russell Sage Foundation, New York, 1955.
[75] Saunders, L. W., *Cultural Differences and Medical Care*, Russell Sage Foundation, New York, 1954.
[76] Clark, M., *op. cit.* p. 216.
[77] Koos, E. L., *The Health of Regionville*, New York, Columbia University Press, 1954.
[78] Friedson, E., *Patient's Views of Medical Practice*, Russell Sage Foundation, New York, 1961.
[79] Linton, R., *The Study of Man*, New York, Appleton-Century Co., 1936, p. 113.
[80] Idem: *The Cultural Background of Personality*, New York, Appleton-Century Co., 1945, p. 76.
[81] Parsons, T., *op. cit.* p. 25.
[82] Newcomb, T. M., *Social Psychology*, New York, Dryden Press, 1951, p. 277.
[83] Saunders, *op. cit.* p. 8.
[84] Homans, G. C., *The Human Group*, New York, Harcourt, Brace and Co., 1950.
[85] Parsons, T., 'Suggestions for a Sociological Approach to the Theory of Organizations I', *Administrative Science Quarterly*, I, 1956, pp. 63-85.
[86] Friedson, E., *op. cit.* pp. 130-131.
[87] Gouldner, A., *Patterns of Industrial Bureaucracy*, New York, Free Press, 1964, pp. 221-222.
[88] Parsons, T., *Introduction to Weber's Theory of Social and Economic Organization*, cited by Friedson, E. in *Professional Dominance op. cit.* pp. 130-131.
[89] Friedson, E., *op. cit.* p. 131.
[90] *Ibid.*, p. 144-145.
[91] Williams, R. M., *Relative Deprivation* in Coser, L. A. (ed.), *The Idea of Social Structure*, New York, Harcourt Brace Jovanovich, 1975, p. 355.
[92] *Ibid.*, p. 364.
[93] Mason, P., *Race Relations*, New York, Oxford University Press, 1970, p. 163.
[94] Grindstaff, G. F., 'The Negro, Urbanization, and Relative Deprivation in the Deep South', *Social Problems*, Vol. 15, No. 3, Winter 1968, p. 325.
[95] Williams, *op. cit.* p. 366.

[96] Hirschman, '*The Changing Tolerance for Income Inequality in the Courses of Economic Development.*' Discussion Paper Number 233, Cambridge, Mass., Harvard Institute of Economic Research, September 1972, pp. 2-6 quoted in Williams, *op. cit.* p. 369.
[97] *Ibid.*, p. 2-6.
[98] Freidson, *op. cit.*
[99] Parsons, T., 'Suggestions for a Sociological Approach to the Theory of Organizations-I', *Administrative Science Quarterly*, I, 1956, pp. 63-85.
[100] Gross, N., Mason, W. and McEachern, A., *Explorations in Role Analysis*, New York, John Wiley and Sons, Inc., 1958, pp. 122, 123.
[101] *Ibid.*, pp. 122-123.
[102] Blau, P., *Bureaucracy in Modern Society*, New York, Random House, 1956.
[103] Freidson, *op. cit.* p. 134.
[104] Riecken, H. W. and Homans, G. C., *Psychological Aspects of Social Structures*, in Lindzey, G. (ed.), *Handbook of Social Psychology*, II, Cambridge, Addison-Wesley Publishing Company, 1954, p. 794.
[105] Gross, et al., *op. cit.* pp. 222-242.
[106] Public Health Papers No. 55, *Modern Management Methods and the Organization of Health Services*, World Health Organization, Geneva, p. 8.
[107] El-Mehairy, T., 'Medical Doctors: Managerial Abilities and Role Definitions, *Middle East Management Review*, Vol. II, No. 1, Dec. 1978.
[108] Gross, N., Mason, W. S., McEachern, A. W., *Explorations in Role Analysis*, London, John Wiley & Sons, Inc., 1958, p. 182.
[109] Blau, P., *Bureaucracy in Modern Society*, New York, Random House, 1956, p. 6.
[110] Freidson, E., *Professional Dominance*, Chicago, Illinois, Aldine Publishing Co., 1970, p. 134.
[111] Merriam, K. H., 'The Employment of Scientifically Trained Women in Egypt, *American Research Center in Egypt, Inc.*, Newsletter, Number 106, Fall 1978.
[112] Kader, S. A., 'The Status of Egyptian Women (1900-1973)', The American University in Cairo Social Research Center report for the Ford Foundation, 1973 and Central Agency for Public Mobilization and Statistics, 'Distribution of Women Graduates Employed in Different Sectors,' 1977, Mimeograph, Cairo, CAPMAS, 1977.
[113] Merriam, *op. cit.*
[114] El-Mehairy, *op. cit.*
[115] *Ibid.*
[116] Scotch, C. B., *Professional Organizational and Sectarian Identification as Factors Influencing Staff Turnover in a Social Agency*. Unpublished doctoral dissertation, Brandesi University, Waltham, Mass., 1969.
[117] El-Mehairy, T., *The Woman Physician—In Perspective*, A paper presented to the workshop on "Women in Management: Future Perspectives", March 25, 1979, American University in Cairo.
[118] Report of the Second Annual International Workshop in Population Program Administration, Pop Case, Department of Health Administration, School of Public Health and Carolina Population Center, University of North Carolina at Chapel Hill, October 1974.
[119] *Ibid.*, p. 5.
[120] Golembiewski, R. T., *Civil Service and Managing Work: Some Unintended Consequences*, in O'Connell, M. E. (ed.), *Readings in Public Administration*, New York, Houghton Mifflin, 1966.
[121] Likert, R., *New Patterns of Management*, New York, McGraw-Hill Book Co., Inc., 1961.
[122] Gross, B. M., *Organizations and Their Managing*, New York, The Free Press, 1964.
[123] Flemming, H., *A Proposed Conceptual Framework for Analyzing Needs for Supervisory Training in Family Planning Programs*, in Teaching Population Program Management, Pop Case, Dept. of Health Administration, The University of North Carolina at Chapel Hill, 1975, pp. 55-76.
[124] *Ibid.*

CHAPTER EIGHT

PSYCHOLOGICAL INFRASTRUCTURE AND JOB SATISFACTION

PERSONALITY VARIABLES

In this section we will examine the physicians' value orientation to the three values of Achievement, Independence, and Recognition, viewed as motivating factors. These values represented in the scale are the most consistent in producing job satisfaction. Differences in the physicians' value orientations from group to group might be due to variations in geographical regions of a culture, to life in the country versus life in the city, to class and economic status, to the location education was obtained or to some other variables. What follows here is a discussion to explore plausible relations between variables. Prior to citing the results of the value scores, a brief introduction of each value will be given here followed by a short theoretical discussion.

Achievement

Achievement values regulate the adaptive performances of any unit in the system from the point of view of their compatibility with the adaptive needs of the system as a whole, while approval-disapproval sanctions reinforce these values by rewarding a given performance or the reverse. It is the fact that these values are "held in common" by the members of the group, i.e. are institutionalized in the system, which makes them the focus of this regulatory process. [1]

The most interesting study concerning achievement motivation is McClellands' attempt to relate achievement motivation to economic growth. [2] McClelland argues that the relationship between early independence training and achievement motivation growth is relevant to the linkage postulated by Weber between the development of Capitalism and the Protestant Reformation.

McClelland states:

> In the first place, he (Weber) stresses, as others have, that the essence of the Protestant revolt against the Catholic church was a shift from a reliance on an institution to a greater reliance on the self, so far as salvation was concerned. The individual Protestant, Lutheran or Calvinist was less dependent on the church as an institution either for its priests or its sacraments or its official dogma. Instead there was to be a "priesthood" of all "believers," in Luther's words. The Protestant could read and interpret his Bible and find his own way to God without having to rely on the authority of the Church or its official assistance. As Weber describes it, we have here what seems to be an example of a revolution in ideas

which should increase the need for independence training. Certainly Protestant parents, if they were to prepare their children adequately for increased self-reliance so far as religious matters were concerned, would tend to stress increasingly often and early the necessity for the child's not depending on adult assistance but seeking his own "salvation." In the second place, Weber's description of the kind of personality type which the Protestant Reformation produced is startingly similar to the picture we would draw of a person with high achievement motivation. He notes that Protestant working girls seemed to work harder and longer, that they saved their money for long-range goals, that Protestant entrepreneurs seemed to come to the top more often in the business world despite the initial advantages of wealth many Catholic families had, and so forth. In particular, he points out that the early Calvinist business man was prevented by his religious views from enjoying the results of his labors. He could not spend money on himself because of scruples about self-indulgence and display, was one reason he prospered. What then drove him to such prodigious feats of business organization and development? Webers feels that such a man "gets nothing out of his wealth for himself except the irrational sense of having done his job well" (22, p. 71). This is exactly how we define the achievement motive. So again, the parallel seems clear, although there is not space to give the argument in full here. Is it possible that the Protestant Reformation involves a repetition at a social and historical level of the linkage that Winterbottom found between independence training and an Achievement among some mothers and their sons in a small town in Michigan in 1950?

To make such an assumption involves a breath-taking leap of hypothesizing so far as the average psychologist is concerned, who is much more at home with a sample of 30 mothers and 30 sons than he is with major social movements. But the hypothesis seems too facinating to dismiss without some further study. It can be diagrammed rather simply. In terms of this diagram Weber was chiefly concerned with the linkage between A and D, with the way in which Protestantism led to a change in competitive business economy. But the manner in which he describes this relationship strongly suggests that the linkage by which these two events are connected involves steps B and C, namely a change in family socialization practices which in turn increased the number of individuals with high achievement motivation. Thus a full statement of the hypothesis would be that Protestantism produced an increased stress on indepence training which produced higher achievement motivation which produced more vigorous entrepreneural activity and rapid economic development. [3]

Hypothetical Series of Events Relating Self-Reliance Values with Economic and Technological Development:

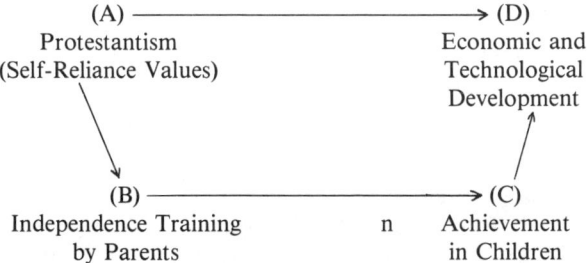

The preceding diagram illustrates the four relationships examined by Mc-Clelland. He hypothesizes that achievement needs precede economic growth and his research has concentrated on these two variables from a number of societies and historical periods. Based on his data he contends that achievement motivation precedes economic development.

How is the value of achievement perceived by the Egyptian physician, a professional practising in a developing nation where the Protestant ethic has not been part of the economic evolutionary process? McClelland's data provides us with relevant evidence that need achievement is an important factor in economic development. We are striving here to determine if geographical, educational and social variables influence achievement behaviour.

Independence

Eliot Freidson, in his discussion of professional values postulated by Parsons states that because of the peculiar nature of the work of the practising professional which encourages a characteristic sense of uncertainty, it reflects considerably more special values than those described by Parsons. [4]

> "One such value is that of independence or autonomy, which is significant for physicians in countries as different as Finland and the United States. Insofar as this value refers to social and economic independence, it reflects the entrepreneural and individualistic ideology of the borgeoise, who are the prime source from which physicians are recruited in virtually all industrial countries. Insofar as the value refers to technical or professional independence—that is, freedom to practise one's craft without interference, advice, or regulation by others—it seems more closely related to a state of mind encouraged by the characters of professional work." [5]

This character of work is demonstrated in that responsibility for success or failure in treating the patient is his individual responsibility.

In an attempt to unravel the interrelating strands of what might be termed the Ideology of Practise, the value of Independence was selected for study. The purpose here is to determine if this value significantly varies quantitatively in the groups studied.

Recognition

According to Parsons, from the point of view of the theory of action, the actor is in part a "goal-directed" entity. Not only are goals as such the objects of moral sentiments, but this status is also occupied by persons and their attitudes to the actor, by things and their relations to the actor, and by social relationships. [6]

> "Closely related to self-respect, indeed in a sense its complement, is what may, following W. I. Thomas, be called "recognition". To have recognition in this sense is to be the subject of moral respect on the part of others whose opinion is

valued. To be approved of, admired, or even envied, are flattering and satisfying to any ego. As the works of Mead and others have shown, the relations of self-respect and recognition are extremely intimate and reciprocally related. The loss of respect on the part of those from whom it is expected is one of the severest possible blows to the state of satisfaction of the individual." [7]

Would Freidson's observation be applicable to non-western societies? Would the value of independence be equally appreciated and would there be feedback into other segments of the system?

THEORETICAL DISCUSSION

Parsons states that a cathexis (concentration of the psychic energy on some particular person, thing or idea) relates an actor and an object. Specifically it refers on the one side to a motivation—that is, a drive need, wish, impulse, or need-disposition, and on the other side to an object. It is only when the motivation is attached to a determinate object or objects through the cathectic mode of motivational orientation that an organized system of behaviour exists. The most pervasive cathected object is a positive affective response or attitude on the part of ego toward alter or toward himself as object (e.g., approval, esteem). [8]

The work of de Charms stresses the notions of competence and self-determination. He states:

> "Man's primary motivational propensity is to be effective in producing changes in his environment. Man strives to be a causal agent, to be the primary locus of causation." [9]

For de Charms, intrinsically motivated behaviours result from a desire to feel personal causation; he further asserts that this general motive differentiates into specific motives as a result of *experiences with one's environment*. [10]

Attribution theorists' basic assumption is that man is motivated "to attain a cognitive mastery of the causal structure of his environment". [11] Heider in describing this phenomenon states:

> ... the search for relatively enduring aspects of our world, the dispositional properties in nature, may carry us quite far from the immediate facts or they may end hardly a step from them. That is, there exists a hierarchy of cognitive awarenesses which begin with the more stimulus-bound recognition of "facts", and gradually go deeper into the underlying causes of these facts ... Man is usually not content simply to register the observables that surround him: he needs to refer them as far as possible to the invariances of his environment ... The underlying causes of events, especially the motives of other persons, are the invariances of the environment that are relevant to him; they give meaning to what he experiences and it is these meanings that are recorded in his life space, and are precipitated as the reality of the environment to which he then reacts. [12]

The assumption that man is an information seeking organism is also present in Festinger's theory of social comparison.

> "... there exists, in the human organism, a drive to evaluate his opinions and his abilities ... A person's cognition (his opinions and beliefs) about the situation in which he exists and his appraisals of what he is capable of doing (his evaluation of his abilities) will together have bearing on his behavior. The holding of incorrect opinions and/or inaccurate appraisals of one's abilities can be punishing and even fatal in many situations." [13]

It is the physician's *evaluation of his abilities* we will be examining in relation to his behaviour.

Since achievement needs are, in part, attributionary dispositions, we may hypothesize that individual differences in achievement concerns will be related to affective expressions for achievement outcomes. That is, achievement concerns are linked with particular causal attributions which, in turn, determine affective responses.

Experimental studies demonstrate that individuals high in resultant achievement needs work harder, that is to say, they display a greater intensity of performance than individuals low in resultant achievement needs. [14]

Research indicates that attributions of success and failure to ability versus effort influence the rewards and punishments given for achievement outcomes. [15, 16]

It has been demonstrated that teachers' attributions for the success and failure of their pupils have great significance. [17] If the self-perception of low ability is an introjection of attitudes or ascribtions expressed by parents or teachers, it would follow that those physicians who have been sent to Upper Egypt (Minia) because of poor scholastic achievement would perceive themselves as lower in abilities than their colleagues in Cairo and Menoufia. This perception would also be reflected in their negative evaluation of the university preparation.

Results of the Value Tests

Table 8.1 summarizes the results obtained from the value tests (Achievement, Independence, and Recognition) for the three samples (Menoufia, Cairo, Minia).

Analysis of variance ($\alpha = 0.05$) between the three samples for Achievement, Independance and Recognition indicated that there is a significant difference between the scores of each group. The results of such analysis are summarized in Table 8.2.

It should be noted that such difference is most significant in the case of Independence and least significant in the case of Recognition.

Table 8.1

Results of the Value Test

Menoufia n = 49	Achievement	Independence	Recognition
Total Possible Score	1176	980	1076
Total Score	626	591	435
Total Possible Mean	24	20	22
Mean Score	12.8	12.1	8.9
Standard Deviation	± 3.7	± 1.3	± 2.9
Minia n = 49			
Total Possible Score	1152	960	1056
Total Score	482	349	361
Total Possible Mean	24	20	22
Mean Score	9.8	7.1	7.4
Standard Deviation	± 4.2	± 2.4	± 2.2
Cairo n = 35			
Total Possible Score	840	700	770
Total Score	436	365	297
Total Possible Mean	24	20	22
Mean Score	12.5	10.4	8.5
Standard Deviation	± 3.2	± 4.0	± 3.1

Table 8.2

Analysis of Variance of Achievement, Independence, Recognition

Source	d.f.	Sum of Squares	Mean Squares
Achievement			
Among	2	245	122.50
Within	130	1883	14.48
Total	132	2128	

$F = 8.46 > F_{0.05}(2,130) = 3.07$

Independence			
Among	2	615	307.50
Within	130	895	6.88
Total	132	1510	

$F = 44.70 > F_{0.05}(2,130) = 3.07$

Recognition			
Among	2	59	29.50
Within	130	1011	7.78
Total	132	1070	

$F = 3.79 > F_{0.05}(2,130) = 3.07$

Table 8.3 gives the statistical difference between the group mean scores (t-distribution at a significance level of 0.10, justifiable for such high standard deviations of the mean scores).

Table 8.3 confirms the results in Table 8.2, inasmuch as the Independence value test is the most sensitive to the group differences. Menoufia appears to lead in Independence orientation by 10% over Cairo and Cairo by almost as much over Minia. The differences in the recognition values were rather small.

The differences for Achievement were greater than those for Recognition. In Achievement orientation, Menoufia and Cairo could be grouped together in distinction from Minia (difference about 7-8%).

Although differences existed statistically for Recognition between the different groups, they were minimal, thus expressing a consensual definition for this value.

However, it should be noticed that the order in all cases was the same i.e. Menoufia was the highest, followed by Cairo then Minia.

Table 8.3

Results of Statistical Analysis (t-distribution) of Value Mean Scores

Value	Samples	Statistical difference at $\alpha = 0.10$	Statistical difference % of total possible mean score
Achievement	Menoufia > Cairo	0.4	1.7
	Cairo > Minia	1.6	6.7
	Menoufia > Minia	2.0	8.4
Independence	Menoufia > Cairo	2.1	10.5
	Cairo > Minia	2.4	12.0
	Menoufia > Minia	4.5	22.5
Recognition	Menoufia > Cairo	0.5	2.3
	Cairo > Minia	0.3	1.4
	Menoufia > Minia	0.8	3.7

Let us now consider how the actors cognitively sensitized through a series of processes in which generalization, substitution and identification play important parts, define their education, job performance and job satisfaction.

Table 8.4 and Figure 8.1 illustrate how the different groups of physicians perceived their university education satisfactorily, together with the values of Independence, Recognition and Achievement.

The group with higher value scores is the group that contained a higher percentage of physicians that thought their basic university education was satisfactory. If such a percentage is used as an index to express the groups' feeling about their university education, one may conclude that a linear positive correlation exists between this index and each value (Fig. 8.1).

The correlation coefficient varies from 0.6 in the case of Achievement to almost 1.0 for Independence and Recognition.

Table 8.4

Satisfaction with University Education Versus Values' Mean Scores

Sample	Values Mean Scores			% of group satisfied with university education
	Achievement	Independence	Recognition	
Menoufia	12.8	12.1	8.9	62
Cairo	12.5	10.4	8.5	53
Minia	9.8	7.1	7.4	34

Table 8.5 gives the mean scores of self-appraisal relating to how the doctors rate the fulfillment of their job specifications (functions) as set by the Ministry of Health together with the mean scores of the values of Achievement, Independence and Recognition. These are shown graphically in Figure 8.2.

Again it appears that the group with higher value scores (Achievement, Independence, or Recognition) is the group with higher mean scores of fulfillment of functions. The relations are linear with degrees of correlation varying from 0.58 for Achievement to 0.98 for Recognition.

Motivational theory can explain the dynamics of these data. Intrinsically motivated behaviour is behaviour which is motivated by a need for feelings of competence and self-determination. This is manifest in achievement situations. If behaviour is intrinsically motivated, people will seek out challenging

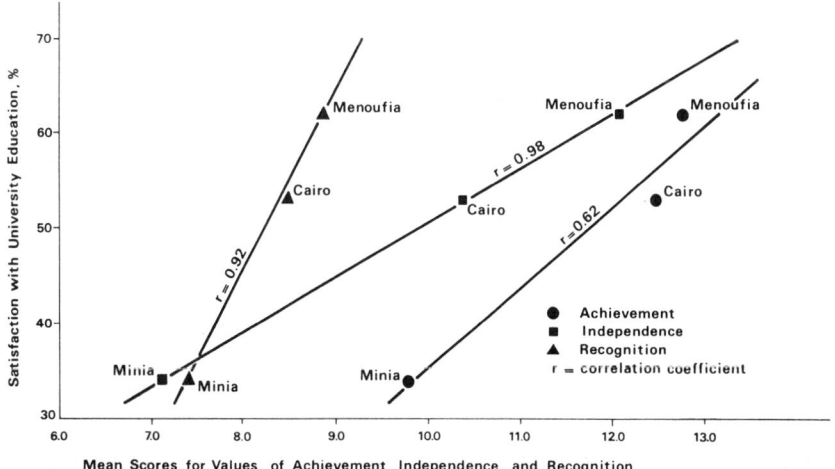

Figure 8.1. Satisfaction with University Education (Percentage of Group) Versus Motivation Value Scores

Table 8.5
Job Fulfillment Mean Scores Versus Values' Mean Scores

Sample	Values mean Scores			Job fulfillment mean scores
	Achievement	Independence	Recognition	
Menoufia	12.8	12.1	8.9	4.2
Cairo	12.5	10.4	8.5	3.9
Minia	9.8	7.1	7.4	3.1

situations. By conquering them, feelings of competence and self-determination are created, as exemplified in the Menoufia & Cairo samples. But if a person attempts too difficult a task he is likely to experience failure and frustration which causes decrements in both intrinsic motivation and performance, as the Minia sample illustrates. This is similar to Piaget's assertion that children seek situations which are assimilable but not completely so, that is they seek challenging situation. However, too challenging a situation will not be assimilable and will be avoided [18]

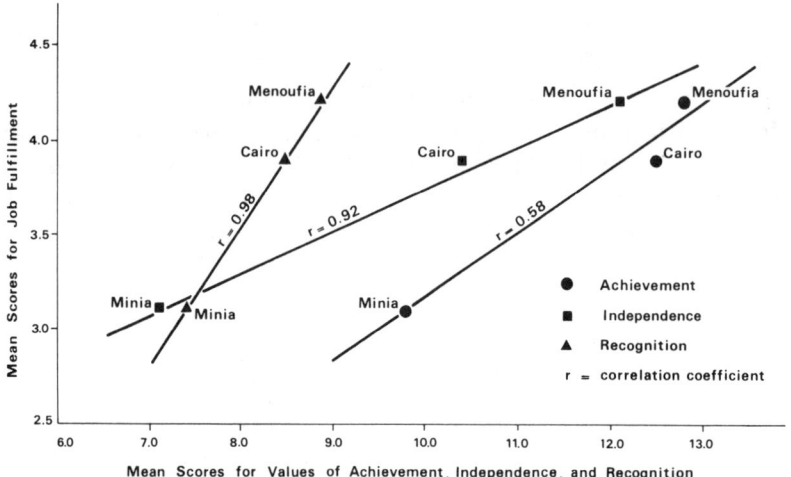

Figure 8.2. Job Fulfillment Index versus Motivation value scores

Performance, motivation, initiative, and goal are so closely related it is often difficult to sort them out in most studies. Atkinson's [19] study used performance as the dependent measure.

Research indicates that negative feedback decreases a persons intrinsic motivation by diminishing his feelings of competence and self-determination. [20] Being sent to Southern Minia could be viewed as negative feedback in this instance. Feelings of incompetence are reinforced by locational determinants, since those physicians who are lower achievers on scholastic exams are sent to more distant areas. Likewise those students who score lower in their final grades go into public health. Students receiving higher grades are accepted into the specialities of Surgery, Obstetrics, or Internal Medicine. This presents problems for improving quality care in rural areas. Those persons selected to study abroad for upgrading rural services, are selected at least partially because of Gemeinshaft relations, and are not as intrinsically motivated as indicated by the substantially lower scores in the motivational factors of the value scores of Achievement, Independence, and Recognition. These initially poor achievers are also poor in English and are incapable of passing qualifying examinations for studying abroad in the public health areas which are desperately in need of qualified personnel. There is a need here to break the vicious circle of negative feedback.

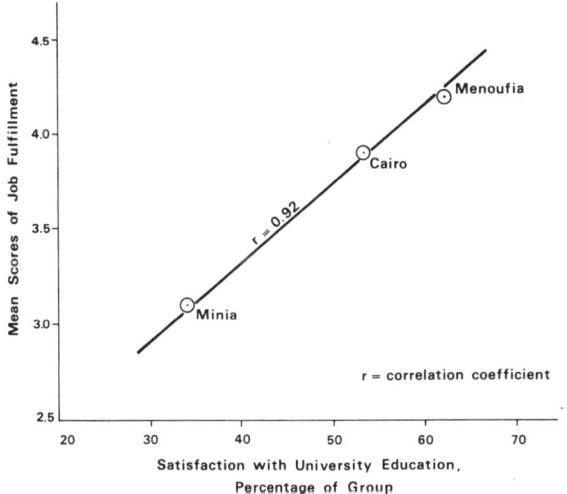

Figure 8.3. Job Fulfillment versus Education Satisfaction

It is also interesting to note from Figure 8.2 that a relatively higher change in the mean score of job fulfillment could be coordinated with a small change in the Recognition mean score in contrast to a higher change in the Achievement score and still higher in the case of Independence. This indicates that the feeling of job fulfillment is most sensitive to Recognition.

Figures 8.1 and 8.2 point out the existence of a linear positive correlation between satisfaction with university education for the performance of the physician's duties and his self-rating of fulfillment of functions are specified by the Ministry of Health. This is clearly illustrated by Figure 8.3 based on the values given in Table 8.6.

Table 8.6

Job Fulfillment Versus Satisfaction with University Education

Sample	Satisfaction with university education %	Job Fulfillment
Menoufia	62	4.2
Cairo	53	3.9
Minia	34	3.1

Job Dissatisfactions as Cognitive Dissonance

By plotting the mean scores of satisfactions against the mean value scores of Achievement, Independence and Recognition in Figure 8.4, the correlation coefficients were all negative and less than 0.6. There is a tendency for the satisfactions mean scores to decrease as the value scales' mean scores increase.

A similar situation was found in correlating dissatisfactions mean scores with the values' mean scores as can be noted in Figure 8.5.

The theory of cognitive dissonance serves as an aid in interpreting these findings.

Cognitive dissonance theory asserts that if a person holds two cognitions which are discrepant, he will experience discomfort and be motivated to do something which will reduce the dissonance.

Zajonc outlines dissonance theory in nine propositions:

1. Cognitive dissonance is a noxious state.
2. In the case of cognitive dissonance the individual attempts to reduce or eliminate it and he acts so as to avoid events that will increase it.
3. In the case of consonance the individual acts so as to avoid dissonance-producing events.
4. The severity or the intensity of cognitive dissonance varies with (a) the importance of the cognitions involved and (b) the relative number of cognitions standing in dissonant relation to one another.
5. The strength of the tendencies enumerated in (2) and (3) is a direct function of the severity of dissonance.
6. Cognitive dissonance can be reduced or eliminated only by (a) adding new cognitions or (b) changing existing ones.
7. Adding new cognitions reduces dissonance if (a) the new cognitions add weight to one side and thus decrease the proportion of cognitive elements which are dissonant or (b) the new cognitions change the importance of the cognitive elements that are in dissonant relation with one another.
8. Changing existing cognitions reduces dissonance if (a) their new content makes them less contradictory with others, or (b) their importance is reduced.
9. If new cognitions cannot be added or the existing ones changed by means of a passive process, behaviors which have cognitive consequences favoring consonance will be recruited. Seeking new information is an example of such behavior. [21]

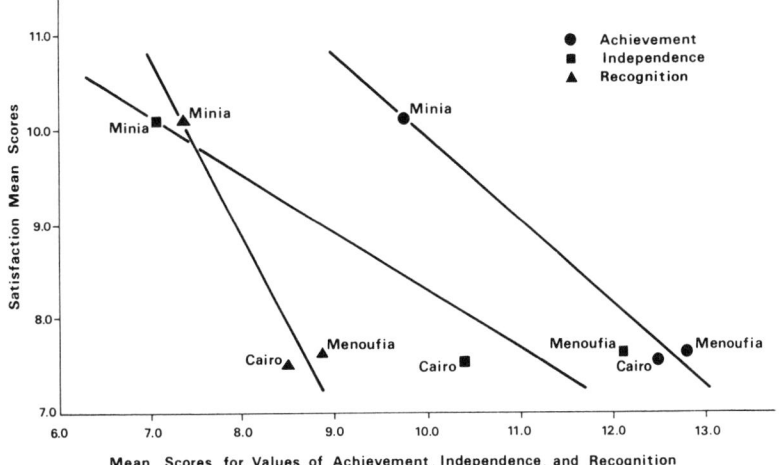

Figure 8.4. Satisfaction mean Scores versus Motivation value scores

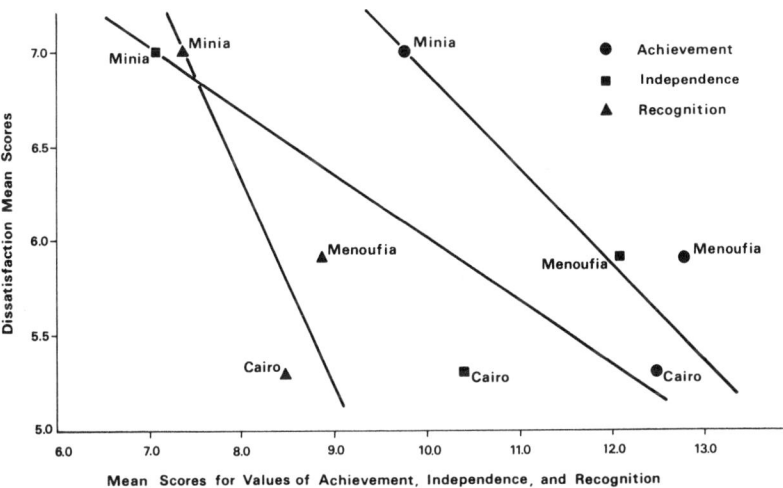

Figure 8.5. Dissatisfaction mean Scores versus Motivation value scores

There are two general mechanisms involved in the intrinsic motivation of behaviour. First, people seek out challenges, that is to say, they seek out incongruity or dissonance. Second, people also attempt to conquer challenges, that is, they seek to reduce incongruity or dissonance. It follows that people may be motivated to engage in a wide variety of behaviours in order to reduce dissonance. According to Festinger, two cognitions are postulated to be in a state of dissonance if "the obverse of one element would follow from the other". Festinger proposed that people prefer no dissonance. However,

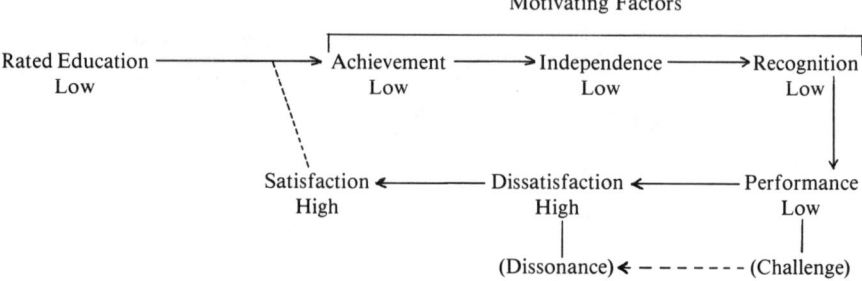

Figure 8.6. Diagram illustrating Minia group.

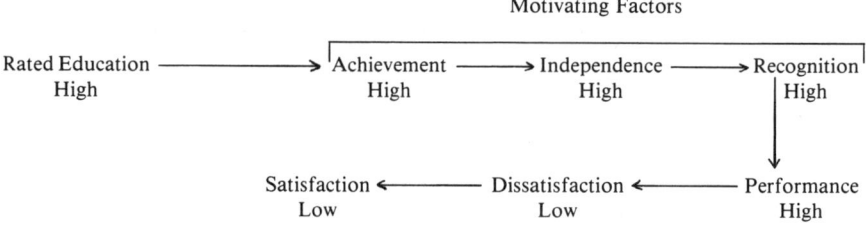

Figure 8.7. Diagram illustrating Cairo group.

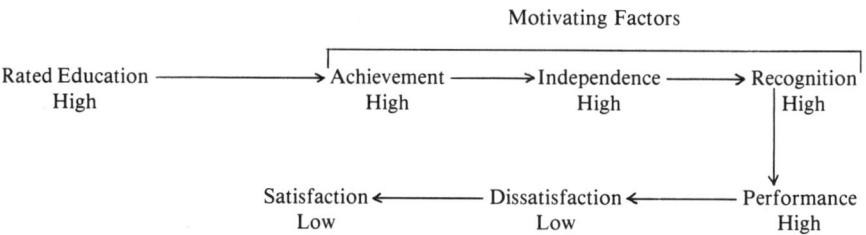

Figure 8.8. Diagram illustrating Menoufia group.

people may seek out incongruity to provide challenge. Then they typically proceed to reduce that incongruity. This action produces the feeling of competence and self-determination. [22]

Contrary to Festinger's argument that because dissonance is uncomfortable, people are driven to reduce that discomfort, Deci postulates that dissonance is not always uncomfortable; sometimes it just represents a challenge [23] However he agrees that dissonance can be at times uncomfortable, as I am proposing that the Minia sample experienced such dissonance as was represented by their high measure of dissatisfaction and failure in performing a task (indicated by low performance index). The incongruity may be very uncomfortable, whereas it probably had not been in his training practice where he had only had to answer to his supervisor.

In most dissonance studies, people are induced to lie, to refrain from doing something they like, etc. Therefore, the incongruity in most studies is typically aversive rather than simply challenging. The most meaningful way to reconcile this is to recognize that dissonance is a subset of incongruity. Therefore, when a person sees that he is unable to behave so as to reduce the incongruity (i.e. to meet the challenge) he will begin to experience discomfort (i.e. dissonance). He then seeks to reduce this discomfort, most probably by changing one of his own internal states, such as an attitude, motive, or emotion. These internal states have a cognitive process of dissonance reduction. [24]

Figure 8.6 schematically illustrates the Minia sample's results and Figures 8.7 and 8.8 explain the results of Menoufia and Cairo for comparison. We can see a feedback loop where the low motivating factors (values) are constantly reinforced. What is demonstrated here is that reduction of incongruity (i.e. challenge) is a mechanism governing the intrinsically motivated behaviour of the Minia sample. If we accept dissonance as a subset of incongruity and the physician fails to meet a challenge, the incongruity which formally represented a challenge becomes dissonance. As a result of experiencing dissonance, he will seek to reduce it by changing one of his internal states (i.e. raise his satisfaction level) and perhaps lower still the motivating factors.

REFERENCES

[1] Parsons, T., Bales, R., and Shils, E., *Working Papers in the Theory of Action*, Glencoe, Illinois, The Free Press, 1953, p. 205.
[2] McClelland, D. C., *The Achieving Society*, Princeton, N.J., Van Nostrand, 1961.
[3] McClelland, D. C., *Some Social Consequences of Achievement Motivation*, in Jones, M. R. (ed.), Nebraska Symposium on Motivation, Vol. 3, Lincoln University of Nebraska Press, 1955, pp. 41-65.
[4] Freidson, E., *Professional Dominance*, Chicago, Aldine Publishing Company, 1970, pp. 96-98.
[5] *Ibid.*, p. 98.
[6] Parsons, T., *Essays in Sociological Theory Pure and Applied*, The Free Press, Glencoe, Illinois, 1949, p. 208.
[7] *Ibid.*, p. 168.
[8] Parsons, T., Shills, E. A., *Toward A General Theory of Action*, Harvard University Press, Cambridge, Mass., 1959, p. 69.
[9] De Charms, R., *Personal Causation: The Internal Affective Determinants of Behavior*, Academic Press, New York, 1968, p. 269.

[10] *Ibid.*, p. 269.
[11] Kelley, H. H., *Attribution Theory in Social Psychology*, in Levine E. (ed.), Nebraska Symposium on Motivation. Vol. 15. Lincoln University of Nebraska Press, 1967, p. 193.
[12] Heider, F., *The Psychology of Interpersonal Relations*, New York, Wiley, 1958, pp. 80-81.
[13] Festinger, L., 'A Theory of Social Comparison Processes', *Human Relations*, 1954, Vol. 7, p. 117.
[14] Atkinson, J. W., 'Motivational Determinants of Risk-taking Behavior,' *Phychological Review*, 1957, 64, pp. 359-372.
[15] Lanzetta, J. T., and Hannath, T. E., 'Reinforcing Behavior of "Naive" Trainers,' *Journal of Personality and Social Psychology*, 1969, Vol. 11, pp. 245-252.
[16] Weiner, B. and Kukla, A., 'An Attributional Analysis of Achievement Motivation', *Journal of Personality and Social Psychology*, 1970, Vol. 15, pp. 1-20.
[17] Crandall, V. C., *Sex Differences in Expectancy of Intellectual and Academic Reinforcement*, in Smith, C. P. (ed.), *Achievement-Related Motives in Children*, New York, Russel Sage, 1969, pp. 11-45.
[18] Piaget, J., *The Origins of Intelligence in Children*, New York, International Universities Press, 1952.
[19] Atkinson, *op. cit.*
[20] Deci, E., and Krusell, J., *Sex Differences, Positive Feedback, and Intrinsic Motivation*, Paper presented at the meeting of the Eastern Psychological Association, Washington, D.C., May 1973.
[21] Zajonc, R. B., *Cognitive Theories in Social Psychology*, in Lindzey, G. and Aronson, E. (ed.), *Handbook of Social Psychology*, Vol. 1 (2nd. Ed.), Reading, Mass., Addison Wesley, 1968, pp. 360-361.
[22] Festinger, L., *A Theory of Cognitive Dissonance*, Evanston, Ill., Row, Peterson, 1957, p. 13.
[23] Deci, E. L., *Intrinsic Motivation*, Plenum Press, New York, 1975, pp. 161-186.
[24] *Ibid.*, pp. 161-186.

CHAPTER NINE

SUMMARY AND PERSPECTIVES FOR THE FUTURE

Summary

The study described and discussed in the foregoing text leads to the following conclusions, which should be regarded within the context of the Egyptian Society. These conclusions need not apply to other parts of the world, even to developing countries, without appropriate modifications based on researchwork.

Certain results embodied in this study indicate that the medical student's anticipatory expectations of the mandatory rural health service do not differ widely from reality as perceived by the physicians in the field. Both indicated the shortcomings of a medical education system borrowed from Western practice and predominantly designed for an urban populace. The rural health physician has defined his role as therapist, manager, educator, and mediator. However, there is no doubt that his medical education has not fitted him for the latter three roles.

It would appear that bridging such a gap between medical education and rural health realities should start at the university; naturally to be followed by on-the-job training at different stages of professional development.

The ultimate aim of any health service is to provide any patient with the necessary services for optimal health care; it would seem, logically, that such a desideratum depends on the physicians' experiencing at least a modicum of role satisfaction. The results of this study indicate that there is a certain correlation between motivation and job satisfaction and that geographical, educational and social variables influence the motivation behaviour and hence job fulfillment. To the goal of revealing to what extent such variables can lead to optimal motivation, the present study could be considered as a contribution inasmuch as it was possible to confirm the applicability of certain value scales, developed recently in Egypt for the Egyptian Society, to the Egyptian physician.

The following hypothesis were accepted within the context of health care. Incumbents of a position will rate their university preparation (fulfillment of role expectations) relative to their scholastic achievement. Incumbents of a position which is geographically isolated will define their role performance less critically than incumbents of a similar position in less isolated or more urban areas; a possible explanation for the above is the marginality of the role and the lack of visibility of role performance. An incumbent of a position will scale down his aspirations if severe conflict is present so that his goals can be satisfied ("attempts at role integration").

This research indicates that what is ultimately needed is a body of cross-cultural sociomedical data that will enable us to go some way towards the construction of a relatively efficient and workable paradigm.

Perhaps the most salient aspect of this research is the inapplicability of Western models in Eastern situations. Although Parsons' formulations are useful if viewed within their sociocultural frame of reference, they have many limitations. His model is mainly dependent upon that of psychotherapy of Western psychiatry and is culture and class bound. It would have to be radically altered to be applicable to the Egyptian case.

The role of the physician is a process rather than a fixed pattern of attitudes, and is subject to redefinition as expectations change. Such a role, as this study indicates, is vulnerable to changes in the organization of medical care, medical fashions and the culture or subculture studied. There is no single physician's role; rather there is a continuum of roles embracing varieties of location, values and significant others in the structure of the Egyptian health delivery system.

Perspectives for the Future

The Education of the Physician

It would seem necessary to incorporate family planning studies into the obstetrics and gynecology course. It should include the social and psychological aspects in addition to Islamic doctrine. This would supplement the ill-attended course of General Health and place family planning within the more prestigious section of obstetrics.

Management training should also be incorporated into the medical curriculum. In view of the many disciplines involved in health, training and experience in multidisciplinary team projects would be extremely valuable.

A course specifically tailored for Rural Health Care should be given in the fifth (final) year. This would include field visits for all students.

The physician should receive some instruction in the techniques of teaching and training subordinate personnel, stressing the team approach. This should be incorporated into the early years of professional education so that the physician might be able to develop his instruction skills as he develops his medical knowledge.

Behavioural sciences should be included in the earlier years of study so that he/she has the opportunity to coordinate them in relation to specific clinical problems.

The present examination system has tended to test the student's capacity to reproduce material learned from textbooks (Western) and lectures rather than his/her capacity to discriminate. The student should, therefore, be encouraged to integrate the instruction he receives in order to ensure that she/he would visualize the patient as a whole and not a collection of systems. This would include integrated teaching, and group clinical teaching.

The Practising Physician

It would appear that the distribution of physicians for the mandatory service should encompass all areas irrespective of the final academic scores. This would eliminate the stigma and labelling of those physicians placed in the equally important distant areas, and ensure a supply of highly motivated physicians to such areas.

Workshops and management development seminars for those already in the field could be coordinated with existing institutions already experienced in management training.

It should appear highly desirable to establish a 3-6 week motivation training course to increase achievement needs for those physicians in Public Health (these physicians have generally ranked lower in their final scores), in which participants learn about thoughts and actions as associated with achievement behaviour. This would include a programme of self-study.

Because of the present emphasis on memorization, the passing of English comprehension examinations is rendered difficult. Since education and/or training abroad rests upon the ability to pass this type of examination, candidates in public health are often unable to pursue further training. It is, therefore, recommended that until the basic approach is changed:
1) English abilities could be determined by oral examinations citing case histories.
2) Candidates may be given a "crash course" (specially designed) in English with frequent examinations similar to the final English qualifying exam.

Suggestions for Further Research

Because of financial constraints as well as an attempt to do an in-depth study of the physician, this research has been limited in scope to the physicians' role, their analysis of their own abilities, and those problems facing them vis-à-vis their subordinate personnel. For future work it is recommended that additional research be done with the attitudes of subordinate personnel as they themselves interpret their problems as well as a skill measurement of male/female physician job performance. In addition, a follow-up study should encompass more provinces and an increased number of respondants from the Cairo and/or Alexandria Governorate. More research is indicated for the consumer of the health delivery system, especially those women in child-bearing years, so that services might be better tailored to their needs as they perceive them.

The work previously described appears to indicate that further research is required in order to understand the physicians' belief systems regarding family planning as well as uncover the forces promoting and obstructing change in health services. Finally, we must find out the beliefs with which medical faculty approaches their job inasmuch as this affects different aspects of medical education and career promotion.

APPENDIX I

PHYSICIAN QUESTIONNAIRE
ENGLISH VERSION

Instructions: This information is being collected for a study of Egyptian Physicians' interests and opinions. Your cooperation is greatly appreciated. Please answer all the questions and return the form in the enclosed envelope. Your answers will be treated as confidential.

GENERAL INFORMATION (Do not sign your name)

1. Place of birth: Village _____ City _____
   County _____ Governorate _____
2. Year of birth _____ 3. Sex _____ 4. Marital status: (Check One)
   Single: _____ Married: _____ Widow: _____ Divorced: _____

EDUCATION

5. Grade school attended: Village _____ City _____
   County _____ Governorate _____

6. What was the year of your graduation from the Faculty of Medicine?
   _____

7. Give the name and location of the university where you obtained the degree: Name _____
   Location: City _____ Governorate _____

8. What is the most advanced course that you have completed (Check one)
   ☐ Bachelor's degree in Medicine & Surgery
   ☐ Master's degree in Medicine, another branch, or graduate studies diploma
   ☐ PhD degree in medical science or another branch
   ☐ Other (specify) _____

9. Do you feel that your university education adequately prepared you for your profession? (check) Yes _____ No _____
   Why? _____

10. Do you feel you need additional education or training to carry out your present work more effectively? Yes _____ No _____

11. Would you like to receive additional education or training to improve your position in the medical profession? (check)
Training _____ Education _____ None _____

12. If your answer to question 10 or 11 is positive, what kind of education or training would you need?
Education (specify)
Training (specify)

13. On a scale of 1-5 rate why you *originally* entered the faculty of medicine:
    (a) Fascination with the subject of
        medicine (Least) 1-2-3-4-5 (Most)
    (b) Prestige (Least) 1-2-3-4-5 (Most)
    (c) Financial reward (Least) 1-2-3-4-5 (Most)
    (d) Family encouragement (Least) 1-2-3-4-5 (Most)
    (e) Desire to help others (Least) 1-2-3-4-5 (Most)
    (f) High Thanawia Amaa grade (Least) 1-2-3-4-5 (Most)
    (g) Other (specify)

EMPLOYMENT

14. What is the title of your present position? e.g., Head of rural Health Unit, Specialist, Head of hospital/division _____
_____

15. How long have you been in the above position? _____

16. Are you presently fulfilling the 1-year mandatory service? Yes ____ No ____

17. What do you consider is the *MAJOR* function in performing your work? (check one of the following, if possible; otherwise, specify)
    ☐ administration
    ☐ supervision
    ☐ teaching (staff and patients)
    ☐ medical care
    ☐ other (specify) _____

18. What other important functions do you perform?

19. The Ministry of Health specifies the functions for each physician's job description. On a scale of 1-5 rate how well you are fulfilling the func-

tions given for your position. (Least) 1-2-3-4-5 (Most) Explain why ____
_____

20. How many hours do you work per day? ____ How many days per week? ____

21. State the approximate *weekly* number of persons you receive for:
    (a) Out-patients   _____
    (b) In-patients   _____
    (c) MCH   _____
    (d) Family planning   _____
    (e) Private clinic   _____
    (f) Other _____   Specify   _____

22. State the general level of competence of other subordinate personnel at your unit in the following (check one)
    history taking   good ____ fair ____ poor ____
    counselling   good ____ fair ____ poor ____
    clinical procedures   good ____ fair ____ poor ____
    follow-up care   good ____ fair ____ poor ____

23. Which of the following items do you regard as *disadvantageous* in your present employment situation? (check as many as you feel apply)
    a. ☐ Conditions of work: isolation, inconvenient working hours, etc.
    b. ☐ Excessive managerial responsibilities, bookkeeping
    c. ☐ Prejudice against women in medicine
    d. ☐ Problems of family arising from career
    e. ☐ Lack of prestige in the profession
    f. ☐ Mechanical aspects of medical work, repetition, tediousness
    g. ☐ Low salary
    h. ☐ Community problems surrounding your work
    i. ☐ Relations with supervisors
    j. ☐ Lack of equipment and supplies
    k. ☐ Inadequate staff
    l. ☐ Other (specify) _____

24. Which of the following problems are you encountering in your general environment that are affecting your private life? (Check as many as you feel apply)
    a. ☐ housing
    b. ☐ transportation
    c. ☐ childrens' education
    d. ☐ cost of living
    e. ☐ other (specify) _____

25. Which of the following items do you regard as *advantageous* in your present employment situation (check as many as you feel apply)
    a. ☐ Job fulfillment
    b. ☐ Professional development
    c. ☐ Promotion opportunities
    d. ☐ Prestige
    e. ☐ Financial rewards
    f. ☐ Social relations
    g. ☐ Contribution to the health and welfare of the people
    h. ☐ Other (specify)

26. As a male or female physician, what are the problems you are encountering in performing your job?

    a. From the people in the community: _____

    Examples _____

    b. From subordinate staff: _____

    Examples _____

    c. From the supervisors in the Governorate: _____

    Examples _____

    d. From the Administrators in the Ministry of Health: _____

    Examples _____

27. Do you think that being a female (male) is considered an advantage or disadvantage in the execution of your work? (check one)
    Advantage _____ Disadvantage _____ No effect _____
    Why? _____

28. What cultural traditions are facilitating your work? _____

29. What cultural traditions are impeding your work? _____

On a scale of 1-5, rate the extent to which you are satisfied with the following:

30. Your career or occupation (Least) 1-2-3-4-5 (Most)

31. Your future job prospects (Least) 1-2-3-4-5 (Most)

32. Family relationships (Least) 1-2-3-4-5 (Most)
33. Leisure time recreational activities (Least) 1-2-3-4-5 (Most)
34. Social relationships (general) (Least) 1-2-3-4-5 (Most)
36. Social status (Least) 1-2-3-4-5 (Most)
37. Relationships with colleagues (Least) 1-2-3-4-5 (Most)
38. Effectiveness of the Medical Syndicate (Least) 1-2-3-4-5 (Most)

ADMINISTRATIVE AND SUPERVISORY SKILLS

Rate yourself on a scale of 1-5 for the following administrative and supervisory skills (Circle one)

39. Ability to plan, organize, manage, and evaluate services of the unit or clinic (Least) 1-2-3-4-5 (Most)
40. Ability to plan, implement and evaluate the nursing and midwifery staff (services, resources, in-service training, etc.) of the unit or clinic (Least) 1-2-3-4-5 (Most)
41. Ability to coordinate the medical component with services (Least) 1-2-3-4-5 (Most)
42. Ability to supervise, counsel, guide and support staff and to interpret their needs (Least) 1-2-3-4-5 (Most)
43. Ability to promote the leadership skills of staff undergoing practical training (Least) 1-2-3-4-5 (Most)
44. Ability to help staff to develop and advance professionally (Least) 1-2-3-4-5 (Most)
45. Ability to record information, use data, and make comprehensive and comprehensible reports (Least) 1-2-3-4-5 (Most)
46. Ability to recognize problems, arrive at decisions based on a critical assessment of the situation, initiate a course of action (with or without the aid of others), and evaluate own performance (Least) 1-2-3-4-5 (Most)
47. Ability to exchange views and cooperate with colleagues and superiors (Least) 1-2-3-4-5 (Most)
48. Ability to exchange views and cooperate with local leaders in your community (Least) 1-2-3-4-5 (Most)

The following is a number of items each containing three alternative personal views concerning aspects of life, people's feelings, people's behaviour and people's interaction. Please read each item carefully, and then choose the one of the three alternatives which coincides most with your personal views, and identify it with an x mark in the corresponding bracket. Remember that you have to choose only one view in each item, that is the view you believe represents your behaviour or interaction with relevant situations. If you find that you can choose more than one view, please mark only the best one, expressing your views. Please remember too that there are no correct answers as known in classical tests; here the correct answer is the one mostly expressing your views. There is no time limit to answer the questions; however, do not hesitate much in marking your views.

The following is an illustrative example:
When dealing with others we must be
— honest ☐
— cheerful ☐
— patient ☒

The respondent chose the third alternative by marking x in the space between the brackets after "patient". He could have chosen "honest" or "cheerful" since we cannot describe his choice as right or wrong. He chose this alternative because it represents his view when dealing with others.

Complete the following:

49. The most I hope for is to be:
— sincere to my colleagues at work ☐
— organized in my work ☐
— doing my utmost in the work I am doing ☐

50. To excel in work requires:
— dealing intelligently with superiors ☐
— independence in taking decisions ☐
— support from colleagues ☐

51. The most important duties of the State which I appreciate are represented by:
— establishing some organizations which develop the discovery of creative people ☐

— concentrating their efforts on the expansion of economical projects so that prosperity prevails ☐
— interest in political affairs leading to a wider horizon in dealing with other countries ☐

52. When executing a certain job, I prefer to be:
    — organized while I am about to do the job ☐
    — executing the job in a way better than others ☐
    — finished with the job before the time limit ☐

53. A person must teach his sons:
    — utilization of others' experience ☐
    — formation of their own views concerning their lives ☐
    — paying attention to what they are told ☐

54. We must rejoice in:
    — keeness of others to recognize good works ☐
    — exchange of courtesies between individuals on social occasions ☐
    — interest of our young people in self-employment ☐

55. One of my goals in life is:
    — accumulate good achievement ☐
    — to have a distinguished job status ☐
    — live my own life ☐

56. When taking a decision, one must reflect on:
    — the effect of the decision on others' minds ☐
    — how far to be convinced of the soundness of the decision ☐
    — what he can get back from the decision ☐

57. We must feel happy when:
    — people are concerned about each other ☐
    — a big amount of money is available ☐
    — the authorities honour living creative people ☐

58. Happiness requires:
    — realization of more achievement ☐
    — enjoying life ☐
    — making others happy ☐

59. We must realize that our young people can achieve a lot if:
    — given freedom of action in what they can do ☐
    — directed to what they must do ☐
    — advised about what they would preferably not do ☐

60. I feel very depressed when:
    — people criticize others' work without sufficient expertise ☐
    — we do not abide by oriental traditions ☐
    — our work does not bring its worth financially ☐

61. I look forward to:
    — attracting the attention of others ☐
    — acquiring more wealth ☐
    — using all my capabilities in whatever job I do ☐

62. We must understand that the main objective of education is to create a citizen who can:
    — accept the traditional systems and values in society ☐
    — defend the traditional systems and values in society ☐
    — accept or reject the traditional systems and values in society ☐

63. I always seek:
    — to settle differences between friends ☐
    — thank people who did work worth appreciation ☐
    — avoid problems which cause me distress ☐

64. I achieve most satisfaction if:
    — I supervise others ☐
    — I get acquainted with people of authority ☐
    — I am entrusted with the difficult jobs ☐

65. If a certain principle is to dominate, it should be:
    — freedom of will ☐
    — social cooperation ☐
    — respect for authority ☐

66. In most social stands I try to:
    — follow the existing traditions ☐
    — make new friendships ☐
    — leave a strong impression on others ☐

67. One must always realize the importance of:
    — doing jobs of importance ☐
    — getting friendly with others ☐
    — the love from the opposite sex ☐

68. We should appreciate those who can:
    — express their ideas without hesitation ☐
    — digest others' ideas quickly ☐
    — implement others' ideas efficiently ☐

69. The best a person can achieve is:
    — have a nice reputation ☐
    — citing his work by others ☐
    — have the approval of others ☐

70. Some of my basic principles:
    — respect of others' feelings ☐
    — achieving a high level of performance ☐
    — avoiding the blame of friends ☐

71. We must admit that what differentiates between advanced and backward countries is respect of the former for the principle of:
    — time exactness ☐
    — freedom of thinking ☐
    — respect of expectations ☐

72. One must be dissatisfied by:
    — lack of appreciation for his work ☐
    — hate of others for him ☐
    — greediness of others for his possessions ☐

73. One must feel very happy when:
    — his name is associated with serving others ☐
    — finds himself of attraction to the opposite sex ☐
    — his capabilities of carrying out whatever responsible are given to him in work, are always mentioned ☐

74. One must direct his behaviour through:
    — famous quotations ☐
    — parents' advice ☐
    — personal initiative ☐

75. I always stick to:
    — giving advice to my colleagues when necessary ☐
    — giving courtesies to my colleagues on social occasions ☐
    — referring to great work done by others ☐

76. One must feel very depressed when:
    — he is subject of blame from his beloved ☐
    — he is subject of reprimand from his superiors ☐
    — neglected by his friends ☐

77. When reading books of difficult material, one must:
    — re-read it until he understands it ☐
    — resort to professors to explain it to him ☐
    — request his colleagues to cooperate with him in reading it ☐

78. When I work which I imagine is of high quality:
    — I give myself some rest ☐
    — I seek to know others' views of this work ☐
    — I feel my distinction over others ☐

79. I am always inclined to solve:
    — friends' problems ☐
    — cross words ☐
    — work problems ☐

80. One must define his objective in view of:
    — what others expect from him ☐
    — what appears to him as realistic ☐
    — what spares him trouble ☐

81. When I do good work it pleases me to have it rewarded as:
    — academic title ☐
    — financial reward ☐
    — professional promotion ☐

82. Our dealing with others should be controlled by:
    — work they can offer ☐
    — their social positions ☐
    — their moral attitudes ☐

83. We must realize that the most difficult professions are those in which one finds himself:
    — restricted by a group of rules which he must follow ☐
    — obliged to define by himself what he should do ☐
    — bound from time to time to stay alone in his work's region ☐

84. The highest I aspire to in my life is:
    — see most of the world ☐
    — my family has an adequate status ☐
    — my work is appreciated by my colleagues ☐

85. My highest goals in life are:
    — leave behind a happy family proud of me ☐
    — my name is associated with a unique accomplishment ☐
    — to be a peace pigeon between people ☐

86. I look forward to a type of superior who:
    — enables us to get what we want ☐
    — diverts us to what he wants ☐
    — makes us avoid what he does not want ☐

87. We must not overlook at all thinking of how:
    — to preserve our oriental traditions ☐
    — to revive religious values in our young people ☐
    — to find a suitable way of honouring our scientists and thinkers ☐

88. I always feel that I am in my best condition when:
    — I find mutual love with others ☐
    — I find others listen to me with interest ☐
    — develop skills suitable for my work ☐

89. One's values should evolve from:
    — his society ☐
    — his family ☐
    — himself ☐

90. The most important principle I have faith in is:
    — there is no adequate mental production without adequate encouragement ☐
    — who has the capability for mental production is not impeded by outside circumstances ☐
    — mental production is only a matter of the right time and the right place ☐

91. I always prefer:
    — difficult work over easy work ☐
    — work which is expected to succeed ☐
    — work which realizes profit ☐

92. Usually it is most difficult for a person to:
    — satisfy his family in what they want him to do ☐
    — revolt against some of the traditions of his society ☐
    — follow the experience of his elders ☐

93. If I have to recommend something, it is:
    — increasing the number of schools ☐
    — changing the system of examinations ☐
    — finding a system to discover contributions of young people ☐

94. One must consider himself lucky if:
    — he enjoys good health ☐
    — accomplished a deed considered great by his colleagues ☐
    — has a good obedient wife ☐

95. When making a plan, one must visualize clearly the extent of:
    — harmony of such plan with others' expectations ☐

— others' welcome of such plan ☐
— his conviction of its effectiveness ☐

96. We must admit that the most important reason behind the inability of individuals to great mental production is:
    — lack of interest of authority in removing many obstacles which are in individuals' way ☐
    — lack of existence of strong incentives to activate their will ☐
    — the sparse support given from others for mental production which requires a lot of effort and cooperation ☐

97. I get the utmost happiness from:
    — people relying upon me in catastrophes ☐
    — commanding respect from my colleagues ☐
    — being pictured by my superior as an example of the productive person ☐

98. When choosing a certain profession, one must choose those:
    — involving definite instructions to spare him making any errors ☐
    — requiring him to think by himself of new systems for work ☐
    — requiring him to listen attentively to experienced people ☐

99. One of the obstacles of mental production is:
    — the absence of a system allowing the discovery of talents at an early stage ☐
    — small financial return to professional intellectuals ☐
    — the absence of capabilities to do such work ☐

100. It must be admitted that one's future depends a lot on:
    — the suitable opportunity ☐
    — one's will ☐
    — support from sincere people ☐

101. One's utmost goal is to have the ability to:
    — execute his ideas without interference from others ☐
    — serve all his loyal friends ☐
    — achieve prosperity for his family ☐

102. One of the things that distress me most in today's youth is their lack of grasping the importance of:
    — respect of traditions ☐
    — giving credit to one who deserves it ☐
    — receiving advice from elderly people ☐

103. One must avoid:
    — loss of friends   ☐
    — waste of effort   ☐
    — misuse of funds   ☐

104. It is not useful to resign oneself in most cases to the fact that one's ideas:
    — are different from others' ideas   ☐
    — are intentionally in harmony with others' ideas   ☐
    — are connected to others' expectations   ☐

105. I have no doubt about the possibility of making quick progress in work, if the responsible people understood the importance of enlightening the individuals to the following:
    — the precise procedures and rules governing their work   ☐
    — efforts will not go unappreciated   ☐
    — what should the relation between superiors and subordinates be   ☐

106. If I have to choose a certain job, it would be the one that gives me:
    — security and stability   ☐
    — affluent living   ☐
    — self-fulfillment   ☐

107. The work one should seek is that which:
    — gives a chance for promotion   ☐
    — helps with stability   ☐
    — encourages distinction   ☐

108. What disturbs me most is courtesy at the expenses of:
    — individuals' comfort   ☐
    — others' efforts   ☐
    — work's budget   ☐

109. When finished with a certain work, one must not miss to:
    — reward himself with an interval of rest   ☐
    — think of what he can do after that   ☐
    — claim a financial gain as a reward for his work   ☐

110. I look forward with great interest to the establishment of a system in every organization which looks after the young at the beginning of their practical life through:
    — early recognition of the efforts of the distinguished   ☐
    — expansion of training programs aimed at enlightening them about work organization   ☐
    — offering them economical assistance   ☐

111. I do not object at all to the enactment of a law through which life years are counted as:
    - the number of years one spent happily enjoying his life ☐
    - the number of years one spends among his family and people ☐
    - the number of years during which one did certain accomplishments ☐

112. We ought to follow some European countries inasmuch as their realization of importance:
    - achieve adequate economical standard for workers ☐
    - inscription of workers' names on the tools they make ☐
    - obliging the workers to enjoy their weekly day off ☐

113. Good work for me is the work which permits the presence of colleagues who are:
    - good in their work ☐
    - easy to coexist with ☐
    - with experience in work ☐

114. I always regard with admiration my class colleagues who were able in a short time to:
    - own a car and bank account leading to stability ☐
    - publish a book or accomplish a distinguished deed ☐
    - visit many countries of the world ☐

APPENDIX II

STUDENT QUESTIONNAIRE
ENGLISH VERSION

This study is part of a research project about the opinions of medical students. All information will be held strictly confidential. DO NOT SIGN YOUR NAME. Your cooperation is greatly appreciated. Thank you.

GENERAL INFORMATION

1. What year are you in medical school?
   Fifth Year _____
   Fourth Year _____
   Other   _____

2. Where did you attend elementary school?
   Village _____ Town _____ City _____

3. Year of birth _____

4. Sex _____

5. Marital status
   Single _____ Married _____ Widow _____
   Divorced _____

6. Have you been to a rural health unit before?
   Yes _____ No _____

7. Was this visit part of your formal education?
   Yes _____ No _____

8. Do you believe that visits such as the above would help prepare you for your mandatory village services?
   Yes _____ No _____

9. Are you looking forward to this service?
   Yes _____ No _____

10. Do you view this service as a form of: (check as many as you feel apply)

    ☐ punishment
    ☐ moral obligation

☐ a means of serving others
☐ a means of repaying society for your education
☐ a means of preventing you from pursuing your academic career
☐ a part of your educational process
☐ a valuable experience
☐ other (specify)

11. Do you believe the villagers share the same cultural background as you?
    Yes _____ No _____

12. What do you understand the villagers "world view" to be? (World view includes beliefs, traditions, values, attitudes)

    List as many as you can recall:
    _____
    _____
    _____
    _____

13. Do you believe an understanding of this "world view" is essential to provide adequate care for the village population?
    Yes _____ No _____

14. Was this knowledge gained in your medical education?
    Yes _____ No _____

15. If no, would you like to see it included?
    Yes _____ No _____

16. Do you believe your education is adequately preparing you to work in rural areas?
    Yes _____ No _____ Why? _____
    _____

17. Does your curriculum include:
    Public Health medicine   Yes _____ No _____
    Preventive medicine   Yes _____ No _____
    Family Planning   Yes _____ No _____
    Social Sciences   Yes _____ No _____

18. Do you believe that your background (upbringing) has prepared you for village service?
    Yes _____ No _____

19. Why is medical care in urban Cairo superior to rural areas? (check as many as you feel apply)
    ☐ More Physicians

☐ More continuing education and professional stimulus for urban physicians
☐ Less problems of time and distance
☐ Superior facilities
☐ Other reasons (specify)_____

Why is medical care in urban Cairo inferior to rural areas?
☐ Less personalized care
☐ Physicians and facilities are less responsive to patients' needs
☐ Less cooperative and coordinated medical community
☐ Other reasons (specify)_____

20. Do you plan to stay in the rural area after your mandatory service?
Yes _____ No _____

21. Which of the following do you anticipate will be *disadvantages* in your rural health service? (check as many as you feel apply)
   a. ☐ Conditions of work: isolation, inconvenient working hours etc.;
   b. ☐ Excessive managerial responsibilities, bookkeeping;
   c. ☐ Prejudice against women in medicine;
   d. ☐ Problems of family arising from career;
   e. ☐ Lack of prestige of the profession;
   f. ☐ Mechanical aspects of medical work, repetition, tediousness;
   g. ☐ Low salary;
   h. ☐ Community problems surrounding your work;
   i. ☐ Relations with supervisors;
   j. ☐ Lack of equipment and supplies;
   k. ☐ Inadequate staff;
   l. ☐ Other (specify)

22. Which of the following items do you anticipate will be *advantageous* in your rural health service? (check as many as you feel apply)
   a. ☐ Job fulfillment;
   b. ☐ Professional development;
   c. ☐ Promotion opportunities;
   d. ☐ Prestige;
   e. ☐ Financial rewards;
   f. ☐ Social relations;
   g. ☐ Contribution to the health and welfare of the people;
   h. ☐ Other (specify) _____

23. On a scale of 1-5 rate why you *originally* entered the faculty of Medicine.
   (a) Fascination with the subject of medicine (Least) 1-2-3-4-5 (Most)

(b) Prestige (Least) 1-2-3-4-5 (Most)
(c) Financial Reward (Least) 1-2-3-4-5 (Most)
(d) Family Encouragement (Least) 1-2-3-4-5 (Most)
(e) Desire to help others (Least) 1-2-3-4-5 (Most)
(f) High Thanwaia Amaa grade (Least) 1-2-3-4-5 (Most)
(g) Other (specify) _____

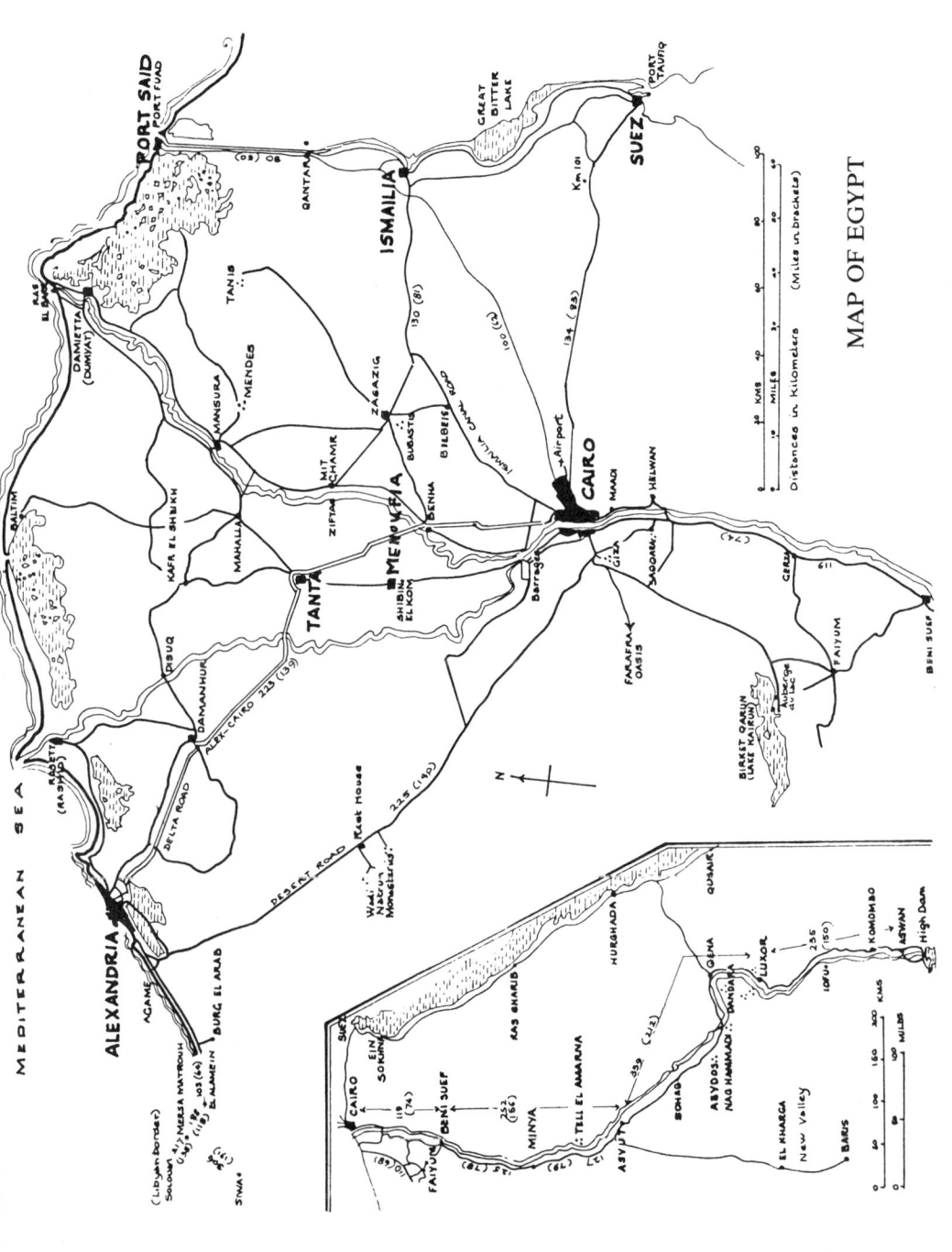

A